SLAUGHTER
AT SEA

SLAUGHTER AT SEA

The Story of Japan's Naval War Crimes

by

Mark Felton

Pen & Sword
MILITARY

First published in Great Britain in 2007 by
Pen & Sword Military
an imprint of
Pen & Sword Books Ltd
47 Church Street
Barnsley
South Yorkshire
S70 2AS

ISBN 978 1 84415 647 4

A CIP catalogue record for this book is
available from the British Library

Typeset in Sabon by
Phoenix Typesetting, Auldgirth, Dumfriesshire

Printed and bound in England by
Biddles Ltd, King's Lynn

Pen & Sword Books Ltd incorporates the Imprints of Pen & Sword
Aviation, Pen & Sword Maritime, Pen & Sword Military, Wharncliffe
Local History, Pen & Sword Select, Pen & Sword Military Classics and
Leo Cooper.

For a complete list of Pen & Sword titles please contact
PEN & SWORD BOOKS LIMITED
47 Church Street, Barnsley, South Yorkshire, S70 2AS, England
E-mail: enquiries@pen-and-sword.co.uk
Website: www.pen-and-sword.co.uk

Dedicated to my grandfather William Felton, who fought the Japanese through the steaming jungles and steep hills of Burma with the Suffolk Regiment, and to his namesake, my son William.

Contents

Acknowledgements

The author would like to extend his thanks to the following organizations and individuals for their assistance during the researching and writing of this book. Many thanks to Brigadier Henry Wilson at Pen and Sword Books Limited for supporting my project, and to my editor, Bobby Gainher. Thanks are due to Jill Durney of the Macmillan Brown Library, University of Canterbury in New Zealand, for her assistance in tracking down exhibits from the proceedings of the International Military Tribunal for the Far East, and to the staff at the Australian War Memorial in Canberra, the Imperial War Museum in London, the National Archives (formerly the Public Record Office) at Kew, and the British Library Document Supply Centre. Many thanks are also due to the staff at the Nanjing Massacre Memorial Hall, and to Ron Taylor and members of the Far East Prisoners of War Association (FEPOW) for their support of this project.

I would finally like to thank my wife, Fang Fang, for her strong support of my work. Her practical advice and keen eye for detail have been invaluable throughout the process of researching and writing this book.

Introduction

*The Navy of the Great Japanese Empire will not try to
punish you all with death. Those obeying all the rules and
regulations, and believing the action and purpose of the
Japanese Navy, cooperating with Japan in constructing the
'New order of the Great Asia' which lead to the world's
peace will be well treated.*
Japanese Naval Regulations for Prisoners of War

Borneo, Netherlands East Indies, July 1945. After surrendering to
Japanese forces in 1942, about 100 former members of the
Netherlands East Indies Army, along with their wives and children,
had been permitted limited freedom within the town of Samarinda
in present-day Indonesia. On the morning of 30 July all of the
Dutch residents were suddenly rounded up by Japanese troops and
taken before an officer. Without explanation the officer declared
that the entire white population was forthwith sentenced to death,
and soon afterwards the hapless Dutch nationals were forced at
gunpoint into trucks and driven to a mine at Loa Kulu just outside
the town. On arrival the men and women had their hands tied
behind their backs, and the men were forced to their knees in a tight
group to watch the execution of their wives and children. The
Japanese soldiers attacked the women with swords and bayonets,
and quite literally hacked their victims to pieces in front of their
husbands and fathers. Younger children and babies were thrown
to their deaths down a 600-foot mine shaft before the Japanese
turned their attention to the men. Forced to kneel before their
tormentors, Japanese officers beheaded each man in turn with
swords, before the remains of the men and women were pitched
unceremoniously down the same mine shaft where the broken

bodies of their children lay. Weeks later the remains of the bodies were discovered by Australian troops, who had captured Borneo and begun a search for its missing European residents.[1]

The crimes committed by the armed forces of Japan between 1931, when the cloven hoof of Japanese militarism first marched onto Chinese soil, and the final surrender of the Empire in August 1945 after the Americans had visited atomic warfare upon the cities of Hiroshima and Nagasaki, were some of the greatest organized atrocities in human history. Millions of civilians and the military personnel of a dozen nations perished in an orgy of sadistic violence not witnessed in Asia since the Mongol hordes had surged westward under Genghis Khan.

Why the Japanese armed forces consistently behaved with such sadism and brutality towards the populations of the nations it fought against is a topic that still generates intense debate among historians today. Even in Japan, a nation not generally known for its willingness to confront its troubled wartime past, a few academics have risked the violent attentions of ultra-right-wing nationalist groups and published books reassessing the country's wartime record (a position often at variance with the Japanese government). In the same way that Western writers have tried to answer the question of why the Germans murdered millions of Jews and other peoples of Europe willingly and often with great brutality, some Japanese have tried to explain why their service personnel committed such sadistic outrages against defenceless people everywhere the Imperial armed forces went.

This book recounts a series of Japanese naval atrocities committed between the high-water mark of the Empire's expansion in early 1942 and the final weeks of the war in 1945. Most were committed at sea by surface and submarine forces. Many of the massacres were committed on land, on distant Pacific islands such as Wake to the sprawling metropolis of Manila in the Philippines. In most cases hardly anyone survived to bear witness to what had occurred, for the Japanese Navy was thorough in the destruction it wrought. When brought to account for its crimes at the International Military Tribunal for the Far East in Tokyo in 1946, and at a number of other war crimes trials throughout Asia, a sufficient number of survivors gave evidence against former Japanese naval officers, which was allied to the interrogation reports of surrendered Japanese service personnel. Many of the naval personnel responsible for the slaughters recounted throughout this book were successfully prosecuted, and subsequently executed or imprisoned. Inevitably, however, many were not, and they were able to disappear into Japan to begin quiet post-war lives.

Arriving inside the Nanking Massacre Memorial Hall on a gloomy, rainy day in 2005 in the former Chinese capital city of Nanjing, the evidence of what the Japanese military had done to the local population in 1937–8 lay all around me. An enormous mass grave has been excavated and preserved, where 10,000 skeletons of men, women and children lie in enormous piles, just a tiny fraction of the over 300,000 murdered by Japanese forces in this single city as they advanced into China. The skeleton of a small child with a long, rusty nail driven through its skull spoke volumes about the barbarity and sadism of the wartime Japanese military. Looking at this one tiny collection of bones that was once someone's child piled upon the bleached bones of countless others, I wondered at the mentality of an army that would murder a child by hammering an iron nail through its face. When I came to research and write this book I soon discovered that what I had seen in Nanjing, emotive and difficult to comprehend as it was, was only the beginnings of Japanese military barbarism that would spread across Asia and the Pacific like a demonic plague as war in China gave way to war across all of Asia and the Pacific. As recently as 1994 Japan's Justice Minister, Nagano Shigeto, was quoted as declaring that what the author and millions of others from all over the world observed in Nanjing at the Massacre Memorial had never occurred, that 'the Nanjing Massacre is a fabrication.' In 1990 a former Japanese cabinet minister named Ishihara Shintaro had gone even further, declaring in an interview, 'The Nanjing Massacre is a lie made up by the Chinese.' Such attitudes are common in Japan today, even at the highest levels of government and academia, but it is perhaps one of the central reasons that many of the terrible deeds that appear across the pages of this book have been swept under the metaphorical 'historical carpet' by successive generations of Japanese, many of whom refuse to confront their country's dark past.

Post-war prosecutions for war crimes and genocide would serve as the epitaph of Japan's disastrous experiment with empire. The majority of these legal punishments were directed against members of the Imperial Army, but the Imperial Japanese Navy (IJN) was found to have been intimately involved in countless atrocities throughout the territories of Asia and the Pacific under Japanese occupation. The extent to which the Japanese Navy committed atrocities has often been sublimated into the greater sum of murder committed by the rampaging Imperial Army, and often naval crimes have been blamed incorrectly on the army. The victims and the victors found difficulty in discriminating the arm-of-service of a green-uniformed Japanese loping along with rifle and bayonet, for in the field very little visual clues signified a demarcation between soldier and sailor.

This book aims to demonstrate, in a small and intentionally limited way, that the IJN was as equally guilty alongside the Army in the planning and execution of many terrible and unnecessary atrocities across Asia and the Pacific, often for reasons that remain unclear or illogical to a modern audience even over sixty years after the events. A selection of war crimes committed both at sea and on land by the IJN are discussed throughout this book, both to demonstrate the heinous nature of the acts in themselves, the sadistic behaviour of the officers and men concerned, and also the geographical breadth of the IJN's crimes. This is only a selection of hundreds (perhaps even thousands) of Japanese naval war crimes, some infamous in history, most of the others almost forgotten except by a few elderly survivors whose dreams still echo to the sounds of gunshots, bayonets driven through helpless flesh and the swish of a samurai sword.

As will become evident from many of the massacres recounted in this book, the Japanese servicemen who committed them appeared inventive in the methods used to 'dispose' of prisoners, and to have been deliberately sadistic in the manner of execution they chose. The IJN very often mirrored the Army in creating despicable methods for killing people who had offered no resistance or threat to its rule. The Navy was as prone to sadism and indiscriminate murder as the Imperial Army. As mentioned, the many crimes of Japan's wartime Navy have often been overlooked when dealing with Japanese war crimes per se, but the Navy's role in such affairs was as equally enthusiastic as the Army's. At sea, Japanese surface vessels and submarines sank Allied naval, Red Cross and merchant vessels, and then tried to murder any survivors who were in lifeboats or were found floating in the sea. Allied aircrew were often rescued from the ocean or picked up on small islands and then tortured to death on the decks of Japanese warships or imprisoned and later killed, and sometimes the Navy collected its victims on land and took them to their deaths out at sea. On land, Japanese sailors and special naval landing parties equalled and often surpassed the brutality of their army counterparts in the administration of captured territories, and were responsible for hundreds of thousands of murders throughout Asia and the Pacific. In some places Japanese naval personnel raped women and girls, and often subsequently killed them. They routinely bayoneted people or beheaded them. Others they beat to death with iron bars or sledgehammers. Many victims were crucified, or burned alive; others drowned, hanged or left to die lonely deaths at sea as live bait for sharks. Some were buried alive, or cut to pieces, and on several occasions both the Army and the Navy used prisoners of war and local civilians as guinea pigs in perverted medical experiments that equalled the horrors committed by SS doctors in German concentration camps (see Appendix 3). Groups of people were often executed by rifle and machine-gun fire, though this seems to have been viewed as a waste of ammunition by many superior officers and death by shooting was often deliberately avoided in place of more mediaeval tortures. On occasion Japanese naval personnel even committed ritual cannibalism, eating selected parts of white prisoners they had specifically murdered for this reason. It is widely acknowledged that the Japanese treated Allied service personnel who became their prisoners with unequalled brutality, enslaving hundreds of thousands of prisoner of war, and subjecting them to a regime of terror in which tens of thousands died from abuse, disease, overwork and starvation. Certainly, due to the fact that the victims were white, this slice of history has entered the common consciousness in the West today, especially through film, whereas the sufferings of the native peoples enslaved alongside their former masters are only now being generally acknowledged.

The Japanese also shared much in common with the Germans, the Japanese Army and Navy plundering entire countries of their wealth, looting national gold reserves and art treasures, and wantonly laying waste to thousands of years of history and culture. No book can do justice to the inhumanity of Imperial Japan towards the peoples it conquered or captured because the scale of the brutality was so vast. The best that can be hoped for are little windows into a dark world gone mad, windows into the soul of a military rabid with a seemingly insatiable bloodlust.

If it was not for the apparently limitless cruelty perpetrated by units of the IJN there would be much to admire in the service. The Imperial Navy fought with unparalleled ferocity, tenacity and bravery during the course of the Second World War. From the brilliantly conceived and executed carrier aircraft strike on Pearl Harbor in 1941, through a string of enormous naval battles such as Midway in 1942, and on to the bitter final battles around the island of Okinawa in 1945, the personnel of the IJN, even when thrown onto the defensive across the Pacific, nonetheless never gave up hope of an ultimate victory over their enemies. Ships, aircraft and men were increasingly sacrificed in a hopeless struggle as the war turned inexorably against Japan after the Battle of Midway, and the commitment of the IJN to preventing the Allies from gaining a foothold in the Home Islands actually increased in ferocity as the Americans pushed ever closer to ultimate victory. But beneath the incredible fighting spirit and individual courage exhibited by Japanese sailors in the best traditions of any of the wartime navies was a self-serving honour. Only the deeds and sacrifices made by the IJN in the name of the God-Emperor Hirohito were worthy of praise or acknowledgment. The foes they met on sea and on land, and the conquered peoples made subject to their rule, were both considered less than nothing in the eyes of the Japanese Navy. 'They', these conquered, subjugated or captured peoples, had no honour or they would have died protecting it instead of surrendering, and so they could be exterminated because they were essentially worthless, their lives without value. The lives of the prisoners belonged to the Emperor and his minions, the armed forces. Such single-mindedness bred a naval service with a piratical disregard for International Law and human rights.

Not all Japanese sailors were war criminals, but although undoubtedly courageous, a great many Japanese sailors involved themselves in war crimes, and not always because they were ordered to do so. Most of the criminal acts recounted in this book were committed by ordinary young men willingly and without question. Only a few Japanese sailors flatly refused to take part in atrocities perpetrated by their units, and then only officers with sufficient seniority to avoid serious censure by their

6

superiors. For modern generations reading about these crimes from the comfort of the twenty-first century, it is difficult to understand the motivations of the sailors who perpetrated mass murder in the dark days of the Second World War. It is harder still to penetrate the thought processes of the Japanese military culture, alien as it was to the Allied nations and their own military codes of conduct. The Imperial Navy certainly possesses the blackest copybook of any of the naval forces involved in the Second World War, though instances of massacre were not solely the habitat of the Japanese Navy. All the navies of the Second World War committed acts which could be construed, with the benefit of hindsight, as war crimes, but none committed them on such a vast, organized and cold-blooded scale, and it can be stated that in no other navy was murder the rule rather than the exception.

One aspect of Japanese naval cruelty is not discussed in this book – what have come to be called the 'Hell Ships'. Allied prisoners of war were routinely moved about the Japanese empire as slave labour as the need arose. Transportation was more often than not by sea. For example, thousands of American POWs were reportedly transported to work in the Philippines, Japan, China, Thailand and Korea in twenty-three prison vessels. They were packed so tightly many could hardly do anything but stand in the inadequately ventilated holds of filthy cargo ships. The prisoners were fed almost no food and given very little water. Unfortunately, American and other POWs were subjected to attack when their prison ships, which the Japanese did not mark in direct violation of international law, were attacked by American submarines. Terrible loss of life occurred aboard these overcrowded ships when they were struck by torpedoes and often sunk. One of the worst cases was that of the *Arisan Maru*, with 1,800 American POWs packed into her holds. Torpedoed by the submarine USS *Snook*, only five American prisoners survived the sinking. Another attack that caused major loss of life among POWs was the sinking of the *Shinyo Maru* by the submarine USS *Paddle*, which resulted in the deaths of all but eighty-two of the 750 American prisoners aboard her. Japanese guards often shot surviving prisoners as they floated in the sea rather than bothering to rescue them. Many fine histories and autobiographies exist that fully document this

Japanese method for transporting Allied prisoners, and the terrible sufferings wrought upon the victims of this organized neglect and deliberate sadism. Two books in particular deserve mentioning: *Death on Hellships: Prisoners at Sea in the Pacific War*[2] by Gregory F. Michno, and *Ships from Hell*[3] by Raymond Lamont-Brown.

Notes

1. 'George Duncan's Massacres and Atrocities of World War II, Pacific' (including Dutch East Indies) http://members.iinet.net.au/~gduncan/massacres_pacific.html#Pacific.
2. Michno, Gregory F., *Death on Hellships: Prisoners at Sea in the Pacific War* (Pen & Sword Books Ltd, 2001).
3. Lamont-Brown, Raymond, *Ships from Hell* (Sutton Publishing, 2002).

Chapter One

Towards the Setting Sun

It is necessary to have politics, economics, culture, national
defence and everything else, all focused on one being, the
Emperor, and the whole force of the nation concentrated
and displayed from a single point . . . This system is the
strongest and the grandest of all . . . there is no nation that
can compare with our national blood solidarity.
Lieutenant Colonel Hashimoto, Japanese Cherry Society

The ships that flew the Rising Sun and blew the Russian Baltic Fleet
to scrap iron at the Battle of Tsushima in 1904 were mainly British
built; designed, crafted and riveted together in the great shipyards
of Empire on the Clyde and elsewhere in England and Scotland.
The officers who stood proudly upon the decks beside their
'Japanese Nelson', Admiral Heirachiro Togo, had been trained
in the best traditions and tactics of the world's most powerful navy,
the Royal Navy, that bestrode the globe at the time like a huge
octopus, its tentacles of power reaching into every ocean, and along
the shores of every continent. Togo himself had received his officer
training aboard HMS *Britannia*. The ordinary Japanese seamen,
decked out in their square rig, looked for all intents and purposes
like Oriental mirror-images of Britain's 'Jack Tars', and the effect
was intentional. When Japan had begun the construction of a
modern battle fleet in the late nineteenth century, emerging from
over two centuries of deliberate isolation under the feudal
Tokugawa Shogunate, its designers and strategists had carefully
studied and then copied the organization, methods, uniforms and
traditions of Britain's Royal Navy. Admiral Togo told his officers,
'The English navy is very great . . . Study it. See all you can. Learn
all you can . . . All other navies are negligible beside it.'[1] But even

in the early twentieth century, when many British officers served in the Imperial Japanese Navy as advisors and training instructors, these men noted that one important aspect of the ethos of the Royal Navy was conspicuous by its absence. The Japanese, though to all intents and purposes having carefully created a carbon copy of Britain's navy, had failed to inculcate the officers and men with the British traditions of compassion, honourable warfare, civic duty and a care of duty towards those whose ships had been sunk or were otherwise rendered helpless. The Japanese were simply not interested in these concepts as they felt them to be alien in origin and not reflective of Japanese society and military culture. The glorification, as well as the perversion, of the old samurai military honour code called Bushido, that had kept Japan isolated and militarily obsolete for over two centuries, was being carefully cultivated amongst the officers and men of both the new Army and Navy. The combination of modern technology and mediaeval doctrines was an elixir certain to produce unspeakable destruction and barbarity at some point in the future, and Japan's victory over Czarist Russia in 1905 was merely a prelude of what the new power in Asia was capable of, as 'the Bushido spirit would propel Japan on an imperialist course of unparalleled ferocity and brutality.'[2] This would begin thirty-three years after Admiral Togo had scored one of history's most astonishing naval victories when Japan launched a full-scale war against China in 1937, and the slaughter would only end with the almost total destruction of one of the world's most modern battle fleets in 1945.

It was the British, ironically, who actually began the process of encouraging many Japanese into a more militaristic stance. London had cancelled a cooperative naval alliance with Japan in 1921, an alliance that had seen the Japanese Navy protect British colonies in Asia, notably quelling a mutiny by Indian troops in Singapore during the First World War when Britain had sent most of her men and ships west. The alliance with Britain had kept the curb bit firmly between the teeth of the Japanese Army and Navy, and keeping Japan close had made sure that she had remained a friend instead of a potential foe in Asia.

As Britain and the world's second power, the United States, along with a collection of lesser Western Powers with traditional interests in Asia, grew increasingly concerned about Japan's growing naval strength, they convened conferences in London in 1921, and

Washington DC and London in 1930. The intention was nothing less than the limitation of Japan's surface fleet so that Japan was unable to ever tip the balance of power in the Far East in her favour by outnumbering and outgunning the British and Americans on the high seas.

By 1934 Japan was in the throes of a nationalist revolution, with democracy slowly being pushed out of mainstream politics as reactionary elements in the military and philosophical circles expounded the inequalities of British and American 'imperialistic' attitudes towards Japan. Many wanted Japan to challenge the imperialist nations by forging for herself an Asian empire. Sea power was going to play a central role in any future race for empire, as Japan depended almost entirely on imported resources, from iron ore to oil and wheat. The Japanese government soon felt secure and strong enough to ignore the naval restrictions imposed on her in 1930, arguing that such restrictions were unfair and Japan would have difficulty in defending herself if she was to abide by the American- and British-instigated naval reductions. The United States and British governments drew in a collective breath, and wondered what they should do, as Japan embarked on a massive rearmaments programme, shortly to be followed by German rearmament in Europe. Lured back to the conference table in 1935, Japan's diplomats quickly snubbed the negotiations, pointing out the bullying attitude of the British and Americans towards their country and withdrew the next year. Japan was by this stage already a nation flexing her military muscles, as there had been conflict in China in 1931–2, and Japan was almost in the terminal grip of the militarists. In 1932 Japanese Special Naval Landing Parties had fought a long and ultimately successful battle with Nationalist Chinese forces in the Chapei district of Shanghai, as the Japanese demanded to extend their section of the International Settlement by all and any means, and demonstrating to the watching world the potential threat her armed forces now posed to the peace of Asia. Foreigners had watched the Japanese military in Shanghai in 1932, and many had witnessed terrible scenes that presaged much greater savagery to come five years later. An American, Rhodes Farmer, wrote of witnessing early Japanese atrocities: 'A crowd of marines and *ronin* stood beside the two Japanese sentries on the far side of the bridge [Garden Bridge separating the Japanese part of Shanghai from the British side]. One of them bayoneted an old man and pitched his body into the [Suzhou] Creek. I saw several good-looking girls seized by the soldiers and dragged into neighboring buildings.'³

After 1936 the Imperial Navy's fleet would grow steadily as the country began a massive warship construction program that would culminate in the two biggest battleships ever built, *Musashi* and *Yamato*, as well as a strong aircraft carrier force and submarine service. Japanese prime ministers who attempted to curb the ambitions of the militarists were removed from power or assassinated as the Army and the Navy vied for favour with Emperor Hirohito. The Army prevailed initially and was able to engineer a crisis in Manchuria that was turned into a full-scale war with China in 1937. The Chinese managed to resist sufficiently to prevent the Japanese achieving a rapid victory, although by 1938 most of eastern and southern China was under a brutal Japanese occupation. With the fall of France to the Germans in June 1940, many of the European colonies in the Far East, including French Indo-China (now Vietnam, Laos and Cambodia) and the oil-rich Netherlands East Indies (now Indonesia) appeared ripe for the taking. The British had begun to appear militarily weak east of Suez, and downright prostrated east of Singapore. The Royal Navy had withered on the vine in Asia as Winston Churchill withdrew all of the best ships and most of the modern air force to the war in the Mediterranean and Middle East. The Far East was a backwater to the war raging in Europe and North Africa, and Britain only had a finite amount of resources with which to police its empire.

Little regard was given to the barbarous Japanese invasion and occupation of eastern China by the Western powers, even though a mighty chorus of, mainly American, reportage clearly warned the comfortable colonists and their armies of what they could expect in due course from the hungry Japanese war machine. Far from the war in Britain, with its accompanying Blitz, rationing and blackouts, the British in Asia fooled themselves into believing two myths regarding the Japanese military. It was widely held that the Japanese were individually inferior in every way to the white soldier, sailor or airman, short, with bandy legs and bad eyesight, and that although they had trounced the Chinese, when faced with 'real', i.e. Anglo-Saxon, armed forces they would ultimately prove to be second-rate opponents. And many of the whites in Asia also believed that their lives were ultimately worth more than those of their Asian subjects, so when many of them were captured by the Japanese they were genuinely surprised that their captors treated them the same as other Asian captives. Although the mother nations of the region's other great colonial powers, France and the Netherlands, were cloaked under German occupation, their eastern colonists ruled comfortably in territories free of Nazi tyranny. Frenchmen still governed in Indo-China, and Dutchmen still ruled in the East Indies. Alongside the slumbering British, concerns about the Japanese mistreating them should they have pierced the Anglo-Saxon military defences that thinly protected the region, were in the backs of minds rather than at the forefront until it was virtually too late.

The only problem that worried the Japanese was the likely re-action of the United States to any Japanese takeover of South-East Asia. The US Pacific Fleet, based at San Diego, with its advanced base at Pearl Harbor, Hawaii, was enormously powerful and the Japanese realized that it would have to be neutralized at the same time as the Army and Navy moved to conquer the European colonies of Asia. Admiral Isoroku Yamamoto, commander of the Japanese Combined Fleet, had a plan in hand by January 1941, outlining how the American threat could be removed from the equation. Ironically again, the British had provided the Japanese with the initial training and tactics to make their Pearl Harbor strike a reality. Just after the First World War it had been Royal Navy officers who had taught the Japanese about aircraft carriers, and trained many of Japan's earliest naval aviators. And it was the British carrier aircraft strikes against the Italian fleet at Taranto and Cape Matapan in 1940 that had demonstrated to the Japanese how to transfer theory into reality. The Japanese had proved to be extremely competent pupils. At the same moment that Japanese naval planes would batter the helpless US Pacific Fleet into scrap iron at Pearl Harbor, army and naval forces were to attack and occupy southern Thailand and British Malaya (the Empire's second richest colony after India) with the objective of capturing the modern naval base at Singapore. Other Japanese forces were to conquer the British colonies of Burma and Hong Kong, the vast archipelago of the Netherlands East Indies, the American pro-tectorate of the Philippines, the international settlements in the old Treaty Ports of Shanghai and Tientsin (now Tianjin) in China (which up to then had been regarded as neutral territories by

Japanese forces), and the Solomon and Central Pacific Islands. From these initial conquests Japan would push out its defensive perimeter to encompass lonely American outposts in the Pacific, extending the boundaries of the Empire way out into the great blue Pacific, and eventually pushing southwards virtually to the shores of Australia.

One of the most significant second-wave Japanese targets after the conquests of Indo-China, Malaya and the East Indies was Midway Island in June 1942. It was during the Battle of Midway that the IJN first demonstrated its contempt for prisoners taken during the air battle. The Japanese Navy's blitzkrieg also struck the tiny American coral atoll of Wake, and here the Japanese abused and butchered again, on an even greater scale. All across South-East Asia and the Pacific, behind the Japanese defensive curtain, the IJN was killing people long since subjugated. Japan's warships and submarines were entering the early rounds of a sea campaign that would turn increasingly brutal and sadistic as time went on. Togo's Imperial Fleet, that had whipped the Russians in a display of naval strategy to rival Nelson's victory at Trafalgar, was now soiling itself and its reputation with a series of pointless massacres designed to earn it the enmity of all its opponents, and its eventual total destruction and eradication from the fabric of the nation.

As noted in the Introduction, one of the reasons the Japanese Navy was able to commit atrocities and war crimes both at sea and on land was because unlike many of the other combatant navies of the Second World War, the IJN administered vast land territories, particularly in the Pacific. This situation arose from conflict between the Army and the Navy in Japanese society before the war. The two services rarely cooperated until late on in the war, and each had its own agenda regarding the prosecution of the war which was usually at variance with the other. Some territories that were conquered by naval landing forces were subsequently turned over to army governance, but many, including the pre-war South Seas Mandate (which consisted of the former German colonies of the Marshall, Caroline and Marianas Islands awarded to Japan after being on the winning side in the First World War) were governed directly by the Navy. Many port cities captured by the Japanese, including Shanghai, were also under naval jurisdiction. Being both a land and a sea force, the IJN was able to extend its power over the conquered peoples and armies of many nations, beginning with the conquest of the Netherlands East Indies and New Guinea in early 1942.

Notes
1. Herman, Arthur, *To Rule The Waves: How the British Navy Shaped the Modern World* (Hodder and Stoughton, 2005), p. 522.
2. Ibid., p. 522.
3. Dong, Stella, *Shanghai: The Rise and Fall of a Decadent City* (William Morrow, 2000), p. 253.

Chapter Two

Tol Plantation

Those who are about to die salute you.
Telegram from Wing Commander J.M. Lerew on New Britain Sent to RAAF HQ, Melbourne, 23 January 1942

The lush tropical island of New Britain in the Australian Mandated Territory of New Guinea was invaded by the Japanese in early 1942, followed shortly after by strong Japanese landings on Timor and Ambon islands in the Netherlands East Indies. The Allied defensive perimeter protecting Australia began to collapse under Japanese pressure as they swept on from Malaya to invest Holland's huge Asian colony, and in the process thousands of Allied soldiers were left in the hands of the victors.

The Japanese invasion of the Netherlands East Indies began on 15 December 1941 with landings on North Borneo and Celebes Island. By the end of January 1942, following the Battle of Balikpapen, South Borneo and Celebes had been captured. The Japanese aim was to invest Java and cut the Allied defence of the region into two parts. To the west, now that Singapore had fallen to the Japanese, only Sumatra remained free, while to the east Timor provided a last defence line before Australia. In February 1942 Japanese forces captured Ceram, southern Sumatra, and Bali, and also launched air attacks on Darwin in Northern Australia. Java was now cut off in the west with a garrison of around 75,000 men.

On all of these islands, Japanese army and navy troops committed terrible massacres of surrendered Australian military personnel, even though they had successfully conquered this outer ring of Australia's defences with very few casualties. The worst atrocity occurred at Laha Airfield on Ambon Island some time after the actual capitulation of Australian and Dutch forces, and this terrible story is described in the following chapter. On New Britain, Australian prisoners, who had only just been captured by the victorious Japanese, were butchered for no apparent reason other than to satisfy the apparent bloodlust of their captors. The blame for such large numbers of Australian servicemen (and a few servicewomen) falling into the hands of the Japanese on New Britain, Timor and Ambon is often laid at the feet of Prime Minister John Curtin's government in Australia, which had dispatched forces to garrison these islands that were simply too small to hold their own against strong amphibious attacks. Even as piquets designed to slow down a Japanese advance towards New Guinea and Australia the forces were too weak to place a brake on the Japanese Empire's rapid expansion. They were also unable to evacuate themselves once it became clear that they could not perform their missions because of Japanese naval and air supremacy, and these small, isolated garrisons were effectively abandoned to their fates after desultory attempts at resistance. Although many of the men involved in these debacles made it back to Australia, it was only by their own efforts, and not through any organized effort on the part of the Australian military, that they were ultimately spared a cruel captivity at the hands of the Japanese.

Rabaul, capital of Australian New Guinea and the largest settlement on the island of New Britain, was of strategic importance to Australia. Its airfields, seaplane anchorages and position only a few hundred miles from the large Japanese naval base at Truk in the Caroline Islands, made the place worth defending. However, Australia appeared unwilling to send forces to New Britain that could actually do the job, simultaneously committing the same error on Ambon in the Netherlands East Indies, where 'Gull Force', the Australian garrison, was being shipped.

The group sent to defend Rabaul was codenamed 'Lark Force', and consisted of a grand total of 1,400 Australian servicemen. Under the command of Colonel J.J. Scanlon from 8 October 1941, the area commander's 'teeth' units consisted of Lieutenant Colonel H.H. Carr's 2/22nd Infantry Battalion numbering 716 all ranks, 17 Anti-Tank Battery, Royal Australian Artillery under Captain E.D. Matheson, and a couple of 6-inch coastal guns, some anti-aircraft artillery and the New Guinea Volunteer Rifles.

Ancillary troops included Major E.C. Palmer's 2/10th Field Ambulance, Australian Army Medical Corps, and the Royal Australian Air Force (RAAF) sent No. 24 Squadron consisting of ten Wirraway training aircraft and four Hudson light bombers to support the ground troops. Lark Force was pathetically small for the tasks it had been given, under-trained and inexperienced, and woefully ill-supported.[1]

Approaching the beleaguered Australians at Rabaul was a large section of the Japanese Navy's 4th Fleet, otherwise known as the 'South Seas Force', combining army and navy ground troops plus naval warships and aircraft under the overall command of Vice Admiral Shigeyoshi Inouye. The actual attack on New Britain would be made by Major General Tomitaro Horii's 5,000 naval landing troops and army soldiers drawn from the 55th Division. The attack began with Japanese naval aircraft neutralizing the Australian's few coastal guns. In the early hours of 23 January 1942 Japanese naval landing troops began coming ashore, often unopposed as Lark Force numbered too few men to guard every possible landing place. The fight was incredibly one-sided. Only 2/22nd Battalion was an infantry unit, and 716 men could do little when faced with 5,000 Japanese marines and soldiers who enjoyed complete air and sea superiority. The fighting lasted only a few hours, and although many of the units in Lark Force tried to put up a spirited defence, it was ultimately a hopeless situation. Carl Johnson, in his moving account of the destruction of the Australian forces on New Britain, *Little Hell: The Story of the 2/22nd Battalion and Lark Force*, paints a vivid picture of the confusion the ordinary Australian troops faced. According to the diary of one soldier:

> Awakened at 0245 hours. First shot fired about 0350 hours. Mortars keep up heavy fire. Air was alive with darting bullets (tracer) about 0400 hours. Stretcher-bearers came up for Bluey and Peachy. Japs doing a lot of yelling in gullies. Planes arrived with the daylight and the fun really started. Had landed troops behind our Company as well as along the side. Two platoons pulled out at about 0540 hours. We stayed to hold them. Pulled out at 0645 hours with the Japs very close. Had a terrible climb up ridge to get out. Planes were machine gunning all troops.[2]

Colonel Scanlon soon realized that resistance was impossible and futile. He gave an order reminiscent of a captain aboard a sinking ship, in this case a very prescient analogy, telling his troops that it was 'every man for himself'. The Australian defenders broke into small groups and scattered into the thick jungle covering most of the island, hoping to avoid the Japanese encirclement, and make it back to Australia by whatever means they could as no organized evacuation was possible. Most of these men never made it, either dying in the jungle, killed by Japanese patrols or made prisoners of war. Only the RAAF managed to make an orderly evacuation, getting most of its personnel out in flying boats just before the end of Australian resistance on the island. The soldiers were left to fend for themselves, and for several weeks isolated groups of Australian soldiers emerged from the jungle to surrender to the Japanese occupiers, weakened by disease and starvation. The desperate predicament of many Australian soldiers has been recreated by David Bloomfield in *Rabaul Diary: The Escape of a Lark Force Man*,[3] that paints a grim picture of young men far from home stuck in a seemingly insurmountable situation. For some of the Australians who lived and worked in New Guinea before the Japanese invasion, the suffering of the young soldiers was terrible to witness. Kenneth Ryall, a plantation manager at Kokopo, who did manage to escape to Australia, later wrote:

I was 11 weeks on the island after the Japanese landing. I lived on Taro, sweet potato and fish, but the soldiers did not have a chance. They were not accustomed to the native food and went down with fever and dysentery. In every second or third kanaka village all along the way there would be two or three soldiers dying. At the food dump at Malalonga, the soldiers had bayoneted all the tinned food with a view to preventing the Japanese from using them. This meant, of course, when the other Australian soldiers came along the food was poisoned.[4]

Although the sufferings of the cut-off Australian troops continued for several weeks after the Japanese invasion and occupation of New Britain, it was the fates of many of the troops captured on the first days that were also a tragedy. Tending to the sick and wounded, the personnel of 2/10th Field Ambulance fell into

Japanese hands as they stood by their posts and continued to do their jobs. One hundred and fifty-eight soldiers, many of them medics, were massacred by the Japanese, a great many dying at Tol Plantation outside Rabaul. Only six men survived the massacres to report what had occurred to the Australian government.

On 4 February twenty-four army medics were captured at Tol, and every one of them was wearing a Red Cross brassard that indicated their non-combatant status. The day before five barges had disgorged a company from 3rd Battalion, 144th Infantry Regiment, under the overall command of Colonel Masao Kusunose, at Henry Reid Bay, an indent of the much larger Wide Bay close to Rabaul. Although army troops, they were under the direct command of the Japanese Navy for the operation, part of Admiral Inouye's South Seas Force. The Japanese troops had set off to round up Australian troops in the surrounding jungle and nearby plantations. The first ten Australians discovered by the Japanese were immediately killed by bayoneting them to death, but the remaining 158 captured over several days were taken prisoner. A party of Japanese troops expertly frisked the twenty-four medics captured on the 4th for anything of value, and also stole their army pay books and identity discs, before the medics had their hands bound with rope. Clearly, from a witness statement made by a survivor of this atrocity, the Japanese intended to kill them all for unknown reasons. Revenge seems unlikely, for the Japanese invasion force had only suffered sixteen men killed during the entire operation. When the medics arrived at Tol Plantation, the Japanese guards ordered them 'to sit down on a slight rise on the track which led from the road to the plantation', according to a survivor, Private Bill Cook of 2/10th Field Ambulance. 'They then began to take the men down the track in twos and threes. I was in the last party which numbered three.' A Japanese officer, unable to speak English, enquired using sign language whether the Australians would prefer to be bayoneted or shot. Faced with this awful choice, the resigned medics asked to be shot, hoping for a quick and painless death. Acting with brutality, 'All three in my group were . . . knocked to the ground, and as our hands were tied behind our backs and we were also tied together we were unable to move.'[5] Apparently the choice between death by bayonet or bullet was some kind of sick joke on the part of the Japanese: 'The escort stood over us and bayoneted us several times. I received five bayonet wounds, but I held my breath and feigned death though still alive. As the Japanese were moving off the man next to me groaned. One of the Japanese soldiers came running back and stabbed him once more. By this time I could hold my breath no longer.' The witness took a deep breath, trying to control the pain from his injuries, but the Japanese guard heard him. 'When I drew a deep breath the soldier heard me and inflicted six more bayonet wounds. The last thrust went through my ear into my mouth severing an artery on the way. The member of the escort seeing the blood gushing out of my mouth assumed that I was at last dead, covered the three of us with coconut fronds and vine leaves and left.'[6] Private Cook bravely recalled of his horrific injuries, 'Each of the wounds which I received had not hurt a great deal, except the last, which grated across the cheek bone and, when he withdrew the bayonet, it lifted my head.'[7] At nearby Waitavalo Plantation, another thirty-five Australian prisoners were shot to death by rifle and machine-gun fire, and their bodies were left where they fell. Cook survived by staggering the 50 yards to the sea after chewing through the rope binding his hands and bathing his appalling wounds in the salt water. Later that day he managed to link up with some other survivors and soldiers in hiding, and they eventually escaped to Australia.

For the remaining Australians who were captured and not killed by the Japanese, a slow agony as slave labourers awaited them, initially imprisoned at Rabaul itself before being loaded aboard a Japanese transport for shipment to the Home Islands. Over 800 died when the ship they were packed aboard, the *Montevideo Maru*, sailing unmarked, was torpedoed and sunk by the American submarine USS *Sturgeon* on 1 July 1942 off the north coast of Luzon in the Philippines.

Colonel Kusunose, the officer responsible for the killings of 158 Australian soldiers, was never brought to trial for his actions. He committed suicide by the unlikely method of starving himself to death over a period of nine days before the Australian authorities could lay their lands on him. Instead, in July 1945, the bleached bones of the men executed at Tol and Waitavalo plantations were discovered strewn about the areas where they had been brutally killed over three years earlier, for the Japanese had not even bothered to bury the bodies.

We will return to the similar fates of Australian and Dutch

forces defending Ambon Island shortly, where Japanese naval forces exacted a terrible price in blood from their prisoners some time after capturing the island.

Notes

1. Gamble, Bruce D., *Darkest Hour: The True Story of Lark Force at Rabaul – Australia's Worst Military Disaster of World War II* (Motorbooks International, 2006).
2. Johnson, Carl, *Little Hell: The Story of the 2/22nd Battalion and Lark Force* (History House – Jenkin Australia Publishing Ltd, 2004).
3. Bloomfield, David, *Rabaul Diary: The Escape of a Lark Force Man* (Australian Military History Publications, 2001).
4. Minute to the Secretary, Department of the Army, 16 May 1942, NAA A5954 Item 532/1, (Australian War Memorial).
5. Russell of Liverpool, Lord, *The Knights of Bushido: A Short History of Japanese War Crimes* (Greenhill Books, 2002), pp. 104–5.
6. Ibid., p. 105.
7. MacArthur, Brian, *Surviving the Sword: Prisoners of the Japanese in the Far East, 1942–45* (Random House, 2005), p. 52.

Chapter Three

Laha Airfield

After watching a dozen more beheadings and feeling
somewhat uncomfortable witnessing such mass butchery,
Kanamoto avers that the constant shouts of jubilation from
watching marines mixed with ribald scorn as some prisoners
begged for their lives became too much for him.
Interrogation of Warrant Officer Keigo Kanamoto
Sugamo Prison, Tokyo, 1949

The Netherlands East Indies (NEI) was of vital significance to the
Japanese. A vast area encompassing most of present-day Indonesia,
the NEI contained huge oilfields located on the islands of Dutch
Borneo, Sumatra and Java. Japan needed Dutch oil to fuel its vast
war machine, and so after the conquests of British Malaya, Burma,
Hong Kong, the American-controlled Philippines and vast sections
of the Pacific, the second stage of the Japanese war plan was
directed against the NEI.

The Dutch had placed themselves on Japan's 'hit list' by siding
with the United States and Britain in imposing an oil embargo
against Japan in late 1941 in an effort to curb her warlike stance
towards South-East Asia, and to stop her war in China. It was
inevitable, however, that the Japanese military and naval war
machine was going to require Dutch oil, and the Japanese were in
no mood to trade with a country whose colony was militarily weak
and very difficult to defend, because of its size and geography,
especially from a determined enemy with naval and air superiority.

The Japanese Army and Navy would be able to achieve a swift
capture of the NEI for several important reasons that were not lost
on the Allied powers at the time. Firstly, the Netherlands had been
under German occupation since 1940, and the Dutch royal family

23

and government were in exile in London. Germany and Japan were allies, and the Germans had no immediate ability to assert control over the far-flung colonial possessions of occupied nations, such as France, Belgium and the Netherlands. A second factor was the Dutch forces defending the NEI, who were low in numbers and overwhelmingly consisted of native troops led by white officers. Thirdly, the Royal Netherlands Navy, although relatively strong in the Far East, was tiny when compared with the IJN, and quite outdated. Other factors in Japan's favour were the inability of the British and Americans to effectively assist their ally. United States forces were bottled up in the Bataan Peninsular and on Corregidor Island in the Philippines fighting for their lives with no hope of reinforcement or relief. British forces had surrendered at Singapore in February 1942 following the mismanaged and tragic campaign to defend the Malayan peninsula and its vital rubber industry, and what units that had managed to escape to Java in the NEI were worn out, demoralized and underequipped. The Royal Navy had virtually ceased to exist in the Far East after the battleship HMS *Prince of Wales* and the battlecruiser HMS *Repulse* had been lost to Japanese land-based bombers early on during the Malayan campaign. The US Navy was in no better shape following Pearl Harbor. Only the Australians were ready and willing to keep the Japanese away from their back door in Borneo, and veteran Australian troops on their way home from fighting the Germans and Italians in the Western Desert were diverted to Java to stiffen Allied resistance. Fresh, but untried, troops were also sent directly from Australia to various parts of the NEI.

The main target for the Japanese invasion of the NEI was the large island of Java. As well as being the headquarters of General Sir Archibald Wavell's ABDA (American, British, Dutch, and Australian) command, Java was also the seat of colonial government for the Dutch and home to the majority of the NEI's European population. If Java fell it would tear the heart out of the NEI, and the rest of the vast archipelago would collapse under Japanese military pressure. Defended by a mixed force of 30,000 Allied troops, and an unreliable locally raised Home Guard of 40,000 men, Allied air power on the island was extremely limited, although a mixed naval force of eight cruisers and sixteen destroyers in various states of repair or refit were available to launch a pre-emptive strike against the Japanese invasion force.

24

To Allied planners, the naval option appeared to be the best solution to preventing the Japanese from obtaining a foothold in the NEI, and so on 27 February a combined British-American-Dutch-Australian naval force attempted to intercept the Japanese Navy's eastern invasion convoy. The attempt went disastrously wrong when the Allied force instead clashed with the powerful Japanese covering force of battleships and heavy cruisers. Several Allied warships, including two Dutch cruisers, were lost in what was subsequently named the Battle of the Java Sea. What was left of the Allied naval force scattered, most units heading for Australia. Two heavy cruisers, the Australian HMAS *Perth* and the American USS *Houston*, made for Batavia but were both sunk when they stumbled into and attacked the Japanese western invasion convoy, heavily protected by another powerful covering group of warships. With the failure of the Allied combined naval operation to prevent the Japanese from landing, the defence of Java was militarily a lost cause. Battle-hardened Japanese troops, although outnumbered by the island's defenders, overcame confused Allied defensive strategies with ease after landing on 1 March. Java surrendered eight days later, and thousands more Allied soldiers were herded off to uncertain futures as prisoners of the Japanese.

A Dutch force consisting of a brigade group remained on the island of Sumatra, defending its northern provinces, and there were scattered Dutch units throughout the rest of the NEI, however they could do little but sit and await the arrival of strong Japanese ground forces. Imperial forces duly mopped up these pockets of resistance over the following weeks. Only one group managed to hold out. On the island of Timor, at the eastern end of the NEI island chain, a combined Australian and Dutch force continued sporadic resistance in the island's interior for over a year, fighting a guerrilla-style campaign against the Japanese occupiers until they were successfully withdrawn in early 1943. The Japanese completed the occupation of most of Timor by 20 February 1942, completely isolating Java. It was at this point that the remains of the region's Allied navies attempted to prevent a Japanese landing on Java as mentioned above. The battles of the Java Sea and Sunda Strait ended with Japanese victories, and Java's fate was sealed. The Japanese landed at three different points on the long island of Java and the understrength Allied troops were hard pressed to prevent them. Batavia was defended by a strong garrison, and a hastily constructed mobile strike group named 'Blackforce' moved to block the Japanese advance from the west. Everywhere else the Japanese brushed aside Allied resistance with relative ease. Blackforce was steadily pushed east and eventually cut off at Bandoeng. All Allied forces on Java surrendered to the Japanese on 8 March 1942.

Towards the white civilian populace of the NEI, the Japanese showed their usual contempt, murdering many for no apparent reason, and committing countless outrages against defenceless women and children. The civilians were interned in camps only slightly better than the conditions in prisoner-of-war camps, even though they were non-combatants and not a direct threat to the occupation forces. A horrific example of the attitude of the occupying Japanese towards local Dutch residents is demonstrated by the case of 21-year-old Jan O'Herne interned at Ambarara, Java, along with thousands of other white women and children. The Japanese decided to force some of the girls into becoming 'comfort women', a term they used for the enforced prostitution of local women throughout their conquered empire. The Dutch girls and young women would become sex slaves to provide amusement for Japanese officers. All girls aged seventeen and above were ordered to report for an inspection at the camp in February 1944. Seven girls, deemed the most attractive by the Japanese, were picked out from the group, told to pack, and were placed on a truck and driven to a large former Dutch residence in the town of Selarang. The house, known subsequently as the 'House of the Seven Seas', was a military brothel. O'Herne and her compatriots were to endure repeated rapes and beatings night and day at the hands of Japanese military and naval officers, and those girls who unfortunately became pregnant were also beaten until they suffered miscarriages. After four months of enduring continual sexual assault and violence at the hands of the Japanese – who in the words of Australian Army war crimes investigator Captain J.G. Godwin (who conducted the interrogations of naval personnel involved in the Laha Airfield Massacres recounted shortly), 'relished the opportunities to humiliate and ravish prisoners, particularly women and girls of European origin' – they were released back to their families. Warned that if they ever told anyone about what had been done to them both they and their families would be killed, the civilian internees were eventually released when Japan capitulated in mid-August 1945. The occupation of the NEI would also witness the Japanese Army and Navy brutalize and kill thousands of ordinary Indonesians and persons of mixed race. No one was exempt from the rapacious, and capricious, Japanese need to humiliate and often kill those peoples who were under their control.

One of the great mysteries of the Second World War unfolded at sea just as the Japanese were landing on Java. At the end of the war in 1945 the US Navy was unable to account for the disappearances of four of its destroyers. Listed as missing, presumed lost, the Navy simply had no idea what had happened to the vessels and their crews. One of these vessels was the rather elderly USS *Edsall*, the ship vanishing during operations off the island of Java in March 1942. It was 1952 before anguished relatives were first informed that a handful of crewmen's bodies had been discovered on Celebes Island in the NEI, and 1980 before the full story of the vessel's end came to light from Japanese sources. It was a story of great courage by the crew of the *Edsall*, who literally went down fighting against overwhelming odds, and of the murder of survivors from the gallant little ship by the Japanese.

The *Edsall* was a Clemson-class destroyer launched in 1920, an old four-stacker, 314.5 feet long, named for a gallant American seaman named Norman Edsall who had died attempting to save his wounded commander during a shore action on Samoa in 1899. Armed with 4-inch guns the vessel had served all over the world before the Second World War erupted in the Far East, serving with particular distinction off Turkey when they expelled Anatolian Greeks from Izmir in 1922. In 1925 the *Edsall* had joined the Asiatic Fleet, becoming a regular visitor to the Philippines, Hong Kong, Shanghai and Japan, helping to protect American interests up and down the China coast. When the Japanese bombed Pearl Harbor, the *Edsall* was based at Balikpapen, an oil port on the south-east coast of Dutch Borneo. With a British liaison officer aboard her, the *Edsall* was one of the ships that had searched for survivors from HMS *Prince of Wales* and *Repulse*, sunk by the Japanese on 10 December as they invaded Malaya.[1] The *Edsall*, under Lieutenant Commander J.J. Nix, sailed to Surabaya and joined a force led by the heavy cruiser USS *Houston* charged with escorting Allied supply ships into the northern Australian port of Darwin. It was whilst employed on this task that the *Edsall* participated in the sinking of the Japanese submarine I-124 on 20 January 1942, alongside Australian naval forces. Nix was awarded the Legion of Merit for this action.[2]

The *Edsall* was damaged on 19 February when one of her own depth charges exploded aboard her whilst she was conducting another anti-submarine attack. Leaking badly, the *Edsall* limped into Tjilatjap for repairs. She was a fast ship, capable of sprints of 35 knots, but the damage and hasty repairs cut her top speed which was ultimately to contribute to her demise at the hands of the Japanese.

Japanese forces were advancing rapidly through the Netherlands East Indies, with very little to stop them. The USS *Langley*, the US Navy's first aircraft carrier now converted into an aircraft transport ship, was loaded with thirty-two Curtiss P-40 Warhawk fighters from Australia and ordered to deliver them, along with their pilots, to Java in an effort to wrest back air supremacy from the Japanese. The *Edsall* and another destroyer, the USS *Whipple*, were assigned as escorts. The little flotilla of ships was spotted by the Japanese fleet on 27 February, and a strong aerial attack witnessed the *Langley* and all the precious aircraft destroyed by bombs. The two escorting destroyers saved 485 men from the *Langley*, and then finished off the historic ship with torpedoes and gunfire before rendezvousing with the oiler USS *Pecos* at Christmas Island. The survivors, except the thirty-two pilots, were offloaded onto to *Pecos*, the *Edsall* receiving instructions to take them to Tjilatjap where it was hoped aircraft would be waiting for them.

Nix set a course north towards Java, and that was the last anyone heard of the *Edsall* and her crew for ten years. The truth, when it began to surface in the early 1950s (and in detail in 1980) was an amazing story of a 'last stand' at sea. Japanese naval landing forces and Imperial Army troops had begun landing on the north coast of Java on 1 March, and it was clear that Allied resistance on the island would soon cease. The US Navy sent radio messages to its vessels at sea to turn around and rendezvous south of the island and then steam in company back to Australia. Nix evidently received these new instructions, for when the Japanese came upon his ship he was heading south. The Japanese were one step ahead of Allied naval forces, and Admiral Chuichi Nagumo and the Carrier Strike Force had entered the Indian Ocean to block any Allied naval withdrawal to Australia. Aside from the carriers *Soryu* and *Akagi*, Nagumo's force included the battlecruisers *Hiei* and *Karishima*, and the heavy cruisers *Tone* and *Chikuma*, a massively formidable fleet the Allies were incapable of matching.[3]

On the afternoon of 1 March, as Japanese troops waded ashore on Java, the *Tone* identified a lone warship 15 miles to the northeast of her. The *Chikuma* spotted the same vessel twelve minutes later, and both heavy cruisers soon identified the warship as an American vessel, probably a light cruiser or destroyer. Aboard the *Tone* officers were convinced from her silhouette that the ship on the horizon was an Omaha-class light cruiser. At 5.30pm the *Chikuma's* huge 8-inch guns opened fire at a range of 21,000 yards, the heavy shells screaming over the *Edsall* to fountain in the ocean all about her. In a display of supreme courage, and knowing that he had nowhere to run to, Nix turned his ship head-on to the *Chikuma* and began powering his vessel towards her until his own puny 4-inch guns were in range. It may also have been a ploy to frighten the larger Japanese ship off as the charging *Edsall* looked as though she was lining up for a torpedo attack. Both ship's failed to register a single hit with their guns, and Nix turned away. A rain squall came up, and Commander Nix used this, and a smoke-screen, to hide from the Japanese cruisers, the *Edsall* disappearing from view at 6.00pm.

The two battlecruisers *Hiei* and *Karishima* had now joined the hunt for the *Edsall*, but Nix tried to use his ship's greater manoeuvrability to outsmart the Japanese gunnery. Because the Japanese warships were firing at extreme range, Nix would have about one minute between observing the Japanese gun flashes on the horizon, and the shells actually arriving. By constantly changing his course and speed Nix hoped to save his ship and escape. The tactic worked for a while, as frustrated Japanese gunners aboard the *Hiei* and *Karishima* fired off 297 x 14-inch and 132 x 6-inch shells at the weaving *Edsall*, only scoring *one* hit. The gunners aboard the *Tone* and *Chikuma* were even worse shots, firing 844 x 8-inch and 62 x 5-inch shells, none of which struck the American ship.

A thoroughly annoyed Nagumo decided to change his tactics, and he ordered an air strike from the carrier *Soryu*, which launched nine dive-bombers, and the *Akagi*, which sent aloft a further eight. The aircraft soon made their presence felt, and between 6.27 and 6.50pm the *Edsall* was struck by several bombs that rendered her a blazing wreck. With a final effort, the *Edsall*'s bows were turned towards the rapidly advancing enemy, before the engines died and the ship was adrift. The Japanese, however, now closed in on the helpless ship and recommenced their gunnery from almost point-blank range. The *Chikuma* demolished the destroyer's bridge and blew off the ship's stern, which caused the *Edsall* to sink at 7.00pm, about 430 miles south of Java.

The *Edsall*'s normal complement was 101 officers and men, swollen by the addition of thirty-two pilots aboard her when she sank. It has been surmised that the vast majority of the crew were killed during the aerial assault and many more when the *Chikuma* came alongside and unleashed her massive firepower. Many would have drowned when the *Edsall* sank, but it stands to reason that a great many men probably made it into the water. Reports vary, but according to the log of the *Chikuma* she only rescued between five and eight survivors, leaving the others to their fate. Whether the Japanese followed their usual practice of machine-gunning other survivors is not known, but certainly some men were abandoned to lonely deaths in shark-infested waters as the Japanese force sailed away.

For those rescued by the Japanese, all of them were brutally in-terrogated aboard the *Chikuma* virtually as soon as they were clear of the water, as the Japanese showed no compassion to fellow sailors who had fought heroically against huge odds, beating infor-mation out of them with alacrity. The survivors gave their tormentors the name of their ship (which the Japanese entered as *Edosooru* in the ship's log), and also explained how Commander Nix had been able to outfox the combined firepower of two battle-cruisers and two heavy cruisers for over an hour. The prisoners were then corralled below in airless compartments along with twenty-five other prisoners, merchant seamen from a Dutch freighter sunk earlier, as the *Chikuma* sailed to Celebes Island in the NEI.

After their arrival at Kendari prisoner-of-war camp, the survivors from the *Edsall* disappeared. In 1952 a unit from the US Army War Graves Commission followed leads given to them by locals on Celebes, and they began excavations at the abandoned and overgrown Kendari camp. Gruesome discoveries were soon made by the army investigators, revealing a little more of the story of the *Edsall* survivors. An unmarked grave was discovered containing the decapitated bodies of five American sailors whose identity tags showed them to be crewmen from the *Edsall*. The bodies of Sidney Amory, J.R. Cameron, Horace Andrus, Larry Vandiver and Donald Watters lay piled on top of one another, evidence that the men had all been executed by beheading with swords. Nearby the army investigators discovered an even larger mass grave containing the decapitated bodies of the twenty-five Dutch seamen who had been held alongside the *Edsall* survivors aboard the *Chikuma*. Why the Americans and Dutch sailors were executed remains a mystery to this day, and perhaps more survivors' bodies have yet to be discovered at Kendari. The Japanese have remained tight-lipped about the details of the destruction of the gallant *Edsall* and its brave crew, but for a nation that inculcated its soldiers and sailors with the belief that true courage was fighting to the death, their harsh treatment of enemy sailors who had put up a terrific resistance virtually to the point of their own destruction was difficult to understand. One possible reason why the *Edsall* survivors were executed in such a ritualistic way probably stems from the loss of face Nagumo's fleet had suffered in attempting to sink one single little American destroyer. The IJN often took out its frustrations upon those enemy soldiers, sailors and airmen unfortunate enough to fall into its clutches.[4]

Back on land, the IJN was now in control of vast areas of the Netherlands East Indies. According to the investigations conducted before the Tokyo War Crimes Trials convened in 1946 the Japanese Navy was implicated in the murders of many Dutch prisoners of war before the butchery they committed on Ambon Island in February 1943. In March 1942 Dutch prisoners were gathered together at Kota Radja shortly after the fall of the NEI. They were loaded aboard sloops, which the IJN then towed out to sea. Once a considerable distance from the shore, the guards began shooting the bound Dutch prisoners, and throwing them dead or wounded into the sea where all of them perished. When Tarakan fell to Japanese forces in January 1942, local Dutch forces were herded aboard a Japanese light cruiser, which took them to the spot where a Japanese destroyer had been fired on during the battle. Japanese naval officers and NCOs then set about beheading the unfortunate prisoners and pitching their corpses overboard as 'punishment' for their earlier legal resistance to the Japanese invader. Beheading with swords was to become a common method of execution employed by the Japanese Navy, and was the sole method used during the horrific and extensive Laha Airfield Massacres of early 1943.

The big island of Ambon in the Moluccas was an important air and sea link between Australia, New Guinea and the northern NEI, and with this in mind the Australian and Dutch governments came to an agreement regarding its defence in 1941, a few months prior to the Japanese attack. An Australian infantry unit, the 2/21st Battalion, was dispatched direct to Ambon, numbering with attached anti-tank, engineer, medical and other supporting units 1,100 men, to assist a local Dutch garrison force numbering 2,600 men. In addition, the Australian government dispatched No. 2 Squadron, RAAF, a Lockheed Hudson bomber unit, to provide the Australian and Dutch defenders, known collectively as 'Gull Force', with some air cover. All of the troops were placed under a joint command headed by a Dutch army officer, Lieutenant Colonel J.R.L. Kapitz, with Australian army Lieutenant Colonel L.N. Roach as second-in-command.[5]

Colonel Roach, commanding the Australian forces, divided his men into two echelons, sending one to defend Laha Airfield (one of two airfields on Ambon, the other located at Liang), sited on the west side of the island. The second echelon was dispatched to dig in east of Ambon Bay, to the south of the main town of Ambon, where any Japanese landing was predicted to come ashore. When it appeared off the coast of the island, the Japanese Ambon invasion force consisted of the aircraft carriers *Hiryu* and *Soryu*, assorted escorting warships and about 5,300 Japanese troops consisting of sailors from the 1st Kure Special Naval Landing Force and Imperial Army troops of the 228th Infantry Regiment, which consisted of three battalions. From the beginning Roach had asked his government in Canberra for more artillery and machine-gun units, but Australian army headquarters ignored these requests. In fact, Roach made so many requests for more men and equipment in the face of a predicted Japanese invasion, even asking that if his men could not be reinforced they should be withdrawn to Australia, that he was removed from his command and sent home in disgrace having committed the cardinal sin of putting his men's lives ahead of political considerations. His replacement as second-in-command of Gull Force was a far more amenable 53-year-old staff officer named Lieutenant Colonel John Scott who arrived on 14 January

1942. This was an unfortunate appointment, because Roach was a far more competent and experienced officer than Scott. As Roach had warned, it soon became apparent that the Dutch and Australian troops of Gull Force were completely inadequate for the task that lay ahead of them, being too few in number and under-equipped to prevent the Japanese from conquering the island. It was exactly the same situation as that already faced by Lark Force on New Britain.

Colonel Scott reconfigured the island's defences. Ambon is shaped like an hourglass or figure of eight. With this geography in mind Scott believed that a Japanese landing would come in the north, for the south of the island was considered too inhospitable to make any attack a practical proposition. This was another error. The Japanese invasion began with a softening up of Ambon Island and its defenders with carrier-based aerial attacks and naval bombardments from cruisers and destroyers covering the carriers, preparatory to an amphibious assault. The Allied force's only air cover, No. 13 Squadron, was ordered to withdraw by command in Australia, and bereft of mastery of the skies the Dutch and Australians were hard pressed to prevent the Japanese landing on 29–30 January 1942. The main Japanese landings came in the south of the island, while all the Allied defences pointed north. After twenty-four hours ashore, Japanese naval landing troops and soldiers had managed to surround many of the Dutch positions, and Colonel Kapitz and his officers attempted to fight their way out of numerous encirclements and coalesce on Ambon City. An urban environment offered more chance of a static Dutch defence holding out until relieved, rather than being outmanoeuvred by rapid Japanese movements to flank them in the open countryside (a tactic the Japanese had already mastered fighting the British in Malaya).

But the Japanese were one step ahead of Allied defensive moves, and a second amphibious assault was launched from the task force, with several thousand more Japanese troops coming ashore in the north. The Allies had made plans to withdraw into the northern neck of the hourglass-shaped island, but this was dashed by the appearance of strong Japanese units behind them. The second echelon of Australian troops defending the eastern shore of Ambon Bay and the approaches to Ambon City were first engaged by the Japanese on 1 February. The story of Driver Thomas Doolan of the 2/21st Battalion exemplified the desperate fighting around the island's main settlement, and the bravery of the outnumbered Australian soldiers. Doolan was stationed at a large Australian food dump located at Kudmati on the town's outskirts. The arrival of the Japanese in force caused the Australian section covering the dump to withdraw back towards the town as they were heavily outnumbered and outgunned. Doolan, however, refused to leave, and all alone he decided to take on the Japanese single-handed. After concealing himself in some undergrowth, the plucky Doolan, armed with his Lee-Enfield rifle, a revolver and six hand grenades, engaged the first Japanese troops that advanced on the dump with a withering fire. A few days after the surrender, Australian prisoners discovered Doolan's body where he had fallen, fighting to the end, and in a rare display of respect the Japanese allowed the prisoners to give Doolan a proper Christian burial and to erect a wooden cross over his grave. Doolan's personal sacrifice probably appealed to the Japanese military spirit of holding a position until killed.

It was the turn of the Australian troops dug in around Laha Airfield (now bereft of any serviceable Allied aircraft) on the north-western shore of Ambon Bay under the command of Colonel Scott to receive the attentions of the Japanese. On 1 February the Japanese attacked, and during sporadic fighting fifteen Australians were killed and over thirty-five wounded. After two days of fighting Scott assessed the situation, coming to the conclusion that the tactical situation was now hopeless and he would be wasting his men's lives by continuing to defend an abandoned airfield. On 3 February Scott ordered *all* Allied troops, Australian and Dutch, to lay down their arms and surrender to the Japanese.[6]

Australian and Dutch resistance on Ambon therefore ended in an ignominious unconditional surrender. If the men had known what horrors awaited them at the hands of their Japanese captors it is probable that they would have fought to the end like Driver Doolan rather than have submitted themselves to a terrible captivity. By the end of the war in 1945 nearly 75 per cent of Gull Force had perished while prisoners of war. This astonishing figure includes over 300 Australian and Dutch soldiers who had been tasked with defending Laha Airfield, who were put to death by the Japanese Navy in an orgy of brutal and sadistic murder some time after their actual surrender. The Japanese then attempted to cover up what they had done with a wall of silence among themselves after the war, for we are only able to reconstruct the events at Laha from the interrogations of two Japanese who did talk to Australian Army investigators as not one of the 312 Australian and Dutch soldiers present lived to tell what happened.

Laha Airfield in February 1942 was garrisoned by the 1st Kure Special Naval Landing Force. Naval landing forces were the Japanese equivalent of the marines found in most other navies, though with some important differences. The Japanese Navy did not possess a force of naval infantry on a par with either the British Royal Marines or the US Marines. All navy personnel had received basic infantry training as part of their initial seamanship and trade courses before going to sea – Japanese sailors were expected to be proficient in the use of infantry weapons and to know simple battlefield tactics and formations. However, they remained primarily sailors and not sea soldiers. Up until the late 1920s, when the need arose, and particularly as the Navy was averse to using army troops due to a deep distrust between the two services, sections of a ship's company, or indeed an entire ship's complement, would be re-equipped with infantry weapons and steel helmets and sent ashore to perform a specific mission. This could be anything from engaging in a full-scale battle with enemy land forces to garrison duties in one of the many land locations under naval control throughout the empire. Using navy seamen directly off warships was not a satisfactory answer for the Imperial Navy's requirement for efficient and effective land forces.[7] To address the problem, from the late 1920s the IJN began forming so-called Special Naval Landing Forces (SNLF), basing their organization and training along army lines. Each unit was the equivalent of an army battalion in size and composition, and the four main naval bases in Japan at Kure, Maizuru, Sasebo and Yokosuka each raised several SNLF's that carried their name. Other SNLF were raised in China at Hankow (now Hankou) and Shanghai, as well as within the administrative region of the Kwantung Army, garrisoning the ports of Dairen and Ryojun. Each SNLF was between 650 and 1,200 men strong, and eventually the Imperial Navy created twenty-one of them. Because of their land-based role, the officers and sailors of an SNLF dressed in a version of the Imperial Army's uniform, but theirs was a much darker green and they used naval rank insignia as well as a fouled anchor badge on their steel helmets. Otherwise, they were equipped in the same fashion as Japanese soldiers, using the same infantry weapons, webbing and equipment though they were often seen sporting specially designed bullet-proof vests. A further difference from the Imperial Army was a lack of heavy weapons, such as tanks and artillery. An SNLF often was employed in conjunction with an army regiment, supported by army heavy equipment and weapons on operations.

The SNLF soon built a reputation for fearsome courage under fire and dogged determination. Known for their suicidal bravery, the SNLF often suffered very heavy casualties during battles with American forces. This was illustrated later in the war during the Battle of Tarawa in 1943 where the 7th Sasebo SNLF made a last stand against the invading US Marine Corps on the island. Almost the entire 1,500-man force was wiped out during the battle, but they managed to inflict over 3,000 casualties on the attacking US Marines in the process.[8]

Within the SNLF were units of infantry, as well as technical and construction personnel in special engineering and pioneer units, and the Navy's equivalent of the much-feared military police, the Tokei Tai. Some SNLF units also received parachute training. In fact, the Imperial Navy's parachute troops made more combat drops and saw more action than the Army's 1st Parachute Brigade. However, brave and resolute though the SNLF were, they shared in common with their army colleagues a complete lack of respect for their enemies, and the reputation of the Imperial Navy's 'marines' was to be stained with the blood of countless victims of the war crimes they perpetrated throughout South-East Asia and the Pacific, from the island of Ambon in 1942 to the streets of Manila in 1945.

In February 1942 preparations were under way on Ambon to kill all of the Australian and Dutch prisoners who the Japanese had captured defending the airfield during the invasion. According to the interrogation of Rear Admiral Koichiro Hatakeyama, the commanding officer of the 24th Naval Base Special Force, he ordered his namesake, Captain Kunito Hatakeyama, commander of Combined Forces, to execute all Allied prisoners of war on the island's Hitoe Peninsula. Captain Hatakeyama in turn ordered Lieutenant Nakagawa to conduct the actual killings using men from his 1st Kure Special Naval Landing Force.

The first group selected was forty-six prisoners led by Major

Newbury of the Australian 2/21st Battalion, and a working party had moved to a quiet location in woods on the edge of the airfield in preparation for this group's 'disposal'. Two large circular pits had been dug, each 6 metres in diameter and approximately 3 metres deep. Testimony of what occurred there on the evening of 6 February comes from the post-war interrogation of IJN interpreter Suburo Yoshizaki.[9]

The naval personnel who would conduct the executions had all willingly volunteered for the task. The sailors involved in the first massacre of Major Newbury and his men numbered about forty, under the command of Lieutenant Nakagawa and Warrant Officer Yamashita. A 25-man detachment came from the Yamashita Shotai Platoon and another fifteen from the Yoshiwara Shotai Platoon; the motive given to Australian investigators for the killings was established 'to be revenge for the death of members of SASHEO Units killed in LAWA River Battle, in particular WO [Warrant Officer] Yoshiwara [during the Battle of Ambon].'[10]

Yoshizaki had left his barracks in company with another interpreter, Terada Okada, and Petty Officer 1st Class Tasuki Yamashita, and together they walked to the execution ground. Standing around the edges of the pits were one or two naval officers and about twenty enlisted men of various ranks. Although both Yoshizaki and Okada were technically civilians, they wore officer's uniforms minus badges of rank, and each carried a sword. Before the executions commenced an enlisted man walked over to them and asked to borrow a sword. Yoshizaki lent the man his, and the sailor thanked him and returned to the pits. Yoshizaki missed the earlier executions of Major Newberry and his men, but he did witness the second execution of the night, when a second group of prisoners consisting of Wing Commander Scott and personnel of the RAAF, Australian army troops and Dutch soldiers totalling fifty-nine men were beheaded. It is believed that Captain Hatakeyama was also present, but the actual execution party was commanded by Warrant Officer Kakitaro Sasaki, officer commanding Machine Gun Company No. 1 of the Kure Special Naval Landing Force.[11] It is likely that Flying Officer William White was among the RAAF personnel about to be killed. White, a Hudson pilot with No. 2 Squadron, had been stranded on Laha Airfield when his unit had withdrawn after his aircraft had sustained serious damage on 20 January. As the military situation deteriorated around the airfield, defended by Colonel Scott's first echelon of 2/21st Battalion, White and ten other RAAF personnel had decided to get off Ambon altogether rather than become prisoners of the Japanese. The party set off in a requisitioned boat across the narrow straits that separated Ambon from Ceram Island to the north-west, where arrangements had been made for their rescue by an RAAF aircraft. Unfortunately White's boat was intercepted by a Japanese patrol vessel, and all the airmen were made prisoners. Hauled back to Ambon, White and his comrades were all beheaded at one of the executions that took place at Laha Airfield. It was no understatement that the secretary who informed White's mother of her son's fate in 1946 wrote that the pilot had 'died in circumstances which are an affront to civilization'.[12] William White, although he never knew it, was posthumously awarded the Distinguished Flying Cross for his daring and skill during the aerial battle of Ambon, the medal being presented to his mother after the war, along with the terrible news of her son's pointless murder.

The first prisoner, an Australian, was led forward to the edge of one of the pits and he was forced to his knees and his head was pushed down exposing his neck. His uniform was tattered and dirty, and he was shaking with fear, his arms securely bound behind his back. Warrant Officer Sasaki stood behind and to the left of the prisoner and slowly raised his *katana* samurai sword high over his head, both hands gripping the hilt. Silence descended among the onlookers, and then Sasaki brought the blade down swiftly, severing the Australian's head from his body. The head rolled into the pit, and as arterial blood pumped in a shower from the corpse, other Japanese sailors pushed the still twitching body over the edge of the hole. A great cry went up from the Japanese sailors, demonstrating admiration for Sasaki's skill. For the bound prisoners waiting further back in the woods under a heavy guard who had just seen their own fate played out before them, the mental anguish these men suffered is impossible to imagine. There was nowhere to run to, the Japanese would not listen to reason and exhibited no compassion whatsoever for the sufferings they were inflicting upon helpless men. All would react in different ways when their turn came to be led away like animals to be slaughtered, and Japanese witnesses remembered how many had understandably cried out or pleaded for mercy. Others were probably so overcome by fear and despair that they said little, while many would have been crying for mothers, wives and children they would never see again; others accepted their fate with stolid silence. Many would have prayed, together and individually, and said their goodbyes to their brothers-in-arms.

As soon as Sasaki had beheaded the first prisoner, another was dragged forward and forced into position by the Japanese guards. Sasaki dispatched four prisoners in quick succession, and then the ordinary sailors who were queuing up eagerly around the pit clutching borrowed swords came forward one by one to commit murder. After each decapitation, the sword blade was carefully wiped clean of blood and the weapon was passed to others waiting their turn, as the sailors laughed and joked with each other, and coached one another on the correct way to hold the sword and make the cut. With the light fast fading from the sky, battery-powered torches were broken out, and the beams used to illuminate the necks of successive victims. Most of the common sailors knew little of swords and the correct methods for using them so that many of the executions were terribly botched. For the prisoners awaiting a quick death their agonies were multiplied by these incompetent swordsmen who slashed at necks and often failed to decapitate their victim cleanly on the first cut. Some unfortunate prisoners, according to Yoshizaki, were pushed into the pits while they were still alive, slowly bleeding to death from botched sword cuts across their necks, heads and shoulders.

The interpreter's sword was later returned to him by the young sailor, who commented that it was now blunt, and that the blade was slightly bent after the decapitation of a 'giant of a fellow'. Yoshizaki and his companions left the scene of the executions before the completion of the massacre and walked back to their barracks. By the end of the night all 105 Australian and Dutch prisoners were dead and the pits were covered over with earth. The methodical executions were to presage a much bigger massacre perpetrated against Allied prisoners later that month, also on the edge of the same airfield.

Evidence of what occurred during the second execution conducted on the night of 24/25 February is chiefly derived from the interrogation report of Warrant Officer Keigo Kanamoto, officer commanding 'L' Repair and Construction Unit, which was part of the Kure No. 1 Special Naval Landing Party.[13] Kanamoto's unit was stationed close to Laha Airfield at Victoria Barracks. On 24 February, he was informed that approximately 220 Australian and Dutch prisoners of war would be put to death that night, or 'punished' as the Japanese commanders termed it. The executions were scheduled to commence at 6.00pm, and being interested in watching Kanamoto decided to attend. He took along with him two enlisted volunteers, Seamen 1st Class Teruji Ikezawa and Shikao Nakamura.

When Kanamoto and his companions arrived at the execution ground it was dark, and the slaughter was already well underway. Once again a working party had dug two large circular pits about 5 metres apart that would serve as mass graves. Several large bonfires had been lit, flames dancing among the trees and across the terrified faces of the prisoners standing under guard close by, waiting to be led to the edge of the pits. This vision of Hell was completed by the impish men with swords who stood gathered around one of the pits, chatting and laughing as successive prisoners met their end kneeling in their comrades' blood. Around thirty Japanese sailors of various ranks were doing all the killing, and Kanamoto watched, fascinated, as a young Australian, his arms bound, was dragged kicking and screaming to the edge of the pit and roughly forced into the execution position. The sailors laughed at the Australian's pleadings, but silence soon returned when his head was severed and his crumpled body was kicked into the hole. Within seconds another prisoner had been decapitated on the opposite side of the pit. Once again, torches were shone on the exposed necks of the victims as the light from the bonfires was not strong enough.

After he had watched his colleagues kill twenty Allied prisoners, curiosity impelled Kanamoto to step forward to peer into the execution pit. What he saw disturbed him, and according to his post-war interrogation report: 'Some corpses were headless but several bodies with heads half-attached were jerking feebly and making faint gurgling moans.'[14] Captain J.G. Godwin, Investigating Officer of the 2nd Australian War Crimes Section, recorded in 1949 that 'Kanamoto avers that a feeling of revulsion mixed with pity swept over him, but he could not interfere in the punishments that had been ordered by the Japanese High Command in the area.'[15]

The reason why these Australian and Dutch prisoners were being killed has never been fully established. The Japanese who were interrogated said it was because a Japanese minesweeper had been sunk in Ambon Bay after running over an Allied mine, and the crew was permitted to take their revenge against local prisoners of war. Certainly, Kanamoto commented that most of the executioners that night were crew of the sunken minesweeper. Post-war Australian investigations have established that a party of at least 100 Japanese sailors from a minesweeper under the command of Sub Lieutenant Fukuda, acting on direct orders received from Admiral Hatakeyama, acted as the executioners.[16] As mentioned, the Japanese Navy used the term 'punishment' in place of 'execution' when referring to what occurred at Laha Airfield. They punished the prisoners by transposing responsibility for the destruction of their minesweeper onto them. In this case, 'punishment' entailed mass murder.

Many of the Japanese present that night may very well have been revolted or upset by what they were ordered to do, and what their comrades were willingly doing all around them. Certainly, this was a line taken by several Japanese who were carefully interrogated later by Australian investigators. It was fair also to assume that due to the levity, banter and ribald comments constantly being made by the Japanese taking part in or watching the executions, most were not viewing their victims as human beings, but as playthings in what was degenerating into a twisted form of sport. Kanamoto, whether he was genuine or not (and Captain Godwin harboured doubts about Kanamoto's claim that he did not participate in the executions), was right in his assertion that he felt unable to speak out and put a stop to the massacre. The Japanese military culture of total obedience of a superior's orders, regardless of their nature, was deeply instilled in every Japanese soldier and sailor. In a culture that glorified sacrificial death for the Emperor and castigated surrender as dishonourable, prisoners of war were nonentities. The Japanese group ethic, which dominated (and still largely dominates) all aspects of life meant it was social suicide to stand outside of the group and challenge the legitimate authority of one's superiors. Such a stance was unforgivable and rarely did a Japanese soldier or sailor dishonour himself or his family by an exhibition of what might well be termed 'disloyalty' by his masters.

When approximately forty executions had occurred Seaman 1st Class Nakamura could no longer restrain himself by merely watching the proceedings and at his urgings Kanamoto lent him his sword. Nakamura beheaded four Dutch prisoners in rapid succession, and then he passed the weapon to Seaman 1st Class Ikezawa. This sailor cut the heads off three Australians and then in turn passed the sword along the line to others of his comrades who were awaiting their turn. Kanamoto's sword was used to kill three more prisoners, but the final execution was botched. A sailor struck a prisoner twice with the sword before decapitating him, and the second blow produced a strange sound and sparks. When Kanamoto recovered his sword and examined it by torchlight, he found that there were nicks in the blade and the weapon was slightly bent.

Kanamoto watched as the executioners continued their work. The shouts of jubilation, as Kanamoto described them, made by the sailors and their ribald comments when prisoners begged for their lives, apparently disturbed him. He and his companions eventually left the scene, and although Kanamoto told other comrades that he had decapitated prisoners, he said he made these claims in order to save 'face'. By any account the executions were completed by 1.30am on 25 February, and 227 headless corpses lay piled inside their earthen graves. The pits were filled in and the Japanese sailors returned to their normal duties about the airfield.

Many Australian prisoners were spared being massacred at Laha Airfield, but ended up dying anyway. Herded into unsanitary prison camps at Ambon, they were transported to the island of Hainan in China, but at both locations they were worked as slaves, exposed to every tropical disease in the book, barely fed and routinely abused by their sadistic captors. On 25 October Colonel Scott and 500 Australian and Dutch prisoners had been herded into the bowels of the 'Hell Ship' *Taiko Maru* and transported to Hainan. Scott proved to be singularly unpopular amongst the prisoners, largely because he bizarrely enforced Japanese-style punishments against prisoners over matters of discipline, instead of King's Regulations. As Dr Peter Stanley of the Australian War Memorial has remarked of the whole sorry Ambon affair, 'Three-quarters of the Australians captured on Ambon died before the war's end. Of the 582 who remained on Ambon 405 died.'

In 1946 the largest of the Second World War's war crimes trials was convened by the Australian government on Ambon, its purpose to bring to trial those responsible for the Laha Airfield massacres. Ninety-three former Japanese naval personnel were arraigned and placed on trial for their lives. Many were convicted and four Japanese were sentenced to death for their parts in the massacres. Rear Admiral Koichiro Hatakeyama was charged with having ordered both massacres of Australian and Dutch soldiers at Laha Airfield in 1942 – he would undoubtedly have been found guilty and sentenced to death. Unfortunately, he managed to cheat the hangman as he died before his trial could begin. Captain Kunito Hatakeyama, the naval officer who had directly commanded both of the massacres, was found guilty and hanged. But, as in so many other similar cases across Asia and the Pacific, the great majority of the murderers, those enlisted men and NCOs who had wielded the swords, were never brought to account for their actions and they escaped justice completely.

Notes

1. *Dictionary of American Naval Fighting Ships*, vol. II (US Naval Historical Center, 1963), pp. 327–8.
2. Full details of this action can be found in the author's *The Fujita Plan: Japanese Attacks on the United States and Australia during the Second World War* (Pen & Sword Maritime, 2006).
3. *Dictionary of American Naval Fighting Ships Online (DANFS)*, http://www.hazegray.org/danfs/destroy/dd219txt.htm.
4. 'Two Mysteries of the Edsall', USS *Edsall*, 'Josh', DD-219, http://www.geocities.com/CapeCanaveral/Galaxy/3070/jjedsall.htm.
5. Beaumont, Joan, *Gull Force: Survival and Leadership in Captivity 1941–1945* (Allen & Unwin, 1988).
6. Harrison, Courtney T., *Ambon Island of Mist: 2/21st Battalion AIF (Gull Force): Prisoners of War 1941–45* (T.W. & C.T. Harrison, 1989).
7. Nila, Gary, *Japanese Special Naval Landing Forces: Uniforms and Equipment 1932–1945* (Men-at-Arms, Osprey, 2006), pp. 4–5.
8. Ibid., pp. 6–12.
9. Executions of Australian and Dutch POWs, Laha Airfield, Ambon Island, February 1942, 'Interrogation report of Yoshizaki, Saburo', File 85H. 851, 85K, 2nd Australian War Crimes Section, 1949.
10. Summary of Japanese massacres of Australian POWs in Ambon 6–20 February 1942, NAA A 705/15 Item 166/43/989 (Australian War Memorial).
11. Ibid.
12. Official Notification of the death of F/O William White DFC, 28 June 1946, NAA A705/15 Item 166/43/989, (Australian War Memorial).

13. Executions of Australian and Dutch POWs, Laha Airfield Ambon 1942. Continuation of investigating a second massacre, 'Interrogation report of Kanamoto, Yoshizaki', File 85H. 851, 2nd Australian War Crimes Section, 1949.
14. Ibid.
15. Ibid.
16. 'Summary of Japanese massacres of Australian POWs in Ambon 6–20 February 1942', NAA A 705/15 Item 166/43/989 (Australian War Memorial).

Chapter Four

In Enemy Hands: The Midway Pilots

After attacking Midway by air and destroying the enemy's shore based air strength to facilitate our landing operations, we would still be able to destroy any enemy task force which may choose to counter attack.
Admiral Chuichi Nagumo, Strike Force
Commander at Midway 1942

The Battle of Midway on 5 June 1942 would end with Japan's vaunted carrier fleet in ruins, and Japan placed on the defensive at sea. It was also one of the Second World War's three great turning points. The other two were the British defeat of Rommel's Afrika Korps at the Battle of El Alamein, also in 1942, and the Soviet victory over the German 6th Army at Stalingrad in 1943. Only half a year before Midway, the US Pacific Fleet had been devastated by the stunning Japanese carrier strike against Pearl Harbor, masterminded by Admiral Yamamoto. Although the Japanese had inflicted serious damage on the American battleship fleet, Yamamoto's pilots had failed to locate and destroy the American aircraft carriers, which even at that stage of the war were the key to naval supremacy in the Pacific. For the Japanese it meant that they would eventually have to deal with those carriers in a major fleet engagement, and failure to destroy them a second time would mean that Japan would be thrown on the defensive in the Pacific theatre.

The Japanese decided to take the initiative and place the American carriers in a position from where they could be destroyed. Central to their plan was an attack on Midway Island, a lonely American outpost in the mid-Pacific, to provide a lure that the American carrier fleet commanders could not resist reacting to. A Japanese victory would secure them naval supremacy until at least late 1943 and push Japan's defensive perimeter still further from the Home Islands. As it happened, American penetration of Japan's naval codes enabled Admiral Chester Nimitz to trap the Japanese Fleet instead.

Midway was the battle that decided who would ultimately win in the Pacific, and it was the first carrier-versus-carrier battle in history, where none of the ships of the two great fleets sighted each other. The American aircraft carriers USS *Enterprise*, *Yorktown* and *Hornet* faced a much larger Japanese fleet consisting of the carriers *Soryu*, *Akagi*, *Kaga* and *Hiryu* close to Midway Island. The fate of American aircrew who were shot down during the terrific air battle to destroy these carriers, and were captured by the Japanese, only came to light after the war, when the US Navy obtained a copy of Vice Admiral Chuichi Nagumo's Japanese fleet action report.[1] The fates of three men in particular caused the Americans to launch an investigation into possible war crimes having been committed against prisoners of war.

The first story concerns a young American naval aviator who was part of a torpedo-bomber attack on the Japanese carrier force on the morning of 5 June. The torpedo-bomber squadrons suffered the heaviest casualties as they launched virtually suicidal attacks on the Japanese carriers through swarms of enemy fighters and clouds of flak – of forty-one Douglas TBD-1 Devastators that took off on these missions, thirty-seven were shot down. The story of one squadron's battle showed how savage the fighting became and how the Japanese were ill-disposed to grant downed airmen any quarter. Twelve Devastators of US Navy Squadron VT-3 lumbered into the air off the deck of the *Yorktown* and headed for the last reported position of the enemy's carriers. Led by Lieutenant Commander Lance E. Massey, the last aircraft in the formation was piloted by Ensign Wesley Osmus. Osmus, sitting in front of his radio operator/gunner Benjamin R. Dodson, Jr., was in the most vulnerable position, effectively the formation's 'tail-end Charlie'. Osmus had enlisted in the US Naval Reserve in 1940, and this was his first experience of combat.

When VT-3 was 14 miles from their target, the squadron was pounced on by defending Japanese Zero fighters. The Zero's came in behind the Devastators, and although the rear gunners did what they could to try to force them off, it was an unequal fight. According to Osmus's Navy Cross citation:

> Participating in a torpedo plane assault against Japanese naval units, Ensign Osmus, in the face of tremendous anti-aircraft fire and overwhelming fighter opposition, pressed home his attack to a point where it became relatively certain that, in order to accomplish his mission, he would probably sacrifice his life. Undeterred by the grave possibilities of such a hazardous offensive, he carried on, with extreme disregard for his own personal safety, until his squadron scored direct hits on two enemy aircraft carriers.

Shortly after unloading his munitions, Osmus's plane took a burst of Zero cannon fire that killed or badly wounded Dodson, and seconds later the plane's fuel tanks exploded. Osmus unclipped his safety harness and baled out after desperately attempting to get a response from Dodson over the plane's intercom. After jumping clear Osmus watched the burning Devastator as it spiralled away into the Pacific like a huge torch. Osmus floated gently down to the ocean, and once in the water he quickly divested himself of his chute and inflated his lifejacket. He also deployed his emergency life raft and clambered aboard it to await an uncertain rescue.

Unfortunately for the young American airman, he was picked up by the Japanese destroyer *Arashi*, part of Rear Admiral Kimura's Destroyer Division 4, providing an advanced screening force ahead of the main Japanese fleet.[2] Hauled aboard and immediately stripped of his flying equipment, pistol and lifejacket, the young American pilot was taken before the skipper for questioning. At this stage of the battle, with the carrier *Akagi* already ablaze, suspicion was mounting in the Japanese camp as to how many American carriers they were actually facing. Commander Yasumasa Watanabe threatened Osmus with his sword, demanding intelligence on the location, names and numbers of American ships, and promising dire consequences if the pilot refused to talk. Faced with continual slaps and the threat of beheading, Osmus told the Japanese that they were up against the carriers *Yorktown*, *Enterprise* and *Hornet*. This information was immediately sent by Morse lamp to the carrier *Hiryu*. Osmus, believing that his cooperation under extreme duress had probably bought him his life did not realize that as far as Watanabe was concerned the terrified young man was now surplus to requirements, and even though he should have been taken prisoner and treated decently, Watanabe later ordered his execution. Chief Warrant Officer Sato was instructed to carry out this order, and gathering some of his men, they dragged the confused and frightened American towards the destroyer's stern, one of them ominously carrying a fire axe. Roughly ordered to face astern, a Japanese sailor swung the axe at Osmus's neck, but failed to decapitate him with the blow. The axe cut knocked Osmus partly over the ship's rail, but, although in agony he managed to catch hold of the chain railing and clung on desperately, swinging about above the churning propellers as the *Arashi* made way. The axe-wielding Japanese struck Osmus again with the blade, and dead or critically injured, the American pilot fell into the destroyer's wake and disappeared.[3] This war crime remained unpunished, and not a single member of the crew of the *Arashi* was ever brought before a military court for the murder of Ensign Osmus. Most of the Japanese involved in the atrocity perished later in the war, and so building a case was impossible. Osmus, however, was honoured by his country. On 4 November 1943 the destroyer escort USS *Osmus* was launched in Bay City, Michigan, and the Ensign was posthumously awarded the Navy Cross, Purple Heart and the American Defense Medal for his courage in pressing home his aerial assault on the Japanese carriers.

Flying off the USS *Enterprise* Lieutenant Commander C. Wade McClusky led thirty Douglas SBD-3 Dauntless dive-bombers on a mission that would ultimately lead to the destruction of the Japanese aircraft carriers *Akagi* and *Kaga*. The air over the two carriers, which were soon an inferno following McClusky's successful strike, was thick with American and Japanese planes. Dauntless dive-bombers were milling around over the target, many of the pilots 'rookies' who were looking to more experienced aviators to lead them back to the *Enterprise*. Japanese Zero fighters attempted to wreak their revenge for the American success. One of the experienced American pilots was Lieutenant Charles Ware and he managed to gather together five other aircraft into an ad hoc group, ordering them to close up and descend to sea level for the return flight to the *Enterprise*. Zero fighters trailed them away from

48

the burning carriers, making strafing attacks from behind, and Wade ordered the gunners in his formation to concentrate the fire of their twin .30 calibre machine guns on each Zero as it made its attack pass. This tactic prevented the Japanese from causing serious damage to the aircraft, with the exception of the Dauntless flown by Ensign Frank W. O'Flaherty. Japanese bullets damaged O'Flaherty's fuel tanks, and as all the American aircraft were already short of fuel after a long mission against the carriers, the situation became critical for the young pilot.

Ware's formation managed to extricate itself from the Japanese defensive screen and headed off north-east where they hoped to find the *Enterprise*. Unfortunately, the American aircraft were spotted by a formation of Aichi Val dive-bombers from the carrier *Hiryu*, escorted by six Zeros. The Japanese fighters immediately broke away from the dive-bombers and pounced on Ware and his comrades, thinking they were easy pickings. Ware ordered his men into the same formation they had used to beat off the earlier Zero attacks above the carriers, but just before the Japanese fighters were upon them, Ensign O'Flaherty radioed Ware that he was out of fuel and was going to ditch in the ocean. There was nothing anyone could do except watch as O'Flaherty took the Dauntless down to wave-top level and gently belly-flopped his aircraft into the sea. O'Flaherty and his gunner, Bruno Gaido, were observed clambering out of the cockpit before the plane sank beneath them, and they took to their tiny inflatable rubber life raft.

O'Flaherty and Gaido listened as the sounds of battle and aircraft engines retreated into the distance, until they were alone on the expanse of ocean. Rescue, when it came, was to prove their demise. The Japanese destroyer *Makigumo* hove to and the two airmen were hauled aboard to a hostile reception. By now, both sides knew that the Japanese were reeling from a crushing defeat and the sailors were in an ugly mood. Stripped of their equipment, the two Americans were interrogated savagely by vengeful Japanese. Both men were subsequently murdered as an act of revenge for the American victory on the orders of the captain of the *Makigumo*. Undoubtedly, O'Flaherty especially would have been in the possession of some minor tactical information that was probably either beaten or threatened out of him before the Japanese decided to dispose of their prisoners. O'Flaherty and Gaido were both bound with stout ropes, to which weighted fuel cans were tied. Not even having the decency to grant their opponents a quick death by shooting them, the Japanese captain ordered the Americans, so tied, to be dumped overboard by the crew. Amid shouts for mercy and pleading for their lives, O'Flaherty and Gaido were thrown from the destroyer's stern, and immediately disappeared beneath the waves to suffer a horrible death by drowning.

Lieutenant Ware and the remaining aircraft of his formation managed to beat off the Zero attacks, with two of the enemy fighters limping off towards the *Hiryu*, and the other four unable to catch up with the Val dive-bombers that they were supposed to escort. When the Vals launched their attack on the USS *Yorktown*, all except one would fall victim to American anti-aircraft fire or fighters.[4] Ware and the others were lost, for they did not know the exact location of the *Enterprise*, and their fuel situation was becoming more precarious by the minute. Ensign McCarthy radioed Ware that he was going alone on a different course to try to find the American fleet, and Ware wished him good luck. The other rookie pilots decided to stay close to Ware, which proved to be a tragic mistake. The four Dauntless dive-bombers ran out of fuel somewhere out in the empty Pacific, and they all undoubtedly ended up ditching in the sea and their crews taking to life rafts. None of the eight men was ever heard from again, dying lonely deaths far out at sea. Ensign McCarthy was the only one who would make it – and only just as it turned out. Critically low on fuel, McCarthy picked up the homing beacon signal of the USS *Yorktown*, which brought him to the edge of the American fleet. Out of fuel, he crash-landed his plane in the sea, and he and his gunner were rescued by the destroyer USS *Hammann*.

The murderers of O'Flaherty and Gaido were never brought to trial, as the destroyer *Makigumo* struck a mine during operations off Guadalcanal in 1943 and was lost. Perhaps other American pilots and aircrew were also picked up by Japanese destroyers screening the Combined Fleet during the Midway battle, but if they were none lived to tell the tale. The summary, and unnecessarily cruel, executions of Osmus, O'Flaherty and Gaido demonstrated the dishonourable attitude of the Imperial Navy towards its opponents in war, and stood in stark contrast to the treatment of Japanese aircrew who became prisoners of the United States, who afforded them prisoner-of-war status. The full impotent rage and vindictive revenge of Japanese officers who keenly felt their nation's defeat at sea was channelled into the decisions to kill the airmen, perhaps to assuage their own sense of shame in losing the battle upon which Japan had pinned so many of her hopes.

Notes

1. Parshall, Jonathan and Tully, Anthony, *Shattered Sword: The Japanese Story of the Battle of Midway* (Potomac Books Inc., 2006).
2. 'The Japanese Story of the Battle of Midway', ONI Review (Office of Naval Intelligence), 1947.
3. War Crimes Committed by the Imperial Japanese Navy, 'Murder of American Pilots and Aircrew at Midway', http://www.users. bigpond.com/battleforaustralia/JapWarCrimes/TenWarCrimes/War Crimes Jap Navy.html.
4. 'The Japanese Story of the Battle of Midway', ONI Review (Office of Naval Intelligence), 1947.

Chapter Five

Out of Bounds:
Attacks on Hospital Ships

Merle Morton and myself [Savage] were awakened by two
terrific explosions and practically thrown out of bed . . . I
registered mentally that it was a torpedo explosion.

Sister Ellen Savage GM
Australian Hospital Ship Centaur

The port of Darwin in northern Australia assumed strategic importance in the Allied war effort in early 1942. Even before the
commencement of the great sweeping Japanese offensives of
December 1941, which would witness Japan extending its control
almost to the borders of Australia, military planners in Canberra
had realized that in the coming conflict Darwin's airfields and port
facilities would be vital in supplying Australian forces assisting the
Dutch in the defence of the Netherlands East Indies. As we have
seen, Australian troops and RAAF squadrons were already in place
on Java, Timor and Ambon. Later, after these locations had fallen
to the enemy, Darwin's position became even more exposed and
important as the Japanese attempted to invest New Guinea, just a
stone's throw across the Arafura Sea from northern Australia.

The Japanese were also quick to realize the necessity of neutralizing Darwin during their attacks on the Netherlands East Indies.
The Japanese never seriously contemplated invading Australia
(contrary to urban myth), but Darwin, ringed by airfields, and
providing a staging point for supply vessels and warships safe in
the port, had to be targeted. The Japanese would choose air power
to do the job, and it was decided to subject Darwin and several
other northern towns to a series of hard-hitting air raids designed

to wear down Australian offensive capacity and hopefully also lower civilian morale.

The Australians had already taken measures to beef up Darwin's defences before the Japanese arrived, but they lacked the necessary equipment, particularly modern fighter aircraft, to entirely discourage a Japanese attack. The army formed the Darwin Mobile Force, large numbers of anti-aircraft batteries being emplaced around the town and the airfields. The RAAF did what it could and sent north some medium bomber and reconnaissance squadrons, but it could not spare any fighters. This mistake would mean that the Japanese Navy would have immediate air superiority over their targets. The Royal Australian Navy (RAN) strung a huge anti-submarine boom across Darwin's outer harbour to protect merchantmen and warships regularly using the port, and also increased the number of patrol vessels along the harbour approaches. The RAN also established a shore base and long-range wireless station in the hope of detecting incoming Japanese air raids. Australia did what it could to defend Darwin without stripping the defences of Sydney and Melbourne further south, but when the Japanese came it was still an attack of unexpected strength and ferocity that devastated the town.

As related, by 19 February 1942, Australian and Dutch forces on Ambon had surrendered after a short battle, overwhelmed by the enemy's numerical superiority and air power. Australian forces out of Darwin might yet interfere with Japan's invasions of Java and Timor, so a task force of aircraft carriers was dispatched into the Arafura Sea with orders to attack the Australian port and town that day. In the crowded harbour there were forty-seven Allied merchant and warships riding at anchor, including the Australian hospital ship *Manunda*. In a classic case of underestimating one's opponent, the military authorities in Darwin disregarded reliable intelligence reports from coast watchers on outlying islands who reported an incoming Japanese air raid until the enemy's aircraft were actually over the town. In forty-two minutes of mayhem, IJN carrier bombers and fighters managed to sink three Allied warships and five merchant ships inside the harbour, and inflict serious damage to a further ten vessels. Because most people, both military and civilian personnel, had virtually no warning of the impending attack until the first bombs started to fall, thousands of them were caught in the open by the Japanese assault. Bombs fell not only on the ships in the harbour, but plunged into the wharves and residential areas around the docks. This first raid was intended to disrupt the harbour, and the Japanese succeeded in killing 280 people before they turned back for their carriers.[1]

HMAHS *Manunda* had been commissioned as a hospital ship into the Royal Australian Navy in July 1940, with Captain James Garden as master. Between November 1940 and September 1941 the big white-painted liner, with its distinctive large red crosses, had made four trips to the Middle East in support of Australian troops fighting in the Western Desert. On 7 January 1942 the *Manunda* had left Darling Harbour, Sydney and arrived at Darwin a week later. For five weeks the ship had sat in port, conducting training exercises and normal duties with nursing orderlies aboard. Medical staff had also been ashore to local hospitals, and everyone was stunned when news reached them that Singapore had fallen to the Japanese on 15 February.

At 10.00am on Thursday, 19 February nurses were undergoing an examination aboard the *Manunda* when air raid sirens began to wail across Darwin harbour. Men and women rushed to don steel helmets and collect gas masks, but already in the background the crump of exploding Japanese bombs signalled that this was no drill. During the air raid recounted above one Japanese bomb narrowly missed the *Manunda*, but white hot shards of shrapnel flayed her decks, killing several people. A second bomb missed the bridge, but impacted on B and C decks, causing extensive injuries amongst medical staff, as well as damaging the ship. Fire broke out aboard the hospital ship, and the doctors and nurses quarters were soon ablaze. However, throughout the confusion and carnage of the attack the army medical personnel continued to perform their duties, even launching lifeboats so they could go to the aid of injured aboard other ships hit in the harbour, and rescue those flung into the water. Altogether, the Japanese bombs killed eleven aboard the *Manunda* and eighteen were seriously injured. A further forty or fifty medics and crewmen received minor wounds. Matron Schumack, in charge of the nursing sisters on board the ship, was later awarded the Royal Red Cross for the calm manner in which she had continued to organize the treatment and care of the wounded and dying throughout the attack. After the war the Japanese produced documents showing that the attacks made on the *Manunda* were mistakes made in error by pilots in the heat of battle, and that the Japanese in no way condoned attacks on hospital ships. The subsequent sinking of the hospital ship *Centaur* by a Japanese submarine appeared to throw such an explanation into doubt.

As emergency services attempted to deal with the chaos of death, injury, property damage and fire created by the first wave of Japanese carrier planes, unbeknown to the Australians a second wave was departing with a fresh set of targets marked on navigators' maps – Darwin's airfields. Just over an hour after the last of the first wave's bombers and fighters had droned away into the smoke-blackened sky, the second wave struck the main RAAF airfield close to the town. Zero fighters strafed virtually at will, as many servicemen abandoned their positions and fled, thinking the attack was the prelude to a full-scale Japanese invasion. Those who stayed at their posts were hard pressed to inflict much damage on their attackers, and the Japanese quickly destroyed nine aircraft parked on the ground and killed six servicemen. The soldiers, sailors and airmen fought hard and the first two Military Medal's won on Australian soil were won on that day, with civilians often displaying gallantry and heroism far beyond what was expected of them. Japanese bombs wrecked the airfield's hangars, stores and base buildings, cratered the runway and a direct hit on an air-raid shelter next to the Post Office killed many civilians.

Darwin was regularly attacked by the Japanese until November 1943, by aircraft flying from Ambon Island. Although none was as severe as that first raid on 19 February 1942, the Japanese returned sixty-three more times to bomb and strafe. A further heavy attack was made on the port town of Broome along the coast, which also possessed an RAAF station. On 3 March 1942 Japanese aircraft came in at low level, and without warning. They hit not only the airfield, but the port facilities, town, and ships and flying boats sitting in the harbour, killing and wounding dozens of people and destroying twenty-four aircraft. It was only with the arrival of Spitfire squadrons that Japanese raids were finally deterred along Australia's northern coast.

The *Centaur*, formerly a large motor passenger ship, had undergone conversion into a hospital ship in 1943, involving a radical alteration in not just her internal compartments, but also in her outward appearance. HMAHS *Centaur* departed from a crowded Sydney harbour on 12 May 1943 with orders to sail to embattled

Port Moresby in New Guinea. To make sure that no one would mistake her for anything else, the *Centaur* was painted brilliant white and had thick green stripes running along the length of her hull broken halfway by huge red crosses. On her bows was painted the number '47', providing information that any submarine skipper could check in order to find out the ship's identity and purpose. The number was the *Centaur*'s registration that the Australian government had lodged with the International Red Cross in Switzerland (IRC), the IRC having informed the Japanese government of the ship's new role as a non-combatant vessel protected by International Law from any form of attack. Although Japan had not signed the 1929 Geneva Conventions, she had nonetheless agreed *prior* to the outbreak of war to abide by the provisions concerning non-combatant status, and the rules regarding hospital ships that had been established as long ago as 1907 fell into this agreement.

The *Centaur* would sail from Sydney to Cairns hugging Australian coastal waters that were by now regularly patrolled by Japanese submarines preying on inshore commercial traffic, and thence on to Port Moresby to collect wounded soldiers from the desperate fighting along to Kokoda Trail. Aboard her for the journey to New Guinea were 64 medical staff, including 12 Australian Army nurses, who would stay on the ship to treat the wounded, and the 149 men, plus an additional 44 attached personnel, of the 2/12th Field Ambulance. This unit was destined for Port Moresby to provide casualty clearing stations and aid posts for the front-line fighting troops. The *Centaur* had a crew of seventy-five men, making a total aboard of 332 souls all headed north into the war zone.[2]

The captain of the *Centaur* was aware that the Japanese had been informed of his ship's status as a hospital vessel on 5 February, and he knew that their superiors would have apprised any roving submarine skippers of this fact. Whether the Australian government, the IRC, or the captain of the *Centaur* thought the Japanese would abide by the rules is difficult to determine. There was a general Japanese unwillingness to follow any rules concerning conduct in war, other than their own military code. The Japanese left much of the observance of these rules to individual commanders, who reacted depending upon the situation they faced, or the degree to which any such rules meant anything to them. Many officers were simply brutal and very often what we might subsequently define as sadistic in dealing with the enemies of Japan. The *Centaur* was about to run foul of one the Navy's most brutal submarine skippers, a man whose reputation as a killer would later loom large when in command of another submarine, the I-37, in the Indian Ocean in 1944.

Lieutenant Commander Hajime Nakagawa was on his first war patrol to Australian waters as commanding officer of the submarine I-177, a KD7 type completed in December 1942. Nakagawa, along with submarines I-178 and I-180, formed Submarine Division 22, 3rd Submarine Squadron based at Truk. Nakagawa was probably driven to obey orders more obsessively than many other Japanese submarine skippers owing to a bad mistake he had made before the war. On 2 February 1939, when he was commanding the I-60, Nakagawa had been conducting training exercises in the Bungo Straits off Japan when he had accidentally rammed the submarine I-63 in the early morning gloom. The fatally wounded I-63 had immediately sunk, taking eighty-two of her crew with her, and Nakagawa had been placed before a court martial. Found guilty of negligence and suspended from the Navy, in 1940 he was given a second chance when he was given command of the I-58, and then the I-177 which he took to Australian waters. He was a man determined to restore his reputation by showing his superiors how obedient and useful he had become.

On the 26 April 1943 Nakagawa had intercepted and sunk the 8,724-ton British merchant ship *Limerick* off Cape Byron near Brisbane and escaped the resulting attack by the convoy escorts. The *Limerick* was one of five merchant ships sunk between 18 January and 29 April off the New South Wales and Queensland coasts by Japanese submarines resulting in great loss of life among the merchant crews. As the brightly lit *Centaur* crossed Nakagawa's path in the early hours of 14 May 1943 he did not hesitate in ordering a torpedo attack launched against her, even though she was strung with electric light bulbs that illuminated the huge red crosses and IRC number on the bows for all to see. Nakagawa knew absolutely that his next actions were illegal under the rules of war, the Geneva Conventions and International Law, yet he ruthlessly ignored these facts and prepared to launch an attack.

Nakagawa probably rationalized his sinking of the *Centaur* thus: a hospital ship was tasked with collecting wounded soldiers and taking them home for treatment so that some might be returned fighting fit once again to oppose the Japanese advance on Port Moresby. He was therefore removing one of the links by which Australia supported her forces defending New Guinea. Nakagawa was also aware of Allied attacks on Japanese hospital ships. This was properly the fault of the Japanese, who, unlike the Allies, did not properly or clearly mark their hospital ships which led to some cases of mistaken identity (the same problem that caused of the deaths of thousands of Allied prisoners of war, transported in the holds of unmarked Japanese merchant ships that were torpedoed and sunk by Allied submarines).

At 4.10am on 14 May the *Centaur* was off Moretan Island, Queensland when Nakagawa's torpedo struck home with deadly effect. Most of the medical staff were asleep at the moment of impact; she caught fire and started to sink by the stern very soon afterwards. Seaman Matthew Morris of the *Centaur*'s crew recalled those terrifying few moments as the *Centaur* foundered: 'I finished the twelve to four watch and I called the four to eight watch to go down, including me mate. And I was just havin' a cup of tea – and this big explosion, and the ship gave a shudder, and the skylight fell in on us.'[3] Somehow, Morris was able to get clear of the sinking *Centaur*: 'I don't really know how I got out of the mess room . . . and I'd say there was a dozen steps up to the deck. And I really can't remember going up them. But then I was washed off the back of the ship and then I realised I was in the water.'[4] Sister Ellen Savage, one of the twelve nurses onboard, was woken up by the torpedo explosion. 'Merle Morton and myself [Savage] were awakened by two terrific explosions and practically thrown out of bed . . . I registered mentally that it was a torpedo explosion.' Stumbling through passageways searching for a way up onto the boat deck, Savage recalled that:

> we ran into Colonel Manson, our commanding officer, in full dress even to his cap and 'Mae West' life-jacket, who kindly said 'That's right girlies, jump for it now.' The first words I spoke was to say 'Will I have time to go back for my greatcoat?' as we were only in our pyjamas. He said 'No' and with that climbed the deck and jumped and I followed.[5]

The *Centaur* sank in about three minutes, giving the crew and passengers virtually no time to abandon ship in an orderly fashion, and certainly no time at all to launch any of the ship's lifeboats. Hundreds of terrified soldiers and sailors simply leaped overboard into the roiling sea. The suction created by the ship plunging into the depths dragged many of the swimmers deep underwater into a whirling vortex, including Savage.

Eventually surfacing in a patch of oil, and suffering from an assortment of painful injuries after having been tossed and battered in the underwater whirlpool, Savage gasped for air at the surface. She had broken ribs, perforated eardrums and severe bruising all over her body. Her nose was also broken, along with her palate, but somehow she had survived. The I-177 was seen to surface close to the point where the *Centaur* had gone down. The Japanese, however, stayed away from the survivors, and shortly afterwards the submarine was seen to submerge and depart from the scene leaving the survivors to their fate.[6]

For most of the men and women who had managed to throw themselves clear of the *Centaur* there was to be no hope. Many could not swim and drowned after failing to don life jackets when woken up on the ship, or to find life rafts in the water. The noises emitted by the sinking *Centaur*, as well as the thrashing of survivors in the sea and the taste of blood everywhere attracted dozens of large oceanic sharks. The sharks would have scavenged the floating bodies first, and then moved on to the swimmers and survivors clinging to flotsam. High-pitched screaming continued for hours after the sinking as people were killed by the sharks and their bodies devoured.

Morris and Seaman Teenie drifted on a small raft amid the horror, comforting one another as the horrific night drew out, until the dawn light revealed a much bigger raft drifting close by. It was on this raft that Ellen Savage had managed to haul herself, along with many others, to get clear of the sharks and rest. Morris and his companion managed to join the others aboard what came to be christened 'Survival Island'. Second Officer Rippon of the *Centaur* was the senior officer to have survived the sinking and he took charge of the raft. Rippon knew that no distress call had been sent before the *Centaur* sank, as there simply had not been time. The survivors possessed only a little food and fresh water, and no medical supplies with which to treat the many injured lying around them on the rafts. Most of the survivors were dressed in night-clothes and would suffer from exposure and hypothermia over the coming hours. Sharks constantly patrolled the waters all around, attacking an occasional person who was unfortunate enough to be still in the water, and dragging below the surface any corpses they discovered floating at the surface.

Rescue came thirty-six hours later and in the meantime still more of the survivors who had managed to get off the ship and onto a raft died. Morris lay next to a badly burned soldier who had ceased moving. Knowing that she was a nurse, he caught Savage's attention and said, 'I think this young chap's dead.' Savage leaned over and closely examined the man, confirming Morris's suspicions. Morris recalled: '[I] took his identification disc off him and his name was John Walder . . . I gave his . . . disc to Sister Savage and she said: "Will you answer the Rosary?" And I said: "Yes, I'll do my best."'[7] Private Walder was one of many buried at sea, though most likely this was more of a gesture than a possibility because of the patrolling sharks.

The American destroyer USS *Mugford* found the rafts on 15 May, and Australia was outraged by the Japanese sinking of one of their hospital ships. Of the 332 men and women on board the *Centaur* when she had left Sydney on 12 May, only sixty-seven men and one woman were rescued four days later. It has been estimated that over 200 people survived the actual torpedo strike and made it into the sea, but only a quarter of those would live. Sharks, injury, drowning and despair took care of the rest, including eleven of the twelve nurses who were aboard the *Centaur*. The sinking of the *Centaur* was Australia's worst disaster from a submarine attack. Sister Ellen Savage spent thirty-six hours on 'Survival Island' working tirelessly to ease the suffering and pain of her companions, even though she was badly injured herself and in great discomfort. It was fitting that she was awarded the George Medal. For all the good it would do, Australian Prime Minister John Curtin lodged an official complaint through the neutral powers with the Japanese government over the 'barbaric' attack on an Australian hospital ship. With his blood up, Curtin called upon the Japanese to punish those officers responsible for the attack, but was later forced to tone down his demands as he and other politicians feared that the Japanese might have exacted revenge on the thousands of Australian prisoners of war in their hands throughout Asia.

Notes

1. 'Japanese air raids on Darwin and northern Australia, 1942–43', Fact Sheet 195 (National Archives of Australia).
2. 'The Sinking of the *Centaur*', Commonwealth Department of Veterans' Affairs, http://www.dva.gov.au
3. Ibid.
4. Ibid.
5. Ibid.
6. Milligan, Christopher S. and Foley, John C.H., *Australian Hospital Ship Centaur: The Myth of Immunity* (Nairana Publications, 1993).
7. 'The Sinking of the *Centaur*', Commonwealth Department of Veterans' Affairs, http://www.dva.gov.au

Chapter Six

A Speck on the Ocean: Murder at Wake Island

Don't fire until you can see the whites of their eyes.
Major James Devereaux, Battle of Wake Island, 1941

I think my trial was entirely unfair and the proceeding
unfair, and the sentence too harsh, but I obey with pleasure.
Rear Admiral Shigematsu Sakaibara,
Commander of Japanese Forces on Wake
Sentenced to death for war crimes, 1945

The Battle of Wake Island is one of the great 'last stands' in military history, where a few hundred defenders, heavily outnumbered and outgunned, held out far longer than anyone expected and exhibited a ferocity the Japanese did not anticipate. The fates of many of those men, both military and civilian, who had resisted the Japanese, is a sorry tale of abuse and murder at the hands of the IJN.

In January 1941 the US Navy had begun construction of a permanent base on the tiny Pacific atoll lying between Hawaii and Guam, measuring only 2.5 square miles, which included a modern airfield. Elements of the 1st Marine Defense Battalion, amounting to 449 officers and men, formed a permanent garrison, and it was supported by Marine Corps fighter squadron VMF-211 operating twelve outdated Grumman F4F Wildcats. There were also sixty-eight US Navy personnel and 1,150 civilian contractors on the island when the Japanese attack came.

Several First World War-vintage 5-inch guns from a defunct American cruiser had been emplaced at strategic points around the atoll, and a variety of anti-aircraft weapons were dug in; all the American forces on Wake came under a US Navy officer, Commander Winfield S. Cunningham. The Japanese first attempted to reduce Wake on 8 December 1941, the same day their carrier planes devastated the US Pacific Fleet at Pearl Harbor (Wake being on the opposite side of the International Date Line). A bomber offensive was launched that managed to destroy eight of the Wildcats on the ground. On the morning of 11 December a Japanese task force, codenamed the 'South Seas Force', approached the atoll, consisting of three light cruisers, six destroyers and a pair of large patrol boats escorting a pair of troop transports loaded with 450 Special Naval Landing Troops. Incredibly, the American defenders were able to send this force packing, sinking the destroyer *Hayate* with 5-inch shells from their dug-in and concealed naval guns, and damaging most of the other ships in a hailstorm of shot and shell. The remaining aircraft of VMF-211 took to the skies and managed to bomb and sink the destroyer *Kisaragi*, forcing the Japanese to place Wake under an aerial siege from land-based medium bombers until a new task force could be constituted. Deeply humiliated, the Japanese invasion force retreated with its tail quite literally between its legs. In the meantime, Admiral Wilson Brown's Task Force 14 had left Pearl Harbor and was steaming towards Wake to relieve the defenders. Brown's force included the aircraft carriers USS *Saratoga* and *Lexington*. The problem was that although the warships were quite swift, they had been forced to match their cruising speeds to a slow and elderly fleet oiler, so that collectively Brown's task force made slow progress towards Wake. Sadly, when the American task force was within a day of reaching Wake Vice Admiral William Pye, Acting Commander-in-Chief of what was left of the Pacific Fleet, had second thoughts about risking his carriers in a showdown with a more powerful Japanese fleet known to be converging on Wake for a second invasion attempt, and he ordered Brown to turn around and return his vessels to Pearl Harbor.[1] The defenders of Wake were abandoned by the American government to their fate, but their refusal to surrender when faced with overwhelming Japanese naval power and to stand and fight to the end proved a huge morale boost to the American public, depressed after the surprise attack on Hawaii.

On 23 December Vice Admiral Sadamichi Kajioka's large

invasion fleet arrived off Wake, and after beginning their landings at 2.35am, by the afternoon 1,500 Japanese naval landing troops had come ashore and slowly began to overcome fanatical American resistance, suffering horrendous casualties in the process.[2] The guns fell silent on Wake on the afternoon of Christmas Eve, 24 December, the day before the British colony of Hong Kong also surrendered after another heroic 'last stand'. Emerging from their defensive positions 1,603 American men, military and civilian, placed themselves into the hands of the IJN. Most probably assumed that the worst was now over for them, and their timely capitulation had saved many of their lives when it became clear to their commanders that further resistance was completely futile. American honour had been served in making such a stout defence of the island, and to continue to the 'last man, last round' was not normally a part of the Western military ethos.

American expectations of decent treatment after having fought so gallantly were swiftly dispelled. The Japanese had lost anywhere between 700 and 900 naval personnel in their two attempts to take the island, and at least another 1,000 had been wounded. Besides the human cost, Japanese naval pride had been damaged by the loss of two destroyers and twenty aircraft. The Americans had come off much better, losing a total of 122 killed, including 49 of the garrison's marines. The Japanese felt that they had been unexpectedly humiliated by this thorn in the side of their otherwise triumphant advance across the Pacific and South-East Asia, and were in a vengeful mood. Collecting up their prisoners, the Japanese found that the majority were actually American civilians, 1,150 employees of the Morrison-Knudsen Company, sent to Wake to construct an airfield, and a seaplane and submarine base for the US Navy before the invasion. The remainder were military prisoners from the US Marine Corps and US Navy.[3] The fact that so many of the Americans who had fought the Japanese were civilians, and not professional military forces, must have further angered the Japanese commanders.

The Japanese Special Naval Landing Force unit that took the Americans prisoner viewed their new charges with barely concealed disgust. Firstly, this motley collection of Americans had repulsed the first invasion attempt and somehow had managed to put up a ferocious resistance when the Japanese had actually managed to land in force. But they had nonetheless surrendered instead of selling their lives dearly for the island, and no Japanese serviceman could understand that. It went against everything the sailors had been taught since their basic training, and they had no respect for men who waved white flags and negotiated their own survival. Ignorant of the cultural differences between the two fighting nations, their officers led the Japanese sailors to believe that the prisoners would be finished off as soon as possible. To this end, the Americans were disarmed and marched under a heavy guard to the shell-scarred airfield runway and ordered to sit quietly in ranks. Machine guns were quickly set up to cover the large group of prisoners, and for many it began to look as though the Japanese intended to mow them down where they sat without further ado.

Although many of the more junior Japanese naval officers were keen to kill the prisoners as soon as possible, Rear Admiral Kajioka, the commander of the Japanese invasion fleet, intervened and forbade any such action. The prisoners were to be kept alive for the time being, and a proper decision would be made higher up the chain of command regarding their ultimate fate. The good news was transmitted to the massed ranks of huddled prisoners, filthy, thirsty and exhausted after the fight of their lives, by a naval interpreter: 'The Emperor has gracefully presented you with your lives,' the interpreter announced to which some wisecracking American shouted, 'Well, thank the son-of-a-bitch.'[4] Such self-confidence was soon to be knocked out of the prisoners as their ordeal began to unfold.

The prisoners spent an uncomfortable three days laying around on the ruined surface of the runway, made worse by the fact that many of them were sick with dysentery, while others were wounded and in need of medical attention. It rained a lot and a fierce wind chilled them further. The Japanese only distributed some bread and water and at mealtimes there was an undignified struggle for food, with fistfights breaking out among the bad-tempered men. Their senior officers, and the contractors' overseers had been taken inside away from their men, and maintaining discipline was a next-to-impossible task. On Christmas Day the prisoners, under escort, were sent off to their former dugouts to collect clothing, tobacco and food, and many were put to work burying the dozens of corpses of their comrades lying all over the island. After completing these tasks over the three days the men were herded into an abandoned barracks complex in the north of the island, and the

Japanese appeared thereafter to relax a little and to treat the men a little better.

For three weeks the prisoners loitered around their barracks, until one morning a large Japanese merchant ship hove to in the lagoon. She was the *Nitta Maru* and her mission was to remove the majority of the men to prison camps in China. The *Nitta Maru* departed from Wake on 12 January 1942, and into her filthy holds were crammed 1,222 American prisoners, with 381 contractors and wounded US Marines remaining behind on Wake. This 'Hell Ship', on which food and water was virtually non-existent for the frozen prisoners huddled together in their own filth in the bowels of the vessel, arrived in Yokohama in Japan on 20 January, and then the ship set sail again for China. The Japanese evidently still felt that they had not been given the chance to take out their frustrations on the American prisoners who had fought them so well, and now away from the gaze of Admiral Kajioka, junior officers plotted a vengeful attack on the defenceless men held down below like animals.

Once out at sea the Japanese guards suddenly bundled five of the prisoners topside. The men, all from the Naval Air Station on Wake, were to be tortured to death in order, said the Japanese, to 'honour their bravery' in the defence of the island. Three Seamen 2nd Class, Theodore Franklin, John Lambert and Roy Gonzales from Patrol Wing 2, and two US Marine Corps NCOs from Marine Fighter Squadron VMF-211, Master Technical Sergeant Earl Hannum and Technical Sergeant Vincent Bailey, were the unfortunate ones selected to satisfy the Japanese version of naval honour.[5] Perhaps the Japanese wanted to make an example of these seamen and marines who had been intimately involved with the valiant American air defence of the island, bearing in mind the damage inflicted on the first Japanese invasion fleet, particularly by the aircraft of VMF-211. The men were tied up, severely beaten and then beheaded with swords by Japanese naval officers. The headless bodies of the five American servicemen were then used by Japanese sailors for bayonet practice, until, mutilated beyond recognition, they were dumped over the ship's side like bags of refuse.

Back on Wake the remaining prisoners were illegally put to work by the Japanese constructing a myriad of defensive positions and obstacles as the Americans pushed closer to the island in their inexorable advance across the Pacific. Worked as slaves, by September 1942, 363 were left alive, and with the completion of many of the defences the Japanese Navy decided to remove more of them to prison camps in Japan. A total of 265 Americans were loaded aboard the *Tachibana Maru* on 30 September and transported to Yokohama. The remainder, ninety-seven of the original force of contractors, would stay on the island and continue working under the direction of Japanese engineers, accompanied by a single medical practitioner, Dr Shank, who bravely volunteered to stay behind and look after the men as best he could.

By the end of September 1942, US Navy aircraft regularly attacked Wake, hoping to prevent the Japanese from using their new airfield, and during the course of one of these raids an American prisoner was killed by 'friendly fire'. In December the atoll's new commander arrived, the relatively young Rear Admiral Shigematsu Sakaibara. Throughout 1943 the US Navy increased the number and ferocity of its raids against Wake, and most of the Japanese defenders, including Sakaibara himself, believed that an American invasion was in the offing. American submarines constantly harassed Japanese shipping attempting to supply the atoll, and what appeared to have tipped the balance for Sakaibara was a raid in force by an American carrier task group that included the USS *Yorktown* on 5–6 October 1943. Two days of unrelenting hell were unleashed upon the heads of the Japanese defenders, naval aircraft stacking up over the island to deposit a total of 340 tons of bombs, accompanied by American cruisers and destroyers battering the shore installations with their main and secondary armaments. Over 3,000 8-inch and 5-inch shells detonated across the atoll, turning the place into a moonscape.[6] At the airfield, so laboriously reconstructed by the prisoners of war, thirty-one Japanese aircraft were wrecked and burning after two days of concentrated attacks, the runway pockmarked with craters and debris.

In Sakaibara's mind the massive raid of 5–6 October was the preliminary preparation for an enemy landing. His men were all stood to and the damaged defences quickly manned. The nagging problem was what to do with the over ninety American prisoners still on the island. Sakaibara knew that he would require all of his men to stand off an American invasion, and men could not be wasted guarding prisoners who had, in his mind, already outlived their usefulness. Lieutenant Commander Tachibana, officer commanding the Special Naval Landing Party's headquarters company, was summoned to Sakaibara's bunker shortly after sundown on 7 October. Tachibana had once been a student of Sakaibara when the latter had been an instructor at the Etajima Naval Academy before the war, and the younger officer liked and admired his commander. After some general discussions had been concluded concerning the island's defences and supplies, Sakaibara suddenly announced a new order, which stunned Tachibana. 'The headquarters company leader is to use his men and shoot to death the prisoners of war on the northern shore.'[7] During his post-war interrogation Tachibana admitted that because he knew the Admiral well, he was confident therefore that such a serious decision would have been weighed carefully in Sakaibara's mind before he had issued such an instruction to any subordinate. Although momentarily stunned by the enormity of the task, Tachibana nonetheless believed that the order was lawful, commenting that 'it was justifiable to execute all the prisoners of war . . . that night.'[8] Fortunately for Tachibana, command of the headquarters company was that very evening being transferred to a more junior officer who had just arrived by aircraft from the Japanese naval base at Kwajelein in the Marshall Islands. Lieutenant Torashi Ito had barely had time to dump his kit in his quarters when he was ordered by Tachibana to take command of the headquarters company and arrange the slaughter of the remaining American prisoners on the beach. In the meantime, Tachibana had the prisoners removed from their barracks and they were marched under guard in the waning light of the tropical evening to the northern tip of the island. Once there the men were roughly tied up and blindfolded with scraps of cloth before being forced to sit on the beach facing the land with a large anti-tank ditch beside them.

Lieutenant Ito arrived to find everything ready; three platoons from the headquarters company had set themselves up behind the long line of seated prisoners, weapons at the ready. At Ito's bellowed command the machine gunners and riflemen let loose a storm of lead at the helpless American prisoners who had no chance of escape. Some did jump up and attempt to run off and amazingly one man (whose name is not known) successfully evaded the massacre and ran off into the island's interior, witnessed by a Japanese sailor. The immobile corpses of over ninety men lay on the blood-soaked sand of the beach as the last shots echoed away, to be replaced by the sound of waves lapping at the sea shore as darkness fell. Working quickly by torchlight, the bodies of the prisoners were tossed unceremoniously into the anti-tank ditch, which was then filled in with sand and the Japanese sailors returned to their billets.

The report of a single American prisoner escaping the slaughter on the beach prompted the Japanese to return to the site the following evening. There, the bullet-shattered bodies were dug back up and carefully counted, and sure enough, one man was missing. It would take the Japanese three weeks to recapture the unidentified American survivor, but his fate was the same as his comrades. Brought before Vice Admiral Sakaibara, the last American prisoner was personally decapitated by the atoll's commander with his samurai sword and his body hastily buried with the others.

The murder of the prisoners was largely forgotten in the course of the next two years, as the war situation deteriorated for Japan, and the Japanese naval garrison on Wake Island starved and waited for an invasion that never materialized. Instead, the Americans had bypassed Wake and allowed it to 'wither on the vine', its garrison denied supplies and reinforcements. Eventually, word reached Sakaibara on 15 August 1945 that his country had surrendered. At this point the Admiral and his staff became concerned about the massacre they had perpetrated two years before. According to the testimony of Commander Tachibana, on 18 August Sakaibara ordered all officers from platoon commander upwards to visit his office for a meeting. His first words were: 'I have just heard over the radio from Melbourne that all criminals of war whether they were ordered or were the officers who gave the orders will be punished.'[9] The net had already begun to close in on Sakaibara and his cronies before the signatures were dry on the unconditional surrender documents signed aboard the USS *Missouri* in Tokyo Bay. On 20 August another meeting was held by Sakaibara ahead of the arrival of an advanced party of US Marines to formally take the garrison's surrender, at which a ridiculous story was agreed upon should any awkward questions be asked by the Americans. To make things a little harder for the American investigators, Sakaibara ordered his men to exhume once again the remains of the prisoners, which he ordered reburied on the eastern shore of the island.

In accordance with the terms agreed to by the Japanese government and the Imperial Rescript, Sakaibara was forced to hold a formal surrender ceremony on 4 September, at which a party of US Marines raised the Stars and Stripes once more over the famous island. American intelligence was interested in locating the whereabouts of the ninety-eight American civilians (including Dr Shank) who were not shipped out to prison camps, but who were nowhere to be found on the island. Sakaibara and fifteen of his officers were promptly arrested by the Americans and brought before interrogators for questioning. They were to be transported to the former Japanese naval base at Kwajelein, and all fifteen would be charged with the murders of ninety-eight American contractors on Wake Island. Remembering the story to which Sakaibara and the others had agreed to in the Admiral's office on 20 August, when individually questioned they began to recount a yarn regarding the demise of the prisoners that actually blamed the Americans for the deaths. According to the officers, during the terrible bombing and shelling of the US Navy raid in force of October 1943, the Japanese had carefully placed the prisoners into two air-raid shelters for their protection. One of the shelters had taken a direct hit from an aerial bomb and all the prisoners inside had been killed. The men in the other shelter, witnessing the deaths of their comrades, had forced their way out of their shelter, killed one of their Japanese guards, broken down the fences to their prison compound and attempted to escape. The other guards had had no choice but to shoot them as they were attempting to escape (which was a legal act under the Rules of War). The bulk of the escapees had been cornered by Japanese troops at the north end of the island and killed. Their bodies had then been buried close by the beach.

The American interrogators did not believe this story and made clear to the Japanese prisoners that further investigations would be made; during the transportation of the Japanese officers to Kwajelein two of the junior officer prisoners committed suicide. By this stage feelings of guilt over what had occurred on the atoll appear to have surfaced among some of the officers, as both men left signed statements that implicated Admiral Sakaibara and others in mass murder. Once the trial got underway, Lieutenant Ito, the man who had commanded the troops who actually conducted the massacre, also killed himself, and in common with the other suicides he too left a statement pointing the finger of guilt for the killings directly at Sakaibara. Confronted with the evidence of his own subordinate officers, Sakaibara confessed that he had indeed ordered the massacre of all ninety-eight American prisoners, and that blame for the crime must lay squarely on his shoulders alone. However, Sakaibara also pointed out in his defence that he had merely followed superior orders, an inadmissible defence in war crimes trials. The military tribunal rejected his excuse, and Lieutenant Commander Tachibana, who also pleaded superior orders, was sentenced to death alongside Admiral Sakaibara. Eventually, after an appeal by the defence, Tachibana's death sentence was commuted to life imprisonment, but Sakaibara's went ahead without interference. Transported to the American island of Guam, Admiral Sakaibara was duly hanged alongside five other Japanese war criminals on 19 June 1947, his last words being: 'I think my trial was entirely unfair and the proceeding unfair, and the sentence too harsh, but I obey with pleasure.'[10]

The Japanese defendants during war crimes trials convened after the Second World War often raised the plea of 'superior orders' when brought to account for their alleged behaviour. On every occasion the plea was rejected as inadmissible by the court. This was based on the ideas outlined in the 1919 Commission on Responsibilities, part of the post-First World War International Commission of Allied Powers questioning the conduct of nations at war. In part, the Commission suggested that civil and military authorities could not be relieved from responsibility for offences just because some higher authority may have been convicted for the same offence. It would be up to future courts to decide whether the plea of 'superior orders' was valid case by case. The German Code of Military Law made it plain that war crimes were punishable offences, even when an individual was following a superior's orders. 'A subordinate who obeyed the order of his superior was liable to punishment if it were known to him that such an order involved a contravention of the law.'[11] A subordinate should therefore refuse to obey the orders of a superior officer if they involved a breach of the law. This is easier said than done, as other factors, such as the group ethic, personal beliefs and peer pressure also play a part in the decision to commit a war crime. Fear of punishment also often leads otherwise law-abiding soldiers and sailors to commit terrible acts during war. The primary duty of the soldier is to obey the orders of his officers, but, as the war crimes trials demonstrated, if the order is obviously illegal, the soldier has an equal duty to refuse to carry it out. The British and American armed forces exercised similar constraints on their men.

The Japanese military code was altogether different and the onus was 100 per cent on unthinking obedience from the junior ranks. Many defence cases rested on the plea that the ordinary troops who partook in war crimes had no knowledge that what they were doing was illegal, and that they simply obeyed their officers without questioning the legality of the orders they were given. Massacring innocent women and children was the same as fighting American Marines, for everything was being done in the name of the Emperor, and it was the absolute duty of the soldier or sailor to obey without questioning orders. A further strong impulse to instil obedience in the Japanese armed forces was the twin concepts of 'face' and shame, absent in Anglo-Saxon armies. The strong Japanese group ethic, the unwillingness to stand out from the crowd, and the loss of face concomitant to disobeying the orders of a superior involved such terrible consequences that very few Japanese officers and men ever questioned what they were ordered to do. To question a superior officer was to question the Emperor, who, as a living god, was above reproach. Grafted onto Emperor-worship was the strict Bushido code, modified from samurai times to fit the exigencies of modern armed forces, which gave every Japanese soldier and sailor a guide on how to behave. Austerity, bravery, death before dishonour and a complete lack of respect for anything or anybody who was not Japanese provided the Japanese soldier and sailor with a belief in their mission not found in other armed forces. The Allied war crimes trials rejected all of these excuses for Japanese behaviour, setting a standard on what was considered morally right or objectionable in military behaviour based upon the traditions of the Western military mind. The gulf between the two cultures was enormous and the military methods of the two so divergent as to be virtually unintelligible to the other.

Notes
1. Urwin, Gregory, *Facing Fearful Odds: The Siege of Wake Island* (University of Nebraska Press, 1997), p. 192.
2. Wukovits, John, *Pacific Alamo: The Battle for Wake Island* (New American Library, 2004).

3. Perrett, Bryan, *Last Stand: Famous Battles Against the Odds* (Weidenfeld Military, 1992).
4. Urwin, Gregory, *Facing Fearful Odds: The Siege of Wake Island* (University of Nebraska Press, 1997), p. 537.
5. 'Total Listing of Casualties and Disposition of Wake Island Personnel, 1941–1945', File 1L (United States Marine Corps Historical Archives).
6. Hubbs, Major Mark E., *Massacre on Wake Island*, http://www.ussyorktown.com/yorktown/massacre.html
7. Russell of Liverpool, Lord, *The Knights of Bushido: A Short History of Japanese War Crimes* (Greenhill Books, 2002), pp. 107–8.
8. Ibid., p. 109.
9. Ibid., p. 108.
10. Hubbs, Major Mark E., *Massacre on Wake Island*, http://www.ussyorktown.com/yorktown/massacre.html
11. Russell of Liverpool, Lord, *The Knights of Bushido: A Short History of Japanese War Crimes* (Greenhill Books, 2002), p. 317.

Chapter Seven

Hell's Way Station:
American Prisoners on Truk

Determined to sacrifice himself rather than risk capture and
subsequent danger of revealing plans under Japanese torture
or use of drugs, he stoically remained aboard the mortally
wounded vessel as she plunged to her death.

Medal of Honor citation of
Captain John P. Cromwell, USN

Dark deeds were committed by the Japanese on Truk Island, part
of a collection of beautiful tropical islands in the Carolines. Truk,
headquarters of the Japanese 4th Fleet, stood at the heart of the
Pacific strategy of the IJN, and hundreds of warships and merchant
vessels constantly passed through the crowded anchorage. As the
Americans advanced ever closer to Japan during 1943, Truk found
itself virtually on the Japanese front line. Truk also served as a way
station in Japan's network of prisoner-of-war camps for American
airmen shot down on Rabaul. From Truk they were transported to
Ofuna in Japan as slave labour. Other Americans, including the
unfortunate survivors of a submarine, were also processed through
the Japanese Navy's harsh detention centre, where cruelty and
torture were practised with relish by their captors.

The American submarine USS *Sculpin* was running fast on the
surface in the darkness, her diesels throbbing as the grey-painted
vessel surged through the dark Pacific waters in a race her skipper
was determined to win. Commander Fred Connaway and his
seasoned crew of fifty-four men were all veterans of the war in the
Pacific. It was the ninth war patrol for the boat that had first
entered naval service in 1939, the men quietly and confidently

going about their jobs as submariners as they had so many times before. It was the night of 18/19 November 1943, and out in the darkness somewhere far head was a big Japanese convoy north of the huge 4th Fleet anchorage at Truk, where Japanese ships and military reinforcements had been departing towards the Gilbert Islands and the American invasion of Tarawa. The *Sculpin*, with its squat conning tower, four anti-aircraft machine guns and forward-mounted 3-inch deck gun, along with two other American submarines, was converging upon the convoy at full speed, determined to achieve good firing positions by first light on the 19th. The three submarines would be acting in concert with one another, and aboard the *Sculpin* Captain John P. Cromwell was tasked with commanding what the US Navy termed a 'Submarine Coordinated Attack Group', otherwise known by its more common German derivation of 'wolf-pack'. It was vital that the submarines attack and sink as many Japanese transports and cargo ships as possible to prevent them from reinforcing Tarawa before the Americans came to liberate the island. Hence Captain Cromwell, at forty-two years old an old man aboard the *Sculpin*, was urging Connaway to run his submarine fast down the radar bearing towards the swift-moving convoy. Undoubtedly in Commander Connaway's mind was the recent run of torpedo malfunctions he had suffered on the preceding war patrol along the Chinese coast which had brought Japanese escorts down upon his boat on several occasions.

The previous patrol had begun well for the seasoned *Sculpin* – Connaway had sunk the Japanese transport ship *Sekko Maru* on 9 August in the Taiwan Strait, and had managed to evade strong anti-submarine forces on 16 and 17 August. Four days later Connaway had discovered a small Japanese convoy and launched three torpedoes at a selected target. For some unknown reason all three torpedoes had failed to explode and instead his attack had alerted Japanese escorts that had flung a hail of depth charges after the escaping *Sculpin*. On 1 September another torpedo malfunction had brought a further furious depth-charge assault down upon the submarine.[1] These mechanical failures played on Connaway's mind as his boat continued on its meeting with destiny.

As light filtered into the sky in the early morning of 19 November the lookouts on the bridge confirmed what the radar operator had already reported, a line of ships labouring along at speed, sleek destroyers marshalling the flanks and rear of the convoy like eager sheepdogs. The *Sculpin* closed up for action, Connaway bringing his boat into a firing position on the surface as the range decreased between the low submarine and the oblivious Japanese convoy. Suddenly, one of the lookouts gave a cry of alarm as a destroyer suddenly swung about and began to bear down on them. The conning tower was cleared, and as hatches swung shut to the tune of 'Dive, dive, dive!' over the boat's intercom, the *Sculpin* slunk beneath the waves and managed to evade the attentions of the searching destroyer. The sonar operator reported the convoy changing course and after manoeuvring his boat into a new position, Connaway brought the *Sculpin* back to the surface behind the convoy hoping for better luck. Unfortunately the American submarine popped up only 600 yards from the Japanese destroyer *Yokohama* guarding the rear of the convoy, forcing Connaway to crash dive the *Sculpin* almost immediately. The first string of depth charges, known derisively to the crew as 'ash cans', detonated out of range of the submarine, but the Japanese got the depth right on their second attack, the ash cans throwing the submarine around, knocking out her depth gauge in the process and causing much minor damage. Connaway decided to bring his boat back up to periscope depth, but with a defective depth gauge it was very difficult to judge his ascent, and as the *Sculpin* broached the surface the Japanese destroyer came about for another attack run. Connaway ordered his boat back beneath the surface, but a hail of eighteen ash cans rocked, jarred and blasted the submarine's pressure hull, causing considerable further damage. The crew lost control of the submarine as it began a plunge into the depths, soon running beyond its safe depth. Pipes burst and rivets popped like gunshots as icy jets of seawater pumped into the boat in every compartment. The situation looked grim as the officers and men flayed around waterlogged compartments attempting to stem the ingress of the sea that would kill them all. The only way to maintain depth was to run the submarine at full speed, aiding the Japanese to track and continue to depth-charge the boat. Already leaking like a sieve and almost out of control, further ash can detonations now poked out the submarine's eyes, destroying the *Sculpin*'s sonar equipment. Commander Connaway faced a terrible decision: either stay down and be slowly blown to pieces by the *Yokohama* above, or surface and fight it out in an unequal battle. No one relished the prospect of surrendering to the Japanese, especially one man

76

aboard her. Captain Cromwell, as well as coordinating the American 'wolf-pack' attack on the Japanese convoy, was also in possession of top secret information concerning the details of the forthcoming American invasion of the Gilberts – he knew that he could not be taken alive when the time came.[2]

Blowing all tanks the *Sculpin* came to the surface, the deck gunners running to man the submarine's small artillery piece while the decks were still awash. The *Yokohama* bore down upon them, guns blazing, while some of the crew still inside the submarine set scuttling charges to prevent the vessel's capture by the Japanese. A shell from the Japanese destroyer tore into the conning tower, killing Connaway,[3] Lieutenant Joseph Defrees, Jr.,[4] and the entire bridge watch, and raking the gunners with shell fragments. The senior surviving officer informed Captain Cromwell that he was scuttling the *Sculpin*, Cromwell electing to stay with the vessel as she took her final dive. Everyone else who was still alive was ordered to abandon ship. In Cromwell's citation for a posthumous award of the Medal of Honor, it read in part: 'Determined to sacrifice himself rather than risk capture and subsequent danger of revealing plans under Japanese torture or use of drugs, he stoically remained aboard the mortally wounded vessel as she plunged to her death.'

Forty-two officers and men plunged into the sea as the *Sculpin* slid beneath the waves, many of them wounded. The destroyer *Yamagumo* hove to and the Japanese crew began hauling the exhausted and terrified men aboard. The Japanese quickly indicated their contempt for the American submariners, first rescuing and then throwing back one critically injured man. Rounded up on the deck of the destroyer, the Japanese robbed the Americans of anything of value, and bound their hands behind their backs. The *Yamagumo* immediately sailed to Truk with the bedraggled prisoners where a Tokei Tai naval police unit awaited their arrival for questioning.

Arriving at Truk on 20 November, thirteen of the American sailors were separated from the main group of *Sculpin* survivors and herded into a small cell on Dublon Island. The jail consisted of three cells opening onto a small courtyard between a road and the water's edge. The men were subjected to fearsome beatings with rifle butts and wooden clubs, and even though several were wounded before they were captured no medical attention was provided for them. Naturally, the Tokei Tai wanted the kind of information that Captain Cromwell had taken with him to his watery grave, but none of the survivors possessed any strategic data of any significance to aid the Japanese in preventing an American invasion of the Gilberts. Some of the American prisoners received extremely severe treatment, including three wounded sailors who had legs amputated without anaesthetic, and another who was forced to stand at attention for forty-eight hours. After ten days of mistreatment and torture the Japanese divided the survivors into two groups, assigning the prisoners to the aircraft carriers *Chuyo* and *Unyo* for transportation to labour camps in Japan.

By a strange twist of fate the *Chuyo* was torpedoed just outside Tokyo and sunk by the USS *Sailfish* (originally named the *Squalus*), a submarine the *Sculpin* had helped locate and raise four and a half years earlier when the boat had sunk while working up in 1939. The crew had been rescued by a special recovery vessel while the *Sculpin* had charted the area and assisted in the rescue effort. Of the twenty-one *Sculpin* survivors held aboard the *Chuyo* only one survived the sinking, saving himself by grabbing hold of a ladder draped down the side of a passing Japanese destroyer. The other twenty-one prisoners aboard the *Unyo* were delivered to the Ofuna prison camp on 5 December, and another dose of severe questioning. Eventually released from interrogation, the battered Americans were put to work as slave labourers in the Ashio copper mines for the rest of the war.

The horrors visited upon the survivors of the *Sculpin* were repeated many times at the Dublon Island holding camp as the war intensified and many American aircrews were shot down and captured by the Japanese. Two local men later gave sworn affidavits to American war crimes investigators concerning what they had witnessed at Dublon while employed by the Japanese. In July 1944 Rayphand Rombert, who was employed as a hospital cleaner at the 4th Naval Hospital close by the naval prison, recalled to investigators that he had just finished his cleaning tasks and was walking down the sandy path that connected the hospital with the water's edge, when he saw two American pilots being led out of the prison building. Escorted by Japanese Navy personnel, the pilots were shirtless, with their hands bound behind their backs, and crude blindfolds and gags of dirty cloth had been tied around their eyes and mouths. During his work earlier at the hospital Rombert had seen four American airmen who believed they were going to be treated for wounds they had incurred, but the civilian witness stated that the Japanese had instead tied these men up and had proceeded to beat them severely. Rombert recalled that he was able to hear the Americans crying out in pain as the 'interrogation' was being conducted, and the bellowed questions of the Japanese naval torturers. Interestingly, according to Rombert, all the questions were made in Japanese, and it seems unlikely that the Americans understood a word of what was being asked. The pair of American pilots that Rombert now came upon being led from the prison building under the bright sun were two of the men he had heard being questioned earlier in the day. Japanese sailors armed with rifles and fixed bayonets escorted the prisoners, and as the blind-folded Americans stumbled blindly along the path their guards repeatedly struck them hard blows with the butts of their rifles. Rombert pretended not to see what was going on and wandered into a patch of tropical undergrowth out of sight of the vigilant Japanese guards. He then made his way to a spot from where he could conceal himself and watch what the Japanese were doing to the prisoners.

The two Americans were pushed and struck as they walked up a small hill and then forced to the ground by their guards' rifles. Guards staked the men to the earth with ropes and wooden pegs and then all but one of them hastily rushed back down the hill. Rombert recalled that the single remaining guard busily dug into a pouch on his belt and withdrew a long object from it. The Japanese sailor then lit one end, Rombert realizing with sudden horror that the object was a stick of dynamite. The fuse hissed and fizzled into life and the Japanese dropped the explosives between the two Americans lying on the ground before running as fast as he could back down the hill to rejoin his comrades. Suddenly there was a huge explosion, rock, dirt, bits of trees and human flesh spraying out over a wide area, a thick pall of smoke lifting into the sky to settle back onto the horrific scene atop the hill. According to Rombert the two Americans were still alive, but both men's legs had been blown off by the dynamite. Screaming in agony, the two men writhed on the ground until a Japanese naval officer, Lieutenant Shinji Sakagami, walked back up to where they lay. Kneeling beside each prisoner, Sakagami placed his hands around their throats and strangled them to death.

Two more American prisoners remained alive and incarcerated inside a cell near the hospital, under guard day and night. Rombert knew this because he had seen a guard occasionally collect dirty, stagnant water from a puddle outside the prison building and pass it to the prisoners through a small hole in the bottom of their cell door. On 20 July Rombert stated that he witnessed a Japanese officer, Captain Iwanami, lead a group of his men into the cell building where the two Americans were being confined. They were shortly led out in the same manner as their two comrades who were murdered a week beforehand, bound, shirtless, blindfolded and gagged. Rombert followed discreetly behind and concealed himself once more in vegetation close to where the Japanese decided to execute the prisoners. Led to a spot between two coconut trees, Iwanami had a long iron bar placed between the trees and the prisoners tied to the bar so they were both elevated off the ground. At Iwanami's command one of his subordinates strode forward grasping a spear which he proceeded to drive into both prisoners, causing them to swing backwards and forwards on the bar. Iwanami then ordered his men to form two lines of six behind two officers, Lieutenant Tatsuo Oishio and Lieutenant Shunpei Asamura. The ordinary Japanese sailors took it in turns to practise their bayonet-fighting skills by using the Americans as live targets, lunging and stabbing repeatedly as they let out guttural screams. After both American airmen had been attacked by six bayonet-wielding Japanese sailors, they were dead, and Iwanami had their bloody corpses cut down from the bar. The officers in the party then beheaded both corpses with their swords, the ordinary sailors were ordered to dig two graves and the dead prisoners were unceremoniously rolled into the holes before being covered over with earth.

Another islander, Otis Billyos, later recounted an identical story to American investigators resulting in some arrests and prosecutions for war crimes of Japanese officers on Truk. The Japanese Navy committed several such outrages against Allied aircrews who fell into their clutches following legislation being issued by Tokyo concerning the murder of airmen prisoners soon after the Doolittle Raid on Japan in 1942, which is dealt with later in this book. Out in places like Truk aircrews were supposed to be held until transported to Japan, but many were murdered at the instigation of local commanders such as Captain Iwanami.

Notes

1. *Dictionary of American Naval Fighting Ships*, vol. VI (US Naval Historical Center, 1976).
2. Lavo, Carl, *Back from the Deep: Strange Story of the Sister Subs 'Squalus' and 'Sculpin'* (US Naval Institute Press, 1995).
3. 'On Eternal Patrol – Lost Submariners of World War II': Fred Connaway, http://www.oneternalpatrol.com/connaway-f.htm.
4. Ibid., Joseph Rollie Defrees, Jr.

Chapter Eight

False Confessions:
Extortion and Death in Borneo

When this war is over, the Japanese language will only be
spoken in Hell.
Admiral William Halsey, 7 December 1941

Borneo, the third biggest island in the world, is a land divided, situated in the western Pacific Ocean in the Malay Archipelago between the Sulu and Java seas south-west of the Philippines. Today, one part belongs to Indonesia, another to Malaysia, and the remainder forms the tiny oil-rich nation of Brunei. Sixty years ago the giant island was also divided, but between the two greatest Asian colonizers, the Netherlands and Britain. The British occupied large tracts of the north, consisting of Sarawak and Brunei, while the Dutch controlled the rest as part of the Netherlands East Indies. By 1943 Borneo was in the grip of an extortion campaign created by the Japanese Navy designed to steal the wealth of private citizens and at the same time murder all those who had been the victims of this crime. Thousands perished as the IJN unleashed its secret police arm in an extraordinary criminal operation.

Pre-war Japanese military interest in Borneo was strong, because the island occupied a strategic position lying across the main shipping routes from north of Malaya and Sumatra, and the Celebes and Java. The Japanese wanted British Borneo's oilfields, while occupation of Borneo would also guard their flank during their advance on Malaya and facilitate an eventual attack on Sumatra and western Java in the NEI. In 1941, the defence of Borneo, both British and Dutch, was left, unsurprisingly, to an inadequate collection of forces. If Borneo could have been strongly held by the Allies, forming a bastion in the defence of Malaya and Singapore further to the south, it would have halted or at the least severely hampered the speedy Japanese advance. As it was, in common with parts of the Netherlands East Indies thinly garrisoned by Dutch, Australian and local troops, neither the British nor the Dutch could spare sufficient manpower to pose any real threat to a complete Japanese takeover.

The British had practically their entire Far Eastern forces concentrated in Malaya and Singapore, with most reinforcements also being shipped there at Churchill's request. A smaller token garrison was maintained in Hong Kong, and the Dutch forces, drawn from the Royal Netherlands Indies Army, were predominantly native troops of dubious reliability. All the British could spare to defend British Borneo consisted of 2/15th Punjab Regiment from India, a 6-inch battery from the Hong Kong & Singapore Royal Artillery (a unit of Indian troops with British and Indian officers), and a detachment from 35th Fortress Company, Royal Engineers. Lieutenant General Arthur Percival, commanding Singapore, commented on this pitiful force during an inspection of Sarawak in November 1941: 'Nobody could pretend that this was a satisfactory situation, but at least it would make the enemy deploy a larger force to capture Sarawak than would have been necessary if it had not been defended at all and that, I think, is the true way to look at it.'

When the invasion came a month later, the Japanese captured most of their key objectives, including Brunei's oilfields, without meeting any serious resistance. When they eventually came to blows with the 2/15th Punjabis, the regiment distinguished itself by fighting extremely hard as Lieutenant Colonel Lane pulled the remains of the British forces into Dutch Borneo, the Japanese hot on their heels. In one action, two cut-off Punjabi platoons fought like demons until their ammunition gave out and they were forced to surrender. In a tremendous display of grit and determination these Indian soldiers had killed about 500 Japanese naval troops.[1] But sadly the Japanese murdered all of the prisoners they took from the two gallant platoons in an apparent fit of pique at having been so rudely held up and for suffering such grievous losses (the fault of which must have been Japanese tactics).

The Japanese rapidly captured the major settlements of Dutch Borneo and the outlying islands, and in this they were assisted by local Dayak indigenous tribesmen who were paid by the Japanese to hunt down and kill Dutch soldiers. The Dutch colonial authorities in Borneo were few in number, had gained a bad reputation for trampling all over aboriginal rights and were not in the least sensitive to the large non-white populace. It was, after all, a relationship built upon exploitation. Little wonder that some of the locals were initially at least favourably disposed to collaborate with the Japanese. However, after the dust had settled from the sporadic fighting across all of Borneo between December 1941 and February 1942, and the local inhabitants found themselves to be under Japanese occupation, their former British and Dutch colonial masters began to look considerably more benign than their brutal new overlords. In fact, the Japanese would tolerate no indigenous ideas of self-government, even though 'freeing' fellow Asians from European colonial dominance was often mooted by the Japanese when they spoke of their Greater East Asia Co-prosperity Sphere. Some Japanese still believe this lie, as noted in the introduction to this book by a quote from a Japanese Parliament resolution of 1995 which stated in part: 'The Pacific War was a war to liberate colonised Asia.'

The IJN was placed in overall command of Borneo after the Japanese Army withdrew. Vice Admiral Michiaki Kamada was the de facto naval governor, ruling from his headquarters at Surabaya in Java. The IJN's secret police, the Tokei Tai, was extremely active in the former Dutch Borneo and this force was given extraordinary powers over the civilian population. The Tokei Tai invented a mass anti-Japanese underground movement among the Indonesians, and unleashed two campaigns of extensive abuse and murder against them.

When the Japanese did not kill, they used torture on anyone suspected of resisting their rule. Much has been written about the activities of the wartime Japanese military police, the Kempeitai. The Imperial Navy had its own version of this force which was deployed to root out resistance to naval rule in the occupied territories, whether the threats were real or invented. This was the Tokei Tai, and it had originally been formed as a low-key police and intelligence group to prevent the Army from meddling in Navy affairs. The Tokei Tai was as brutal an organization as the army Kempeitai, a sort of marine Gestapo, and it was especially active in the areas of the South Pacific under IJN control. In common with the army Kempeitei, naval Tokei Tai investigators used extreme tortures to obtain intelligence and confessions, often resulting in death or permanent disablement for the victims. Standard practice was the water torture, where victims had gallons of water forced into their lungs until they passed out; this was then evacuated by jumping on the victim and the process repeated. Suspects were burned with cigarettes on the sensitive parts of their bodies, and women were often burned on their breasts and genitals. Electricity was applied in the same manner, while other lengthy tortures included the knee-spread, where the victim was forced to kneel for hours on sharp objects, and hanging by the arms, neck or legs for prolonged periods of time to cause the maximum suffering to the suspect. Beatings with heavy objects were standard, along with floggings and the removal of finger- and toenails with pliers. The tortures just recounted were not used solely by the trained torturers of the Japanese police state, but also by servicemen at the front at the instigation of their superior officers.

There never was a real 'anti-Japanese' resistance in Borneo, and although many of the locals had no reason to love their new masters, they were wise enough not to express such opinions in public. Borneo, in common with many other areas of the Netherlands East Indies, had a small and relatively well-off Chinese population of merchants and traders, as well as several other nationalities besides the indigenous tribal peoples and Indonesians. There was also several rich and powerful native rulers, or sultans, and, coupled with the wealthy merchants, the Japanese Navy decided to 'acquire' this wealth.

In October 1943 the Tokei Tai reported to Admiral Kamada that Dutch Borneo was harbouring an active 'anti-Japanese' organization, its membership thought to include rich Chinese merchants, native rulers and strangely enough anyone else with money; Kamada dutifully gave his assent for the secret police to begin an 'investigation'. The investigation consisted of the arrest of hundreds of innocent people, who were subjected to all the grotesque tortures that the Japanese Navy could dream up, until the victims signed forced confessions that they had been plotting against the Emperor. In the beginning, the Japanese attempted to make the confiscation of local wealth appear legal, and 'spy' trials were convened. Sixty-three unfortunate victims were found guilty of plotting against Japan at these show trials, and all were executed soon after. Thereafter, the Tokei Tai expanded its operations, and began systematically robbing and killing hundreds of people, dispensing with trials altogether. The Tokei Tai officer in charge of this programme of death was Lieutenant Yamamoto and it was reported that he ordered the trials stopped because the number of suspects awaiting trial was enormous, Yamamoto noting that 'it would have taken two or three years perhaps and there was no time.'

The first Tokei Tai reign of terror against the different nationalities of Borneo lasted from October 1943 until June 1944. Apart from sixty-three people tried and put to death at the beginning, Yamamoto and his men executed 1,000 more at Mandor, 240 at Sunggei Durian, 100 at Katapang and an unknown number at Pontianak, including the Sultan of Pontianak and his two sons, whom the Japanese publicly beheaded. Some local Dutch colonial officials captured in 1942 were also dragged out of captivity and murdered at this time.

The Japanese Navy unleashed a second terror campaign on Borneo in August 1944, this time only targeting the unfortunate local Chinese population. A hundred and twenty Chinese civilians were rounded up by the Tokei Tai at Suigkawang in west Borneo. The Japanese tried seventeen of them for 'anti-Japanese' activities, after torturing them, and unsurprisingly all were found guilty, their money and property was confiscated, they were sentenced to death and beheaded. A further 103 Chinese civilians were spared a show trial and were simply killed by the Japanese so the naval secret police could appropriate their cash and businesses. The Japanese Navy could now add extortion to the long list of its wartime crimes.

Notes
1. Woodburn Kirby, Major General S., Addis, C.T., Meiklejohn, J.F. and Wards, G.T., *The War Against Japan: The Loss of Singapore*, Official Campaign History, vol. I (History of the Second World War: United Kingdom Military) (Naval & Military Press Limited 2004).

Chapter Nine

The German Massacre:
The *Akikaze* Executions

To die for the Emperor is to live forever.
Japanese Army slogan

The citizens of neutral nations and of countries in alliance with Japan often suffered badly at the hands of Japanese military and naval forces. If the Japanese perceived the tiniest threat from an individual or group their response was usually extremely violent and often murderous. A case in question was the 'disposal' at sea of over forty German nationals in New Guinea in 1943 by the IJN.

The Germans in question, Catholic priests and nuns, and Protestant missionaries ministering to the local population, would have been, because of their nationality, under the protection of the Nazi regime, at that time an ally of Japan following the September 1940 Tri-partite Pact signed in Berlin between Germany, Italy and Japan, creating the Axis partnership. The Catholic priests, monks and nuns, as religious representatives were also under the protection of the Vatican in Rome, a neutral nation at war with no one. These legal niceties did not unduly influence the local Japanese naval command in the decision to kill the Germans.

Based at Wewak in New Guinea, the Vicariate of Central New Guinea was led by Bishop Joseph Loerks, and around the region the Divine Word missionaries had been quietly carrying out their work to convert the local tribal peoples to Christianity when the Japanese invaded. The Germans had been in the region for a considerable time, since before the First World War when northern New Guinea had been a German colony. The Treaty of Versailles handed the colony to Australia, under whose control the territory was when the Japanese invaded. The Catholic priests, monks and nuns had maintained good relations with the local indigenous people, but with the arrival of the Japanese in April 1942 all that was about to change. For several decades German missionaries had worked hard not only to convert the locals to Christianity, but they had also endeavoured to improve healthcare facilities for the indigenous tribal peoples, constructing small cottage hospitals and educating local women in child-birthing methods and other health-related issues. The Japanese, seemingly unable, or more likely unwilling, to differentiate between the civilians of friendly and neutral nations from the civilians of enemy powers, immediately ordered that Loerks and his missionaries be imprisoned in an internment camp on Kairiru Island. Allied pilots who had been shot down throughout the region were hiding in the jungle, anxious not to be apprehended by the Japanese, and some had attempted to contact the white missionaries in the hope of gaining aid. Japanese fleet headquarters decided to move the missionaries from Kairiru to Manus. After a short while the Imperial Navy, whose forces constituted the local garrison, removed the Catholic missionaries from their camp and they were herded aboard the destroyer *Akikaze*, whose skipper was Lieutenant Commander Sabe Tsurukichi.

The Japanese then set about destroying all traces of the mission-aries' work that had been carefully constructed over the previous decades. Truck loads of Japanese sailors were dispatched to the mission plantations, where they burned down the churches, clinics and houses, bayoneted converts to death, and made sure that the work of the Divine Word organization was obliterated from the face of the earth, as it represented another unacceptable face of 'white colonialism' that did not fit with the Japanese attempt to create their awkwardly named Greater East Asia Co-Prosperity Sphere. By the end of the war this scorched-earth policy had wiped out over 90 per cent of the Catholic mission plantations. Because almost nothing was known of these crimes until after the Second World War, neither the German nor the Vatican authorities made official complaints to Tokyo regarding the behaviour of their forces.

The *Akikaze* steamed towards Rabaul on New Britain, calling at Manus in the Admiralty Islands, a British protectorate, to pick up more interned missionaries, this time a group of twenty Protestants.

On Manus, relations between the Japanese and the local missionaries had been excellent, a very unusual situation for whites under Japanese control. Manus was garrisoned by only twenty Special Naval Landing troops under the command of Chief Petty Officer Ichinose Harukichi. It was said that Harukichi often invited the missionaries to dinner at his quarters, and seemed to enjoy their company immensely.

Dark forces at fleet headquarters were quietly conspiring to rid New Guinea of the whites the Japanese had inherited, plans that would go further than simply removing them from the area to internment elsewhere. The missionaries were suspected by the Japanese authorities of using concealed radio transmitters to report the movements of Imperial Navy ships to the Americans. The spying story was most probably concocted by the Tokei Tai naval police as an excuse to dispose of the Germans, giving them a reason to kill them within Japanese military law. Forty German Catholics, including nuns and two young Chinese children, had boarded the *Akikaze* at Kairiru Island, and another twenty Protestant civilians (accounts vary as to the exact numbers) were escorted aboard at Manus on 17 March 1943. Chief Petty Officer Harukichi was apparently none too pleased with the order given to him to hand over his missionary captives to Tsurukichi, and as an experienced member of Japan's navy he probably suspected that his friends were facing an uncertain future. Commander Tsurukichi, however, behaved well towards his captives, removing some of his crew from their quarters so the missionaries and children could be sheltered from Allied bombs should his ship have encountered enemy forces. The missionaries were fed, watered and the ship's surgeon was ordered to attend to them.

The *Akikaze* steamed to Kavieng and dropped anchor. No one left the warship and no one boarded her whilst she drifted around her cable. A small motor launch came alongside and a sealed envelope was delivered, with instructions that it was to be given only to Tsurukichi. The order came direct from 8th Fleet Headquarters – it instructed Tsurukichi to kill every civilian man, woman and child aboard the *Akikaze* and to dispose of their bodies at sea. Tsurukichi did not question the legality of this order, but he was visibly shaken. The *Akikaze* got underway again and the skipper called an officers' meeting in the wardroom where he disclosed to them the task his vessel had been given. Tsurukichi read the order aloud to the assembled officers, pale and with his hands shaking, and then told them that although the order was distasteful, it was nonetheless a direct order from Fleet and therefore it must be obeyed.

He detailed more junior officers and NCOs to carry out the task. The Japanese immediately began to make preparations to dispose of the prisoners. On the destroyer's aft deck a wooden scaffold was erected by the ship's carpenters, and ropes prepared. A large sheet was then strung across the deck so that when the prisoners were led out from below they would not see what was being done to their colleagues on the other side of the curtain. Thick woven matting was placed beneath the scaffold to soak up the blood. A group of riflemen and a light machine gun manned by Sub Lieutenant Takeo were made ready to kill the victims.

The prisoners were herded out onto the deck in small groups under a heavy armed guard. One by one, beginning with the men, they were firstly asked some polite questions by an officer, including their name, nationality, marital status and age. This information was then entered on legal notepads, which subsequently disappeared. One by one, the victims, following a calm questioning, were led behind the curtain to their fate.

Once behind the curtain, each prisoner was blindfolded and ropes were attached to each of his/her wrists. Several Japanese sailors then pulled on the ropes in unison, which were all attached to the wooden scaffold, and struggling in agony the prisoner was bodily hauled off the ground and suspended ready for execution. At a given signal the destroyer would suddenly increase speed, the noise of the engines used by the Japanese to disguise the shots coming from behind the curtain. A four-man firing squad then took aim and dispatched the victim with a single volley, along with a burst from Lieutenant Takeo's machine gun. Afterwards, the body was dropped to the deck, untied and pitched over the stern of the ship as she continued on her way. Whether intentional or not, the nature of the prisoners' deaths, suspended as if crucified, was the final indignity to their beliefs.

When all the male prisoners had been killed, it was the turn of the nuns and other women, two of whom were holding small Chinese babies in their arms. Ignoring their desperate pleas of mercy for the infants, Japanese sailors wrenched the children from the nuns' arms and threw them overboard to drown. The women were then subjected to the same treatment as the men – after three hours all the neutral civilians had been shot and thrown overboard. The scaffold was dismantled by the destroyer's crew and also dumped over the side, along with the woven matting, now heavy with blood. A working party was then ordered to scrub the deck clean of any trace of what had been done before Commander Tsurukichi addressed his assembled crew. On pain of severe punishment the officers and men of the *Akikaze* were sworn to secrecy concerning the massacre before Tsurukichi held a short religious service in honour of the recently deceased. The *Akikaze* continued on her way to Rabaul, her mission complete, berthing at 10.00pm that night.

In February 1944 the Japanese turned their attentions to the Vicariate of East New Guinea, consisting of Bishop Wolf, seven priests, sixteen monks and thirty nuns. Gathered together and herded onto a transport ship for delivery to a prisoner-of-war camp, the Japanese did not bother to clearly identify the ship as a prisoner transport. By a terrible twist of fate roving American aircraft spotted the lone Japanese merchantman and proceeded to strafe and bomb the vessel. Bishop Wolf and many of the missionaries were tragically killed during the attack, while those left alive eventually spent the rest of the war in the hell of a Japanese civilian internment camp where some succumbed to disease and the casual violence of their captors.

The Japanese method of taking captives far out to sea and then killing them was not confined to the massacre committed aboard the *Akikaze*. Another example occurred towards the end of the war off northern Java in the occupied NEI. After the Japanese surrender in August 1945 many important documents implicating particular naval officers and vessels in atrocities were deliberately destroyed by the Japanese to prevent their falling into Allied hands. One such case concerns ninety European civilians last seen alive boarding a Japanese submarine at the northern Javanese port of Cheribon in July 1945. Due to the missing documents, the submarine concerned has never been properly identified, but one presumably Javanese-speaking Dutch colonist managed to live long enough to explain what had occurred far out at sea.

The ninety men, women and children were civilian internees from one of the many camps the Japanese had set up throughout the Netherlands East Indies, and quite why they were killed so close to the end of hostilities is not known. The behaviour of the

Japanese towards their captives often indicated that they needed only spurious reasons to commit mass murder – perhaps their deteriorating military situation in the summer of 1945 led them to dispose of extra mouths to feed and guard. It is known that the Japanese intended to massacre all of the prisoners of war and civilian internees in their charge across the Empire as defeat stared them in the face, and perhaps the Cheribon atrocity was part of this master plan. A general order was issued by Vice-Minister of War Shibayama on 11 March 1945 that stated: 'The handling of prisoners of war in these times when the state of things is becoming more and more pressing and the evils of war extend to the Imperial Dominion, Manchuria and other places, is in the enclosed summary.' The summary stated: 'The Policy: With the greatest efforts prevent the prisoners of war falling into the hands of the enemy.' Preventing prisoners and internees from falling into Allied hands by killing them was the interpretation many army and navy commanders placed on Shibayama's rather vague order.

The internees boarded the submarine and, due to their large numbers, were forced to stand on the deck covered by sailors armed with light machine guns. Internees crowded both the fore and aft deck of the submarine, a machine gun covering each group. The submarine cast off at dusk and headed out into the open ocean for several miles. Probably fearing that they were going to be killed by gunfire from the conning tower the prisoners, helpless and tormented by not knowing what was to become of them, stood and waited. Suddenly, their guards disappeared inside the submarine, without warning the ballast tanks blew and the submarine slid below the surface pitching all ninety terrified Europeans into the dark ocean.

Many undoubtedly perished by drowning in those first horrible minutes. The stronger swimmers gathered together and tried to help one another to stay afloat, for they had no lifejackets or flotation devices of any sort. A mass of panic-stricken men, women and children kicking furiously in the sea, coupled with the dead bodies of the drowned sinking into the depths, soon attracted sharks to the area looking for an easy meal. As the Japanese intended, the sharks would finish what the Imperial Navy had begun. Over the next few hours hundreds of sharks congregated at the scene and proceeded to devour all of the internees, whose deaths were more horrible than it is possible to imagine, eaten alive by unseen predators in the dark of night.

One grievously injured European man managed to get clear of the carnage and the next morning, near to death, he was discovered and rescued by a small Javanese fishing boat. When the crew pulled the survivor aboard they knew he only had minutes to live, for the sharks had taken one of his arms and his right foot. Bleeding to death, the man told the Javanese what had been done to the internees by the Japanese, and then he died. The fishermen put his remains back into the sea, not wanting to come ashore with a European body in their boat, for the Japanese would have undoubtedly killed them as well to protect the secret of the massacre they had perpetrated. In August 1945 the Javanese reported what had happened to the British occupation authorities, but an investigation was impossible owing to the 'cleaning' of Japanese files by naval officers *before* they were surrendered for inspection. No justice was possible for the ninety innocents so barbarously left to die in the ocean, and no prosecutions have ever been made in this case, or in the case of the *Akikaze* murders. The wall of silence of Japanese veterans has remained unbroken to the present day.

Chapter Ten

The Butcher Boat

Do not stop at the sinking of enemy ships and cargoes. At
the same time carry out the complete destruction of the
crews of the enemy's ships.

Excerpt from an order of Japanese
1st Submarine Force Truk, 20 March 1943

The I-37 was one of twenty Type B1 submarines produced in Japan
between 1940 and 1943, which became the most numerous
Japanese submarine the Allied navies encountered. The I-37 was
one of the later examples, being launched at the Kure Naval Yard
in March 1943. On the surface the boat displaced 2,584 tons and
was 356.5 feet in length, making her nearly as large as some of the
ships she hunted and sank. Two 12,400 horsepower diesel engines
powered her through the water, giving the I-37 a top speed of 23.5
knots. When submerged and running on 2,000 horsepower electric
motors, the I-37 had a maximum speed of 8 knots.[1] Perhaps the
most incredible aspect of many Japanese submarines, the Type B1
included, was the very great ranges they were able to sail without
refuelling. For example, the I-37, if her skipper kept the submarine
on the surface, cruising at a relatively swift 16 knots, had enough
fuel aboard to cover 14,000 nautical miles without refuelling. It is
no surprise that Type B1 submarines were utilized by the Japanese
when they took part in the secret Yanagi trade with the Germans,
and the I-29, I-30 and I-34 all either attempted or successfully
completed voyages to German-occupied France loaded with raw
materials, weapons and personnel destined for the Nazi war
machine.[2]

A further innovation that placed Japanese submarines into a
league of their own during the Second World War was the mounting

of aircraft on board submarines. The ninety-four officers and men who crewed the I-37 included a pair of pilots and a pair of aerial observers who formed a crew and back-up crew for the submarines small Yokosuka E14Y1 reconnaissance floatplane, which was stowed inside a waterproof hanger on the submarine's deck. Used primarily as a long-range scout for the submarine, the aircraft carried aboard the I-25 in 1942 bombed the coast of Oregon, while others flew hair-raising missions over Allied cities and ports including Sydney, Melbourne and Hobart in Australia, Wellington in New Zealand and Durban in South Africa.[3] One aircraft even found its way to France and was operated by the German Navy. The E14Y1 was sent aloft by means of a catapult built into the deck and the aircraft was recovered by being hauled aboard by a crane after landing in the sea. All in all, the I-37 and her ilk were some of the most formidable submarines ever constructed and as was to be proved tragically correct, they were crewed by some of the most dedicated and ruthless submariners in history.

Commander Kiyonori Otani, the former skipper of the I-18, was assigned to the new I-37 as her captain. On 25 May 1943 Otani took the new submarine out from Kure bound for the island of Penang, lying off the west coast of Japanese-occupied Malaya, ready to operate in the Indian Ocean as part of the 6th Fleet's Submarine Division 14 of Submarine Squadron 8. Sub Division 14 totalled five boats under the command of Rear Admiral Noboru Ishizaki. On 16 June the I-37 attacked and sank the British tanker *San Ernesto* with deck gun shells and torpedoes, and on the 19th found and sank the American Liberty Ship *Henry Knox*.

In the meantime, Rear Admiral Hisashi Ichioka succeeded Ishizaki as commander of Submarine Division 14, fully intending to utilize the Yokosuka floatplane carried aboard his submarines. In September, Otani was ordered to take the I-37 close in to the shore of East Africa to conduct dangerous reconnaissance missions over British colonies in the region. On 11 October the little two-man floatplane evaded detection over the British-occupied northern Madagascan port of Diego Suarez, and six days later managed to penetrate the airspace above Mombassa, reporting on the great number of Allied merchantmen and warships lying at anchor in the harbour. Returning to traditional anti-commerce raiding, Otani and the I-37 struck again on 23 November, sinking the Greek merchant ship *Faneromeni* off Madagascar.

Otani's next target was the 9,972-ton Norwegian tanker *Scotia* which had left Bahrain on 19 November heavily loaded with 13,800 tons of diesel fuel oil destined for British warships waiting at Melbourne. Captain Karl Hansen and his crew of forty mainly Norwegian sailors crossed Otani's path at 5.25pm on 27 November, south-west of a place marked on charts as One and Half Degree Channel. A single torpedo launched from the submerged I-37 struck the *Scotia* in her starboard side near the aft mast. The detonation of the torpedo warhead sent a brilliant flash across the dark sea, as the sun had only just set when the *Scotia* took the hit, grinding rapidly to a halt from the 12 knots she had been making on the calm ocean. The torpedo had blown a huge gaping hole between Nos 13 and 14 tanks, which caused the ship to swing violently to starboard and to list dramatically. The detonation of the Japanese Long Lance torpedo blew the starboard aft lifeboat into matchwood, the ship's deck buckled 8 inches at the starboard rail, the mainmast snapped and crashed down onto the ship's superstructure, and the engine room bulkhead buckled but fortunately did not give way. The *Scotia* could no longer steer and the engine-room telegraph was inoperable.

Captain Hansen ordered the *Scotia* to be abandoned and the crew took to the three serviceable lifeboats and rafts. During hasty operations to launch the boats the port aft lifeboat capsized and three crewmen were dumped into the ocean beside the foundering tanker. Fortunately, they were soon plucked to safety by the remaining starboard boat which contained seven men. The captain went in the third boat with seven men, and twenty crew members crowded into the port motor lifeboat. Captain Hansen held his boat alongside the *Scotia* to give radio operator Kaare Kristiansen time to send distress messages, and 1st Engineer Josef Amundsen also remained aboard for some time after the first torpedo strike. Commander Otani watched the *Scotia* begin to settle and the crew taking to the boats through his periscope, before deciding to finish the tanker off with another torpedo. Fifteen minutes after the first explosion another Japanese torpedo detonated in the engine room, entering the ship on the starboard side. By the light of the fires that had broken out aboard, Hansen and his crew watched the *Scotia* break in two about amidships, the stern section disappearing beneath the dark waters like a stone. The forward section remained sticking up out of the ocean at a crazed angle.

The Japanese submarine motored on the surface towards the little collection of lifeboats and, following Fleet instructions, an English-speaking officer demanded that the captain identify himself. Hansen stood up and his lifeboat was ordered alongside the submarine, where armed Japanese sailors could be seen standing about on the casing. Captain Hansen was in some pain, as he had injured his right arm when the first torpedo had exploded, and he would have had some difficulty in clambering aboard the submarine unaided. With this in mind two Japanese sailors lowered a rope to him, on the end of which was attached a butcher's meat hook. Ordered to put the line around his waist, Hanson complied and Japanese sailors began hauling him aboard. Unfortunately, a knot in the line broke and the meat hook buried itself in Hansen's upper arm. Screaming in agony, the Japanese continued to haul Hanson aboard anyway. Hansen was quickly bundled away out of sight through a hatchway into the I-37. The Japanese now demanded that the radio officer and first officer, Kristiansen and Nils Andersen respectively, identify themselves. After witnessing the brutality of the Japanese in the treatment of the injured Captain Hansen, nobody said anything and sat rigidly in their lifeboats. Andersen was believed by some of the crew to be dead already, as no one had seen him since the sinking; Kristiansen was still aboard the forward section of the *Scotia*, which was at this stage still afloat. Japanese sailors told the men in the captain's boat to remain alongside the submarine, but the other two lifeboats had drifted behind the floating forward section of the *Scotia*, and, sensing the real danger they were in, the men inside had used the darkness to slip further away from the I-37.

Japanese sailors now moved quickly to prepare the submarine's 140mm (5.5-inch) deck gun for immediate action, and after a few deafening reports, the forward section of the *Scotia* was set ablaze. Radio Officer Kristiansen dove overboard and swam to a piece of floating debris as the remains of the tanker sank. The two boats that had managed to slip away into the darkness met up, the crewmen linked the lifeboats together with a length of rope and began sailing in a north-easterly direction, changing to north or north-westerly when the sun rose the following day. The bravery of the radio officer had not been in vain, for at Colombo in Ceylon the British had intercepted his distress calls which gave the position of the attack and information that the *Scotia* was being abandoned.

Two RAF PBY Catalina maritime patrol aircraft were scrambled to fly to the spot and conduct a search for survivors. The Royal Navy whaler HMS *Okapi* had also left port on receipt of the news and would attempt to rendezvous with the lifeboats after the Catalina search aircraft had located their position. On the evening of 28 November one of the Catalinas found the pair of lifeboats and dropped an encouraging message to them that read: 'We have plotted your position. Steer 040° Compass to intercept HMS Okapi. Two more survivors at place of sinking. Good luck.' The following day HMS *Okapi* found them – now began the search for the captain's boat, which was unaccounted for.

The captain's lifeboat was eventually discovered adrift and containing only one man, 23-year-old Able Seaman Thorbjorn Kristiansen, and the ship's dog which, though covered in diesel oil, was in good spirits. British officers immediately questioned Kristiansen to determine what had happened to the rest of the survivors, for they already knew that Captain Hansen had been taken aboard the Japanese submarine. Kristiansen's story was both shocking and difficult for his rescuers to comprehend.

Apart from the captain, Kristiansen and the dog, the lifeboat had also contained First Officer Andersen, Third Officer Arnfinn Strom, 4th Engineer Fritjof Mehlum, Pumpman Bjarne Omdahl, Saloon Boy G. Dias and Ordinary Seaman Victor Purdy. Shortly after Captain Hansen had gone aboard the I-37, and after the Japanese had demanded that the radio officer and first mate identify themselves, a light machine gun located in the submarine's conning tower had suddenly, and without warning or provocation, opened fire upon them. Kristiansen immediately jumped backwards into the water and hid himself underneath the lifeboat. He surfaced on the other side of the boat, which afforded him a little protection from the bullets which peppered the boat and the water to find Andersen and Strom both treading water as well. Both men were wounded, Anderson having been hit in the left leg and Strom in the shoulder. Andersen thought the end had come, but Strom was determined to survive and tried to rally the first mate's spirits. Machine-gun fire found both officers again, and the two men were struck and wounded for a second time. In the meantime, Kristiansen managed to stay under cover on the port side of the lifeboat. The rattle of the machine gun continued, but the men also heard the submarine's diesel engines start up and the boat began to move away from the lifeboat, firing long bursts all the time. The I-37 was manoeuvring in order to get at the three men hiding on the port side of the lifeboat, and realizing the danger he was in Kristiansen dove below the surface again. Coming back to the surface gasping for air, Kristiansen witnessed Andersen's death, as the officer was struck in the side of the head by a bullet and killed instantly. The lifeless body of Strom floated nearby. In a moment of immense desperation and bravery Kristiansen decided that he had to get away from the lifeboat, for the Japanese machine gunner fired burst after burst into it, probably knowing that one or more survivors were using it as cover. Taking a huge breath, the young Norwegian plunged beneath the waves again and swam for all he was worth *under* the I-37, emerging on the opposite side of the submarine where he was able to hang on unseen, as all Japanese eyes were on the lifeboat. After some time the firing ceased, hatches clanged shut as the Japanese disappeared inside the casing, and Kristiansen realized the submarine was about to submerge. Letting go of his handhold, Kristiansen pushed himself away from the huge submarine as the boat's ballast tanks blew noisily, and the I-37 sank beneath him.

After treading water for a while, Kristiansen cautiously swam back to the drifting lifeboat and wearily hauled himself aboard. What he found turned his stomach. Four bodies lay in various positions of death inside the lifeboat which was full of blood. Sitting completely exhausted among all of this gore, with the un-injured ship's dog, Kristiansen decided to commit the bodies of Mehlum, Omdahl, Dias and Purdy to the deep. Summoning what strength that remained in his body, Kristiansen grimly manhandled the broken corpses of his shipmates over the side, noticing that sharks had already arrived at the scene, attracted by all the blood in the water. The lifeboat had been drilled full of holes by Japanese machine-gun bullets and was leaking badly. Kristiansen and the dog sat in the lifeboat for the remainder of the night, shivering in water up to the Norwegian's waist.

When the dawn light broke over an empty ocean the following morning Kristiansen plugged as many of the bullet holes as he could manage and started to bail the boat out. His encounter with the I-37 was not finished, however. Setting the lifeboat's mast into position with the intention of making sail, Kristiansen decided firstly to climb up the mast and take a look around. To his horror he spotted the unmistakable shape of a submarine's periscope close by, and realizing that the Japanese had probably returned to complete the destruction of the crew of the *Scotia* in daylight, he quickly wrapped himself and the dog in the lifeboat's sail, and lay completely still in the bottom of the boat. Quivering with fear, Kristiansen heard the sound of a submarine surfacing nearby, and its diesel engines starting up as the I-37 motored towards his lifeboat. As the submarine's engines throttled down, Kristiansen could hear Japanese voices talking close by. Expecting any minute to be struck by a bullet, Kristiansen lay as still as he could, trying to control his breathing as his mind raced with thoughts of an impending and unpleasant death. After a while the voices stopped and the submarine seemed to go away. By a stroke of immense luck it appeared that the Japanese sailors had looked into the lifeboat and, thinking that it was empty of any human cargo, the I-37 had gone on its way to continue its commerce raiding mission. Not taking any chances on this, Kristiansen lay still underneath the sail all day until darkness fell once again.

Kristiansen and the dog would spend one more night in the blood-soaked lifeboat, alone in the vast Indian Ocean, not knowing if rescue was at hand or whether the daring escape from Commander Otani's clutches would give way instead to a lingering death, adrift and miles from land. Fortunately, Kristiansen's amazing luck came through for him once again when he and his canine companion were rescued by HMS *Okapi* on the afternoon of 30 November. The captain of the *Okapi* continued to hunt for survivors, for it was known that the radio officer, Kaare Kristiansen, had been spotted by one of the Catalina rescue planes – he had waved to the aircraft as it circled above him and the RAF crew had watched him swim towards a rubber dinghy they had dropped from the plane. The *Okapi* found a raft drifting in the ocean from the *Scotia*, lying on top of which was 1st Engineer Josef Amundsen, his dead body and the raft both riddled with bullet holes. Sadly, the rescue ship also came upon an empty RAF rubber dinghy, and although they searched, the British did not find the body of the radio officer, Kristiansen. A service was held aboard the *Okapi* before she headed back to her base at Addu Atoll, 750 miles south-west of Ceylon, and the body of Amundsen was committed to the deep.

On 1 December the *Okapi* arrived at Addu, where injured Able

Seaman Gerhard Larson was transferred to hospital. The rest of the survivors, thirty-one in total, and the ship's dog, boarded a French troopship and sailed to Colombo. The Admiralty convened a board of inquiry into the sinking of the *Scotia* and the attack by the Japanese on her crew. Most of the survivors gave statements which proved that Japanese submarine skippers were ignoring important rules of warfare at sea, and the Allies could expect more of these atrocities to occur.

The IJN had disregarded Article 22 of the London Naval Treaty, signed by Japan in 1930 alongside Britain, the United States, France and Italy, which made it clear that combatant ships, including submarines, were not allowed to sink ships until the crew had been put in a place of safety. Furthermore, this limitation was binding without time limit due to Article 23. Japan had also signed the 1936 London Protocol which incorporated verbatim the provisions of Part IV of Article 22 of the 1930 agreement relating to submarines. From Kristiansen's detailed statement as the only surviving witness to the machine-gunning of members of the crew of the *Scotia* the Admiralty was even able to identify positively the Japanese submarine as the I-37, all useful evidence for later use at any war crimes tribunal. As for Captain Karl Hansen, who had been so roughly treated by the Japanese when he was taken prisoner, nothing more was heard of him until shortly after the end of the war. Held captive inside the submarine, the Norwegian was routinely beaten and an interrogation of sorts was rather crudely conducted. Taken back to Penang, Hansen was transferred to a prison camp at Fukuoka in Japan, where he suffered terrible privations and was lucky to survive his encounter with the Imperial Navy's submarine pirates and their jailors. Many other merchant skippers taken prisoner by the Japanese were never heard of again and the fates of many of them remain a mystery to this day because of the haphazard nature of Japanese prisoner-of-war records, and missing or destroyed documentation.

Returning to Penang, command of the I-37 was given to a new skipper, Lieutenant Commander Hajime Nakagawa, who had previously commanded the I-177, and whom we have already met when he sank the Australian hospital ship *Centaur*. Nakagawa was to see to it that the disgraceful attack on the helpless survivors of the *Scotia* was repeated three more times under his personal command. According to Nakagawa's post-war interrogation, he stated that he committed his crimes with a clear conscience. In his mind he was duty bound to obey a 'massacre order' issued by the commander of the 1st Submarine Force at Truk on 20 March 1943, and as long as he fulfilled this duty, the methods by which his crew 'disposed' of their captives was irrelevant. The order Nakagawa referred to read as follows:

> All submarines will act together in order to concentrate their attacks against enemy convoys and totally destroy them. Do not stop at the sinking of enemy ships and cargoes. At the same time carry out the complete destruction of the crews of the enemy's ships; if possible seize part of the crew and endeavour to secure information about the enemy.[4]

It remains strange, however, that Commander Otani, although he committed a clearly identified war crime against the survivors of the *Scotia*, had not attempted to massacre the survivors of the other two ships he had previously sank, the *San Ernesto* and the *Henry Knox*. Both of these sinkings occurred after the famous massacre order to submarine skippers issued on 20 March 1943. In contrast, Nakagawa attempted to butcher – often accompanied by acts of sadism – every survivor from the three ships he managed to sink while commanding the I-37. For Allied merchant seamen, encounters with Japanese submarines and their subsequent survival appeared to depend far more on the capriciousness of individual skippers, rather than higher orders.

Nakagawa struck first on 22 February 1944 against the *British Chivalry*, a 7,118-ton steam tanker that the Japanese sank with torpedoes in the Indian Ocean. When the survivors took to a pair of lifeboats and two rafts, Nakagawa ordered their execution by machine-gun fire as his submarine approached the site of the sinking. The captain of the *British Chivalry* flew a white flag from his lifeboat in an effort to demonstrate to the Japanese that they were no threat, but Nakagawa simply ignored this device. According to a survivor, 'The submarine closed the boats and waved us alongside. It was noticed that she was manned by Japanese. They intimated that they required the Master to board her, which he did. The boats were then ordered to carry on, and the submarine moved off.'[5] Five minutes later the I-37 came back and 'steered towards the boats heavily machine-gunning them'. An officer on the submarine's conning tower, for unknown reasons, reportedly filmed the massacre with a small hand-held cine-camera. 'Most of the crew dived into the water, and a few lay down inside the boats. The machine-gunning lasted for quite a time, and one boat containing the radio equipment was sunk, and another left in a sinking condition. The sub then made off in a south-westerly direction.'[6] The thirty-eight survivors spent thirty-seven days adrift in an open boat before they were rescued by the MV *Delane* and recounted their terrible ordeal to British authorities. The I-37 continued the hunt for victims.

The 5,189-ton British motor ship *Sutlej* had sailed all the way from the United Kingdom, in the process losing a life raft during a fierce North Atlantic storm. The ship had dodged U-boats all the way, until, after a cruise through the Mediterranean to Alexandria and passage through the Suez Canal, the vessel had arrived in the British fortified harbour of Aden at the entrance to the Persian Gulf. On 15 February 1944 the *Sutlej* had departed for sea once again, this time in a convoy bound for Fremantle in Australia; she was loaded with 9,700 tons of phosphates and mail. After five days of travelling in company with the other ships, under the protection of warships on the convoy's flanks, the convoy dispersed and the *Sutlej* steamed on alone. The dangerous part of the Indian Ocean was considered by the British Admiralty to be the western side washing against the shore of East Africa and extending into the Persian Gulf, for here German U-boats roamed from their bases in Malaya and the Netherlands East Indies. Any Japanese submarine threat was considered minimal, so convoys were dispensed with in the eastern Indian Ocean. On the evening of 26 February, six days after leaving the protection of the convoy, the *Sutlej* continued her passage to Australia, no incidents having occurred outbound. But all this was about to change dramatically.

At 6.20pm the captain and the chief officer, standing side by side on the bridge, spotted the telltale wake of a torpedo fast approaching the port side of their ship. There was almost no time to manoeuvre the ship away from the threat and seconds later the Japanese Long Lance punched through the side of the *Sutlej* between No. 1 and No. 2 holds, detonating with a fearsome ex-plosion. As the ship reverberated from the blast, twisting and shaking like a wounded animal, the captain rang the engine-room telegraph to 'stop engines', and the chief engineer quickly evacuated the engineering personnel as the ship heeled violently to starboard and rapidly began to sink.

The *Sutlej* had become the second victim of the Japanese submarine skipper Hajime Nakagawa, commanding the I-37. As we have seen, Commander Nakagawa had successfully attacked and sunk the *British Chivalry* only four days before, and then callously ordered the machine-gunning of survivors sitting help-lessly in the ship's lifeboats, killing twenty men. The desperate men of the *Sutlej* could expect little mercy from Nakagawa.

The mass evacuation of the crew of the *Sutlej* was accompanied by the frantic klaxon wails of the 'abandon ship' signal which rang out continuously from the moment the *Sutlej* was hit until her super-structure disappeared beneath the waves only five minutes later. The crew, working like men possessed, cut loose the three remaining life rafts, which were unceremoniously pitched into the sea. The captain was last seen in the wireless room, but no distress call was ever sent before the *Sutlej* went down, taking her master with her.

Chief Engineer P.H. Rees tried to take up his station at Lifeboat No. 1, which was located on the starboard side boat deck, but it proved to be an impossible task for 'On getting amidships I was waistdeep [sic] in water, the vessel having sunk this deep already.'[7] Realizing the futility of attempting to get this lifeboat launched, Rees 'turned back to try another boat, No. 4 (port side engine room). I had no sooner mounted the ladder when the vessel started to drop away under me.'[8] Shouting to those crewmen around him to jump for it, Rees followed his own advice and dived overboard. Surfacing next to the 3rd engineer, the two men paddled over to what turned out to be a small auxiliary raft. The two officers managed to haul themselves aboard, where they found a coal boy already lying inside it. Rees and his companions then began to save as many of the swimming men as they could find, eventually plucking several from the water, including the chief cook, who died shortly afterwards of the injuries he had sustained during the torpedo attack.

Meanwhile, the Japanese submarine had surfaced, and was nosing into the debris field searching for survivors. It was now approximately ten minutes after the sinking, around 6.35pm, and from the submarine's conning tower a Japanese officer shouted to them in English, asking for the captain, the ship's name, her desti-nation and her cargo. Rees and the others stayed silent, whereupon the submarine came about and bore down relentlessly towards the rafts full of men, a machine gun rattling away from the bridge. The bows of the submarine tore into rafts and men alike, machine-gun bullets thudding into the rafts and spurting in the water as shouting men tried to swim clear of the homicidal attackers. Fortunately, darkness had already begun to fall, cloaking the survivors from the Japanese machine gunner. Rees recalled that 'The exhausts of the submarine were sparking badly and showed up against the darkness very clearly.'[9]

After the submarine had disappeared into the darkness, having abandoned its futile attempt to kill the survivors from the *Sutlej*, Chief Engineer Rees decided to try and retrieve an upturned lifeboat he could see floating some way off. He was determined to collect as many of the crew as were left clinging to debris at the sight of the sinking before currents and darkness split them up for ever. Fortunately, Rees and his party ran into two larger life rafts that were tied together. The first raft contained the 4th engineer and a naval rating from the *Sutlej*'s small anti-submarine gun, and the second the purser, a Chinese and seven white sailors. Rees made fast his smaller raft to them and they settled down to an uncomfortable night on the open ocean, where wind and driving rain intermittently chilled and soaked them through.

The next morning the men on the little floating island of conjoined rafts spotted another life raft in the distance, with men aboard. 'Owing to distance and weather contact was unable to be made,' recalled Rees. 'On the third morning this raft was lost sight of.'[10] For the survivors there now began a grim ordeal on the high seas with minimal supplies and little hope of rescue. As the senior surviving officer Rees took command and, setting a course northeast with the prevailing wind, he ordered the smallest raft to be stripped of anything useful and then cut adrift. The remaining two rafts would continue to drift and sail in tandem on this rough course. After twenty days, although the survivors sighted two small islands, the prevailing offshore wind and their inadequate sails meant that they were unable to make it ashore. During the several nights it took to pass the islands Rees fired emergency flares from his Very pistol, but no response from the shore made him assume they were uninhabited. The rain continued, which became an excellent source of fresh drinking water, and the survivors managed to catch both fish and seabirds to eat.

Eventually, Rees and the other officers decided that in order to increase their chances of survival, it was better that the two rafts part company – there was at least a likelihood that one of the rafts would be spotted by a friendly aircraft or ship and the men rescued. But as Rees later wrote: 'This decision I may add went badly on the conscience.'[11] On the morning of 13 April an RAF Catalina flying boat spotted one of the rafts and dropped supplies to them. A sea search was launched, the next day both of the rafts full of desperate men were sighted by HMS *Flamingo* and the survivors of the *Sutlej* rescued from their terrible ordeal. Far behind them, the I-37 continued its remorseless hunt for victims, the Japanese skipper with murder in mind.

On 19 February 1944, the British armed merchant ship *Ascot* had pulled away from the bustling docks of Colombo, Ceylon, and set course for Diego Suarez, the main port on the French island of Madagascar which was then under British occupation. After ten days of steaming steadily through the Indian Ocean, the crew and gunners from the Maritime Regiment had settled into a routine, with the gun crews also acting as lookouts around the vessel. The captain and his officers were aware that they had entered dangerous waters, with both German U-boats and Japanese submarines present, so that everyone was extra vigilant.

Around midday on 29 February army gunners on watch on the starboard beam suddenly gave a cry of alarm – the unmistakable wake of a torpedo running fast in the water coming directly for their vessel gave them only seconds to react, but for the *Ascot* it was already too late. Moments later the torpedo impacted against the *Ascot*'s hull and detonated inside the forward section of the engine room. A sheet of flame and debris engulfed the space, killing four of the engineers on duty instantly. The exterior blast from the torpedo's detonation blew the two starboard side lifeboats to pieces, scattering them into the ocean as so much broken matchwood. The *Ascot* immediately slowed to a halt as the power was cut, and the captain, realizing that his vessel was likely to founder, ordered the remaining crew to abandon ship on the port side as the ship took on a pronounced list to starboard. Working fast, the fifty-two men still alive managed to launch the two port-side lifeboats and a large raft, and within minutes everyone was safely away from the ship, which though still afloat, was perceptibly settling into the ocean.

The crew took the two small boats and the raft clear of the *Ascot*, and although after a short time the *Ascot* had ceased to settle, they sat contemplating their next move. So many men crammed into only half the available lifeboats would mean that the small survival stores of water and food carried aboard each would not last very long. Their only consolation was the fact their ship had been hit on a busy sea lane – another merchant ship would probably be along in a day or two and find them. Whilst the crew were sorting themselves out, a large submarine began its ascent to the surface with a hiss of escaping compressed air. The submarine, unmistakable from even a mile away, its large conning tower jutting skyward like an enormous dorsal fin, had come to the surface on the starboard quarter. The crew of the *Ascot* later testified that the submarine carried no distinguishing marks, and the hull was painted grey and covered in rust and barnacles. 'She was about 300 feet long with a high conning tower which had square glass windows in the fore part.' As well as a large deck gun, the submarine 'had a large 20 mm type gun fitted in a perspex blister in the side, and a light machine-gun resembling a Bren, on top of the conning tower.'[12] The machine gun was a Japanese Nambu light automatic weapon superficially similar in appearance to the British Bren gun because the magazine stuck out of the top in the same manner. As to the identity of the submarine, the survivors of the *Ascot*, according to British Naval Intelligence, 'on being shown photographs and silhouettes, all unhesitatingly picked out I – 121 – 124 of Jap submarine'.[13] The identification of the submarines listed as the I-121 to the I-124 was incorrect. Both the I-123 and I-124 had both been sunk earlier in the war, and the I-121 and I-122 had been assigned to training duties in Submarine Division 18, part of the Kure base force in Japan, from 1 January 1944. Neither was officially on operational patrol in the Indian Ocean in February 1944. The Japanese submarine responsible was the I-37 once again, the same submarine that had earlier sunk the *British Chivalry* and *Sutlej*, and had committed crimes against the survivors. The I-37 was then part of the Penang-based Submarine Squadron 8, along with the I-8, I-26, I-27 and I-29.[14]

The crew watched nervously as the submarine began to motor in a large circle around the *Ascot*; the survivors could just make out tiny figures running about on its decks. Suddenly a flat report echoed across the calm ocean, followed immediately by the whine of a high-velocity shell passing overhead. The submarine's deck gun boomed out several times, the crew watching as the armour-piercing shells punched holes in the hull and superstructure of their ship and burst within. Fires had soon broken out all over the *Ascot*. The firing abruptly ceased and the submarine turned its bows towards the little flotilla of lifeboats and motored towards them. Fascination with the pyrotechnic display now turned to horror as the crew got a closer look at the submarine's crew. Dressed in khaki shirts and trousers, and wearing soft-peaked caps with an anchor badge and black piping, hard Oriental eyes peered out from beneath with stony expressions. The crew of the *Ascot* were now at the mercy of the Japanese and no one knew how they might react towards their captives. The crew might have felt some reassurance when they spied a European face among the officers on the conning tower bridge, sporting a German naval officer's cap. This 'observer' was probably a U-boat officer from the joint German-Japanese submarine base at Penang, an island off the west coast of British Malaya overrun by the Japanese in 1942. At this stage of the war several long-range Type IX U-boats were operating in the Indian Ocean and Arabian Gulf, dispatched there by Grand Admiral Karl Dönitz after the failure of the Germans to win the Battle of the Atlantic in the hope of regaining the initiative over the Allies' poorly protected supply lanes east of Suez. The U-boats were involved in both commerce raiding and running supplies between Europe and the Far East, and their skippers had achieved some success against the poorly defended Indian Ocean convoys. In order that these boats could remain on station in the Indian Ocean, the Germans had established a series of small U-boat bases throughout Asia in cooperation with the Japanese Navy. Primarily based at Penang, smaller facilities existed at Batavia (now Jakarta) and Surabaya in the Netherlands East Indies, Singapore and Kobe in Japan. What the German observer thought of what was about to occur, as the Japanese submarine approached the survivors of the *Ascot*, was never recorded.

The submarine's big diesel engines slowed and a voice called out in bad English, asking the captain, chief engineer and radio operator to identify themselves. The survivors remained silent, but the Japanese had methods for ensuring speedy cooperation. A light machine gun chattered angrily and a stream of bullets kicked up the water close to one of the boats. The captain, realizing the danger his crew was in, stood up in his boat clutching an attaché case containing the ship's log and papers, and gave his name. The Japanese ordered the lifeboat to come alongside and the captain climbed carefully aboard. The Japanese were known to be obsessed with the concept of 'face', shame and superior-inferior relationships. The captain's refusal to initially identify himself in the Japanese military mind meant that he was not acknowledging his shame in capture and not behaving in a suitably subservient manner towards his captors. On these occasions, especially when Westerners showed any pride or superiority in front of their Japanese overlords, retribution in the form of extreme violence was usually meted out. The Japanese officer marched over to the *Ascot*'s captain, snatched his attaché case and bellowed: 'So you don't speak English, you English swine!'[15] He grasped first one and then the other of the captain's hands and, drawing a knife, slashed both of his palms deeply. With a hard shove, the captain was pitched overboard, where he was quickly rescued by one of the lifeboats. In retrospect, the captain of the *Ascot* was lucky not to have been executed immediately, but the Japanese were so unpredictable, and prone to so many variations of violence and sadism, that the fate of prisoners was impossible to predict. Following no absolute rules themselves, Japanese capriciousness had become legendary. According to their operational instructions, a Japanese submarine skipper was obliged to take an enemy merchant ship's master and radio operator prisoner for questioning, and to kill the rest of the crewmen. On this occasion, it appears that the documents the *Ascot*'s captain taken aboard the submarine were sufficient information for his captors. A complete disposal of the soldiers and sailors was now ordered by Commander Nakagawa.

A single command was issued and immediately the machine gun again opened up from the submarine conning tower, the fire directed towards the two lifeboats and the raft, idle alongside the I-37. When the first shots were fired all of the British crewmen jumped into the sea and attempted to take cover by sheltering behind their boats out of sight of the Japanese machine gunner. Unfortunately, in those first minutes of confusion and panic, ten crewmen were picked off with bursts of fire as they swam around trying to find cover.

As suddenly as it had begun, the machine gun fell silent and was replaced by the bark of the submarine's 140mm deck gun. Around thirty shells rendered the abandoned *Ascot* a flaming wreck, on fire from stem to stern. The submarine then turned about and motored away from the scene. As it looked to the British as though the submarine was making off, the survivors gingerly climbed back aboard their lifeboats. Whether the departure of the submarine was a deliberate ruse by Nakagawa to tempt the *Ascot*'s crew back into the open is not known, but only half an hour later the Japanese submarine came back at them and immediately opened fire on the survivors with machine guns. Once again, everyone who could jump overboard did so and attempted to shield themselves behind the boats as bullets splintered wood and mushroomed in the sea all around them. On the raft a wounded man named Richardson could not move, and in an act of selfless courage a young solider, Gunner Walker of the Maritime Regiment, decided to stay with him. The submarine constantly manoeuvred around, as the machine gunner searched out his victims. Walker kept up a running commentary from his position atop the raft, telling his shipmates where the submarine was. Inevitably, machine-gun fire eventually peppered the raft, and Richardson was struck again and killed, even as Walker tried to shield him with his own body. Walker was shot through the thigh and leg but survived. His actions were commended by Lieutenant Commander Seward, who later debriefed the survivors of the *Ascot*, the intelligence officer noting that 'this act of gallantry should be suitably rewarded.'[16] Whether it ever was is not known.

The Japanese now tried a new tactic to get the survivors out into the open sea where they could be killed more easily. Manoeuvring around, its big diesels chucking out plumes of blue exhaust smoke, the submarine charged one of the lifeboats, its bows slicing through the wooden craft with a sickening crunch, and the machine gunner made short work of the swimmers floundering in the submarine's wake. The submarine now made for the second lifeboat, into which the *Ascot*'s captain and many of her crew members had climbed. All of the occupants except one man dived into the sea where they were all killed by concentrated bursts of machine-gun fire. The submarine did not ram on this occasion and a member of the crew named Hughson lay absolutely still in the bottom of the boat, feigning death. The Japanese sailors took this lifeboat in tow for ten minutes, presumably to prevent its use as cover by any remaining swimmers, miraculously ignoring Hughson. After cutting the lifeboat free, the submarine rammed it causing extensive damage in the port quarter. Finally, as the light began to fade from the horizon, the Japanese gave up and the submarine moved off once more.

Seaman Hughson lay motionless in the bottom of the leaking lifeboat throughout the entire night until early morning on the next day when he discovered that the Japanese submarine had definitely gone. He carefully raised the lifeboat's foresail and began making his way back to where the *Ascot* had gone down. On 2 March he sighted the raft with seven men lying on it and managed to clamber onto it before his lifeboat finally sank. Commander Seward later singled out Hughson for special mention, writing that he had 'showed courage and fine seamanship'.[17] On the following day, 3 March, the eight survivors were picked up by a passing Dutch merchant ship, the *Straat Soenda*, and taken to Aden. Carefully debriefed by British Naval Intelligence, it was a miracle that any of the crew of the *Ascot* had survived their encounter with the Japanese. Fifty-two men had abandoned the *Ascot* in good order on 29 February, only for the Japanese to murder forty-four of them in cold blood.

Although Commander Nakagawa left the I-37 after the return of the submarine to base, his past would catch up with him when the Allies came to bring the Japanese to account for their wartime crimes – Nakagawa was arrested in Japan and brought before a British military tribunal. He did not deny that he had ordered his men to kill the survivors of the three ships he sank during the course of his patrol in the Indian Ocean during February and March 1944, but he argued that he had only been following orders. Although technically such a plea was absolutely correct, as all Japanese submarine skippers had been ordered by their commander to kill enemy merchant crews after 20 March 1943, the plea of 'superior orders' was not recognized by the tribunal. As outlined earlier in this book, it was not a valid defence where the act committed was, on the face of it, unlawful and in violation of the unchallenged rules of warfare. Nakagawa must have known that his actions contravened the rules of war and were so inhumane that no amount of 'superior orders' could excuse them. Under the rules promulgated by the Supreme Command of the Allied Powers (SCAP) for use in war crimes trials, sub-paragraph (f) of paragraph 16 stated why the plea of 'superior orders' was inadmissible as a defence, but could be considered as mitigating circumstances:

> The official position of the accused shall not absolve him from responsibility, nor be considered in mitigation of punishment. Further, action pursuant to order of the accused's [sic] superior, or of his government, shall not constitute a defence but may be considered in mitigation of punishment if the commission determines that justice so requires.[18]

When it came to sentencing, Nakagawa was only given eight years in Sugamo Prison in 1949. Perhaps reflecting a belief in Japan at the time that their military and naval officers were being unduly punished for what they perceived to have been 'legal' acts of war, just four years later the Japanese government released Nakagawa when the Allied powers withdrew from the occupation of Japan. Four years was a very light punishment considering the dozens of men he had ordered killed in the Indian Ocean and for whose murder he bore the responsibility as commanding officer of the I-37. No other members of the I-37's crew were ever prosecuted over the attacks on the *British Chivalry*, *Sutlej* and *Ascot*.

Notes

1. Combined Fleet, http://www.combinedfleet.com/type_b1.htm.
2. See the author's *Yanagi: The Secret Underwater Trade between Germany and Japan 1942–1945* (Pen & Sword Maritime, 2005) for further details on these extraordinary Japanese voyages to Europe.
3. See the author's *The Fujita Plan: Japanese Attacks on the United States and Australia during the Second World War* (Pen & Sword Maritime, 2006) for further information on IJN aircraft sorties over the United States and Australasia.
4. Russell of Liverpool, Lord, *The Knights of Bushido: A Short History of Japanese War Crimes* (Greenhill Books, 2002), p. 214.
5. Ibid., p. 219.
6. Ibid., p. 219.
7. Statement of P.H. Rees, Chief Engineer, M.V. SUTLEJ, sunk 26 February, 1944, Exhibit 2096, International Military Tribunal for the Far East, MB 1549, vol. 46, Exhibits (MacMillan Brown Library: University of Canterbury, Christchurch).
8. Ibid.
9. Ibid.
10. Ibid.

11. Ibid.
12. Report of attack of S.S. ASCOT, sunk 29 February 1944, Exhibit 2097, International Military Tribunal for the Far East, MB 1549, vol. 46, Exhibits (Macmillan Brown Library: University of Canterbury, Christchurch).
13. Ibid.
14. HIJMS Submarine I-37: Tabular Record of Movement, www.combinedfleet.com/I-37.htm.
15. Report of attack of S.S. ASCOT, sunk 29 February, 1944, Exhibit 2097, International Military Tribunal for the Far East, MB 1549, Vol. 46, Exhibits (Macmillan Brown Library: University of Canterbury, Christchurch).
16. Ibid.
17. Ibid.
18. *Law Reports of Trials of War Criminals*, vol. 1 (His Majesty's Stationary Office, 1947), 'Case No. 6: The Jaluit Atoll Case', p. 76.

Chapter Eleven

Objection to Murder:
The *Behar* Tragedy

I told the Captain that such a course was inhuman and that I
could not be a party to the execution especially in view of
the fact that I had ordered the rescue of the survivors.

Commander Junsuke Mii
Japanese cruiser Tone

The treatment of the crew of the British ship *Behar* at the hands of
their Japanese captors was a preventable tragedy and one of the
few examples where a Japanese officer attempted to intercede on
behalf of civilian and military prisoners to prevent their gruesome
executions. It was all to be to no avail, for the officer concerned,
Commander Junsuke Mii, was unable to secure the good treatment
of the captives held aboard his ship, the cruiser *Tone*, although to
take no part in their executions he nonetheless was forced to stand
helplessly by and allow the killings to proceed. Mii's post-war testimony to the International Military Tribunal for the Far East was
his act of contrition, and his apology for not having done more for
the victims of Japanese barbarism in 1944. His behaviour indicates
that the blanket categorization of all Japanese military and naval
personnel during the Second World War as callous and having little
or no regard for human life is misleading, for some Japanese
servicemen viewed the orders that were issued to them by their
superiors as dishonourable and contrary to well-known international law.

The heavy cruiser *Tone*, under the command of Captain Haruo
Mayuzumi, was sent into the Indian Ocean to assist in anti-
commerce raiding then being conducted by Japanese submarines in

early 1944. The 15,200-ton warship was sailing in company with her sister ship *Chikuma*, the flagship *Aoba* and the destroyer *Uranami*. Collectively the vessels formed a flotilla under the mission title 'SA No. 1'. The *Tone* had received specific orders as part of the 16th Cruiser Squadron under the command of Vice Admiral Naomasa Sakonju that she was to capture enemy merchant ships and crews, effectively to take them as prizes, and not to sink the vessels. Due to the very effective American and British submarine blockade of Japan by this stage in the war, the Japanese merchant marine was rapidly being sent to the bottom of the oceans, and new sources of transport vessels were urgently required to meet the shortfall in merchant vessels. Japanese ship-yards struggled to make good the losses with limited raw materials available to them.

On 9 March 1944 the cruiser, now acting alone as a commerce raider, encountered the British merchantman *Behar* off the Cocos Islands, and as the big warship bore down on the unfortunate freighter Commander Mii, as executive officer and second-in-command of the *Tone*, had speedily mustered an armed boarding party of Japanese sailors and a prize crew. The *Behar* had set sail from Melbourne in Australia on 19 February bound for Britain with a partial load of 796 tons of zinc. The 7,840-ton ship was also carrying passengers, and was scheduled to call at Bombay and other Indian coastal ports.

Commander Mii was on the bridge when Captain Mayuzumi suddenly ordered his gunners to open fire on the British ship, in direct contravention of the standing orders that had been issued to him at the beginning of the operation. The forward turrets, mounting 8-inch guns, boomed, and smoke and flames mush-roomed from the barrels as they flung their huge shells into the distant *Behar*, as Mii desperately remonstrated with his captain to cease firing and so allow his boarding and prize parties to capture the vessel intact. Mayuzumi ignored his executive officer's pleas and the bombardment continued. No time had been given for the crew of the *Behar* to abandon ship, the vessel was soon struck several times and set ablaze, the large armour-piercing shells ripping the soft-skinned merchantman apart like a can opener whilst the merchant seamen frantically launched lifeboats and tried to get clear of the foundering ship. Although the *Behar* was armed, her guns were no match for the 8-inch guns of the heavy cruiser attacking them, and the gun crews, consisting of seventeen soldiers and sailors (with some also manning the ship's Asdic sonar equipment) attempted to abandon ship as well. Three members of the crew, 21-year-old Gunner Stanley Pyecroft of 4 Maritime Regiment, Able Seaman Thomas Robinson of HMS *President* (a naval rating assigned to the *Behar*), and 55-year-old Indian merchant sailor 2nd Paniwalla Noor Khan Emad, were killed by the Japanese shelling. In the meantime, Mii had ordered all of the cruiser's boats, and even the cutter, swung out and launched, as he endeavoured to rescue the crew of the *Behar*.

Conscious that he wanted no harm to come to his captives, Commander Mii related that 'I instructed the rescue party that no rough treatment of survivors would be tolerated.'[1] The junior officers in charge of the rescue apparently did not take Mii's order seriously, for when Mii saw the survivors coming aboard the *Tone*, 'I was surprised to find that they were all bound and haltered.'[2] In fact, the crew and passengers, including two women, had been stripped of most of their clothes before being bound. Mii immediately ordered that the survivors' hands be untied and he reprimanded the officers responsible for their disobedience.

Mii ordered Lieutenant Ishihara to take command of the sailors guarding the prisoners, and as a further humanitarian gesture he ordered the ship's medical officer, Surgeon Lieutenant Commander Nakahashi, to examine each survivor for wounds and treat them accordingly. Lieutenant Nagai, the paymaster, was placed in charge of interrogating the survivors for information, and as he was also the cruiser's supply officer, Nagai was made responsible for feeding the 115 captives. Although they were crowded together on the warship's deck, water, food and medical attention was given to the prisoners, and their guards did not mistreat them whilst Mii was around. This changed later and, after enduring several hours of sitting on the aft deck under the hot sun, the prisoners were herded below into airless compartments where, according to survivor Petty Officer Walter Griffiths, they were subjected to some physical abuse from their guards, now safely away from the watchful eyes of their officers.

In the meantime, Captain Mayuzumi reported the sinking of the *Behar* to the flagship *Aoba* and requested directions regarding what he should do with his prisoners. Later that day the *Aoba* signalled the *Tone* ordering Mayuzumi to 'dispose' of all of the prisoners except two or three key personnel, such as the captain, radio operator and chief engineer. Mayuzumi was also reprimanded by Admiral Sakonju for firstly sinking the *Behar* when she could have been captured and put to use in the Japanese war effort, and secondly for allowing so many enemy survivors to board the *Tone*. Mayuzumi knew that he should have captured some of the key personnel for interrogation and machine-gunned the rest in the water.

When Commander Mii was informed of the 'disposal' order he quickly made known his feelings to his captain. 'I told the Captain that such a course was inhuman and that I could not be a party to the execution especially in view of the fact that I had ordered the rescue of the survivors and saw to it that the order was carried out in spite of the high seas running.'[3] Mii's complaint bought the prisoners a few more hours, and, unsure of what to do, Mayuzumi signalled the *Aoba* that the prisoners were still under investigation.

The following day, 10 March, Captain Mayuzumi, acting on Mii's suggestions, signalled the flagship again to request that all of the prisoners be landed. Because the crew of the *Behar* contained a high percentage of Indians, Mayuzumi recommended that the Indians be split up and used as crewmen on board small Japanese merchant ships, and the European prisoners sent to internment camps for use as slave labour. The reply from the *Aoba* was unequivocal. Captain Mayuzumi must carry out the disposal instruction in accordance with the Japanese Navy standing orders issued to submarines on 20 March, and amended for surface vessels, that stated that warships were to 'carry out the complete destruction of the crew of the enemy's ships'.[4] All of the survivors were ordered to be killed with the exception of what the *Aoba* termed 'those required for further interrogation, in accordance with previous orders'.[5] This was not a popular order amongst the cruiser's officers, who were divided between the duty to follow their orders, deeply ingrained in them from their first day in the Navy, and their own private humanity. The unease was compounded by the fact that Captain Mayuzumi had not made a strong decision concerning interpreting his orders, and the ship's second-in-command, Mii, was outspoken in his refusal to carry out any 'disposal' order. Mii convened an officer's meeting in the wardroom to gauge opinion and found that a majority of the ship's officers were not in favour of killing the prisoners. However,

Lieutenant Tani led the faction who believed that as naval officers they were duty bound to follow the orders of their superiors – perhaps because of a fear of censure from Fleet command and a deeply held sense of duty, a minority of the officers sided with Tani and demanded that the order be carried out. After the meeting Commander Mii went to his captain and told him the feelings of the officers in the hope of persuading him that only a minority were prepared to kill the prisoners. Mii later blamed Mayuzumi for his weakness as a commanding officer, stating: 'There would have been no need for this meeting if the Captain had stated definitely his refusal to execute the prisoners in the first place.'[6]

The *Tone* sailed towards Batavia, capital of the occupied Netherlands East Indies, no decision having yet been taken over the fate of the 115 men and women locked away in compartments below decks. On 15 March the warship arrived at Batavia, and on the following day a conference was convened aboard the flagship *Aoba* which Mayuzumi and Mii attended. Mii was determined to get his prisoners ashore now that they were in port, to avoid the unnecessary spilling of blood. With this in mind he approached Captain Shimanouchi, the 16th Squadron's senior staff officer, and formally requested that the prisoners from the *Tone* be landed. Shimanouchi shrugged off Mii's request and refused to listen to the Commander's pleadings. Mii believed that Captain Mayuzumi also approached Admiral Sakonju on the matter and it appeared that the Admiral was more receptive. An order was received from the *Aoba* to land fifteen prisoners, and Mii managed to get ashore the two women amongst them and a Chinese academic named Dr Lai Yung Li on 16 March. That still left 100 captives aboard the *Tone*, their future increasingly uncertain.

Mii went back to the *Aoba* and requested a meeting with Captain Shimanouchi. Once again, however, he was rebuffed. Desperately searching around for someone with enough seniority to plead his case, Mii approached the commander of the cruiser *Oi*, Captain Katsuo Shiba, and asked him to intervene with Shimanouchi on the prisoners' behalf. Mii also risked further censure by personally asking Vice Admiral Sakonju to save the prisoners' lives. Mii's persistence appeared to pay off, for Sakonju suddenly ordered fifteen of the Indian captives to be transferred ashore to the prisoner-of-war camp located in the city of Batavia. On the afternoon of the 17th Mii acquainted Mayuzumi with this order, and

1. A Japanese officer beheading Chinese prisoners with a sword.

2. Japanese Special Naval Landing Troops celebrating a victory with a collective 'Banzai!' to the Emperor.

3. Australian troops of 'Lark Force', the small and under-equipped Australian force sent to defend Rabaul from Japanese invasion. Most were subsequently captured in January and February 1942.

4. Japanese Special Naval Landing troops conducting a bayonet charge. Japanese 'marines' were famous for their suicidal courage in combat and their brutality towards prisoners.

5. Tantui Barracks on Ambon Island – home to British and Dutch prisoners captured by the Japanese.

6. The USS *Edsall*, sunk by the Japanese after a vicious sea battle. Many of the survivors were killed by the Japanese after being captured.

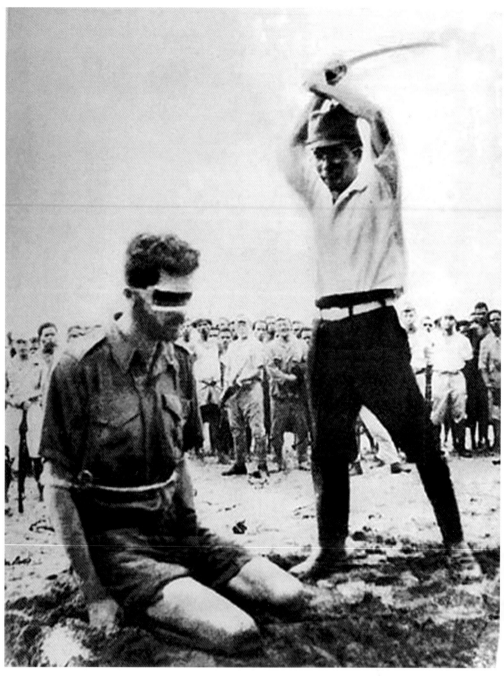

7. Australian Sergeant Leonard Siffleet about to be beheaded by the Japanese in New Guinea, 1943.

8. A US Liberty Ship, one of 2,700 identical cargo vessels constructed during the war. Several, including the *Jean Nicolet, John A. Johnson* and *Richard Hovey*, were sunk by Japanese submarines and their crews murdered.

9. The Japanese heavy cruiser *Tone* on whose aft deck seventy Allied merchant sailors were tortured to death in 1944.

10. The American submarine USS *Sculpin*, sunk by the Japanese in November 1943. Survivors were taken to Truk and handed over to the Japanese Naval Secret Police.

11. A Filipino victim of the Rape of Manila in 1945. After having been assaulted by Japanese naval forces, her tongue had been cut out.

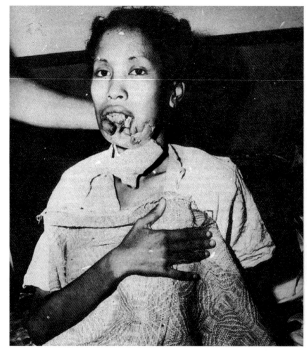

12. A mother and daughter killed by Japanese naval forces lie in the rubble of Manila, 1945.

13. Three young Filipino children bayoneted to death by rampaging Japanese sailors in Manila, 1945.

14. Lieutenant General Tomoyuki Yamashita in American custody. He was tried for 'command responsibility' over the Rape of Manila and later hanged as a war criminal.

flagrantly disregarding his admiral's instructions, bravely doubled the number sent ashore to thirty individuals. He concealed the exact number he had sent ashore from both Mayuzumi and Sakonju – unusually for a Japanese officer, he had deliberately disobeyed orders and saved as many as possible from the slaughter to come.

Still not satisfied with the fact of the imminent mass execution of seventy innocent men, Mii went back to Captains Mayuzumi and Shimanouchi and argued forcefully with both of these superior officers. He told them that 'as my efforts resulted in the release of 15 prisoners [he concealed the true figure of thirty], their concerted efforts [in talking to Sakonju] would produce considerably more releases.'[7] The two captains' argued with Mii, stating that the Batavia prisoner-of-war camp was already full to capacity and there was no more room for further captives. Mii replied that the prison camp may be small, but the island of Java was big enough. 'I also told them that if they made no further efforts they were lacking in human sympathy.'[8] Perhaps because Mii had lost his temper with two senior officers, or perhaps because Admiral Sakonju believed that he had already released into custody as many prisoners as the local camp could handle, the *Tone* received sailing orders for the 18 March, with the remaining prisoners still aboard her. Captain Mayuzumi was ordered to dispose of the remaining captives out at sea during the night. When Mii learned of this irreversible order he declared that he would have nothing to do with such a crime and busied himself on the bridge. Mayuzumi instead ordered Lieutenant Ishihara to take charge of the massacre, and various junior officers from the group originally in favour of the executions would form the chief executioners, assisted by many ordinary members of the crew.

Late in the evening Japanese sailors began hauling the cowed captives to the cruiser's stern, where the victims had their hands bound behind their backs. Captain Mayuzumi did not make their last moments on earth comfortable, nor did he grant his prisoners a quick death. Probably having also turned his back on the prisoners now that Lieutenant Ishihara had been charged with their disposal, the skipper was conspicuous by his absence during the executions. Without Commander Mii present to keep the sailors behaviour in check, the prisoners were treated with the utmost brutality, encouraged by the hard-line junior officers in charge of the seamen. Kicked in the stomach or the testicles by their guards, the moaning and terrified prisoners were thrown to their knees before a collection of junior officers armed with swords, among them Lieutenant Tani and Sub Lieutenants Tanaka and Otsuka, who were later heard boasting of their actions in the ward-room. One by one, the seventy remaining prisoners were beheaded and their bodies dumped overboard for the sharks to clean up.

The resistance of Junsuke Mii to his orders is remarkable and noteworthy considering the more usual slavish obedience to instructions by wartime Japanese military and naval officers. His disobedience perhaps should have been taken as an example by other officers who found themselves in similar situations, for Mii's career was not affected by his strident stance on the fate of the men and women he had saved from the ocean. In fact, Mii was later promoted to captain, demonstrating that the affair did him no harm whatsoever. But it was not in the interests of the IJN to widely circulate the story of an officer who placed his own conscience and personal humanity before his duty to his Emperor. Although he tried everything he could, except physically preventing the executions, for the rest of his life Mii was filled with remorse for his failure to save every survivor from the *Behar*, stating during his interrogation by Royal Navy intelligence in 1946: 'I am profoundly sorry that this atrocity should have happened and I console myself with the fact that through my efforts, I was able to save 30 persons from execution.'[9] Mii feared that by making such an admission that the officers and men of the *Tone* were responsible for a war crime would have made himself and his family in Japan vulnerable to revenge attacks, and it was noted in May 1946 that Mii only gave his affidavit after considerable prompting by British investigating officers. Junsuke Mii did everything in his power to save lives – not many Japanese officers were able to state that when the time came to account for their wartime behaviour .

Most of the Japanese sailors involved in the *Behar* massacre were never prosecuted after the end of the Second World War, and it fell to Allied military tribunals in the Far East to find and prosecute the more prominent officers involved in the crime. Vice Admiral Sakonju, who had consistently refused to spare the lives of most of the survivors even when Commander Mii had pleaded on their behalf, went on to higher things. Promoted to become Chief of Staff of the China Area Fleet in October 1944, he was still in this post when the war ended. Arrested and placed on trial in Hong Kong by the British, Sakonju was found guilty of causing the *Behar* massacre and was sentenced to death. In 1948 he was hanged. Captain Mayuzumi was given a light sentence, even though he too had finally decided to follow Sakonju's orders and had instructed junior officers under his command to execute the prisoners. He pled 'superior orders' with mitigating circumstances. Mayuzumi received a seven-year prison term; after his release he disappeared into Japan and a new life. Commander Mii was acquitted of any involvement in a war crime, though he was forced to live the rest of his life with what he perceived as the dishonour of having sold out his comrades during the trials by testifying against them. Those who actually murdered the survivors of the *Behar* mostly remained at liberty after the war.

Notes
1. Affidavit of Sugamo Prisoner 4A-24 Mii Junsuke sworn on 30 May 1946, Exhibit 2104, International Military Tribunal for the Far East, MB 1549, vol. 46, Exhibits (MacMillan Brown Library, University of Canterbury, Christchurch).
2. Ibid.
3. Ibid.
4. Russell of Liverpool, Lord, *The Knights of Bushido: A Short History of Japanese War Crimes* (Greenhill Books, 2002), p. 214.
5. Affidavit of Sugamo Prisoner 4A-24 Mii Junsuke sworn on 30 May 1946, Exhibit 2104, International Military Tribunal for the Far East, MB 1549, vol. 46, Exhibits (MacMillan Brown Library, University of Canterbury, Christchurch).
6. Ibid.
7. Ibid.
8. Ibid.
9. Ibid.

Chapter Twelve

Eliminate All Survivors

Two Japs were . . . in front of us, one with a revolver and
one with a coil of rope. Again and again they shouted from
the [conning] tower, 'Do not look back, because that will
be too bad for you.'

Chief Officer F. de Jong
S.S. Tjisalak

Japanese submarines continued to attack and sink Allied merchant
ships throughout the Indian Ocean and Arabian Sea throughout
the rest of March 1944. Sometimes submarine skippers appeared
satisfied with an easy kill and left the scene after a ship had
foundered, and importantly they did not order their crewmen to
molest the surviving crew. But, in common with the massacres
perpetrated on the survivors of the *Scotia, Daisy Moller, British
Chivalry, Sutlej* and *Ascot*, some Japanese skippers determined to
follow their orders to the letter and attempted to kill all the Allied
sailors they could lay their hands on. None of these attempts was
completely successful, and men did manage to survive, even when
the Japanese were extremely thorough in taking their time over
executing survivors. The British and Americans were soon to be
able to build up a detailed picture of Japanese submarine war
crimes as each new atrocity was reported to them. Furthermore,
the close observations of survivors allied with captured IJN files
enabled naval intelligence organizations to identify the particular
Japanese submarines and skippers involved in these violations of
the accepted rules of war – information that in many cases led to
post-war prosecutions being brought against them. However, the
carnage and death, as well as the extreme brutality and sadism of
Japanese submariners towards fellow seamen soon became

legendary, and many an Allied merchant ship captain sailing his ship unescorted through the Indian Ocean feared an encounter with Japan's bloodthirsty sea wolves.

The *Nancy Moller* was zigzagging at 9 knots when two Japanese torpedoes struck her side, the first exploded in the engine room on the portside, and the second, a couple of seconds later, blowing up in the deep tank underneath the bridge. The violence of the explosions tore the guts out of the ship and she sank in about one minute, leaving the crew virtually no time to organize an evacuation or to launch the lifeboats and rafts. Three of the ship's lifeboats were still firmly attached to their davits when the *Nancy Moller* sank, but the violence of her end freed a fourth boat and some rafts which floated on the disturbed and debris-littered surface of the water.

The single remaining lifeboat was upside down; much of the survival equipment carried inside the rafts had been lost during the sinking. The men who had made it into the water now thrashed about trying to find something to cling to as the Japanese submarine came to the surface close by and made for them. Second Officer S.K. Chu observed about twenty Japanese sailors on the submarine's lower bridge and fore deck, recalling that the boat 'was painted with dark grayish colour, had no identification mark [and was] mounted with one 4 inch gun forward'.[1]

The submarine motored up to one of the rafts, aboard which were several wet and exhausted officers and crew. Gunlayer Fryers, 2nd Engineer H.T. Shing, Fitter Wong and three Indian seamen watched as their raft bumped up against the Japanese submarine. Ordered to board her, the six men slowly clambered onto the deck of the submarine where they were roughly handled by the well-armed crew. Fryers was led away to an open hatch in the submarine's deck and taken below out of sight of his shipmates. Japanese sailors then forced the remaining five to their knees, facing the bow. Chu watched as 'The 2nd Engineer was shot twice with a revolver, and was kicked into the sea.' The gravely wounded Shing soon drowned as he was not wearing a lifejacket. Another Chinese member of the crew, Wong, was next. 'Fitter Wong received one shot, and as he was wearing his jacket, he managed to struggle in the water and was finally picked up.'[2] The three Indian sailors were not shot – the Japanese simply drove them with their rifles into the sea, where they were all later rescued by other survivors on rafts.

The Japanese now turned their attention to disposing of the other survivors who were lying on various rafts, and a light machine gun appeared on the conning tower. As soon as the gun rattled into life, the survivors crawled off the rafts into the water, and 'were alert enough to hide their bodies under water with hands grasping the becket lines'.[3] All survived the machine-gunning and as the Japanese could see no one alive in the water, they ceased firing and went below. Shortly thereafter, the submarine motored away on the surface and was not seen again.

The survivors decided to get together and, roping the rafts together, they discovered that thirty-two out of an original crew of sixty-five were still alive. The gunlayer had been hauled away as a prisoner to an unknown fate, the captain was dead, killed along with many members of the crew during the torpedo attacks, and the 2nd Engineer had been executed by the Japanese. Together, the survivors numbered four Britons, two Chinese (one badly wounded), a Russian and twenty-five Indians. Such grubby little attacks on unarmed passengers and crews of merchant vessels were to become increasingly common as the Japanese appeared hell-bent on murdering anyone who fell into their hands at sea.

The 5,787-ton Dutch merchant ship *Tjisalak* had sailed from Melbourne on 7 March 1944 fully loaded with over 6,600 tons of flour. Operated by JCJL, her destination was Colombo in Ceylon, and the vessel would work her way along a prescribed route in the Indian Ocean given to her master by naval command in Australia. In common with the other ships sunk by roving Japanese submarines, no escort was provided for the ship, and no convoys had been constituted to make the passage a safer one.

In addition to her cargo, the *Tjisalak* was also loaded with 700 tons of fuel oil and 400 tons of fresh water, sufficient to carry her and the 103 persons aboard her all the way to Ceylon. The crew numbered seventy-six men, with the remainder of the complement being made up of passengers. There were five first-class passengers and twenty-two Indian lascars lodged between decks who had been paid off from another Dutch ship and were hitching a lift home to India. It was not unusual for merchant ships like the *Tjisalak* to carry a few fare-paying passengers and reasonable accommodations had been provided for their comfort on the upper decks. The passengers included an American woman named Mrs Brittan who was travelling to Calcutta to be reunited with her British husband who worked for the intelligence services. There was a sailor, Captain Scotti, of the British Merchant Marine, who was on his way to rejoin his ship after a holiday in Australia, and a young Australian Army lieutenant. The final passengers were two young British lads who had just enlisted and were on their way to report for duty in India.

On Sunday, 26 March the sun rose at 5.25am over a fair sea. The sky was slightly cloudy, with a light westerly wind blowing the water into a slight swell as the *Tjisalak* sailed on. Visibility for the lookouts was 8 miles, and at 5.30am Chief Officer F. de Jong visited the master in his cabin, asking permission to be relieved on the bridge as he wished to take sights on the stars. The captain came onto the bridge and de Jong reminded him that he wanted to begin zigzagging the ship in the morning. The practice of zigzagging was a rather futile anti-submarine drill intended to make a merchant ship less of an inviting target because of its erratic course, making plotting a submerged torpedo attack difficult. The Fourth Officer was sent off to calculate a zigzagging pattern, and de Jong stepped into the chartroom and began calculating his ship's position. All of this early morning routine was about to be rudely shattered. Suddenly de Jong heard the voice of the captain yelling 'Hard to port, hard to port!' through the open door from the bridge; de Jong dropped his pencil and dashed onto the upper bridge. Just as he arrived there, he could see the white wake in the water left by a torpedo and barely had time to take this in before there was an almighty explosion on the port side. Amid the sounds of falling debris, including the radio masts, and hissing steam from broken pipes, the *Tjisalak* leaned precariously over to port, quickly gaining a 20-degree list that appeared to indicate her doom. Then, like some great pendulum, the vessel rolled back 5 degrees and began to settle. The ship's gun crew were already engaging something as yet unidentified, their small gun blasting away without effect. The gunners were all British, drawn from the Royal Artillery and the Royal Sussex Regiment, and numbered ten in total under the command of the *Tjisalak*'s Second Officer.

De Jong and the captain knew that the *Tjisalak* was probably going to founder, and so, after a quick consultation, the two men agreed to give the 'Abandon Ship' signal to the crew and passengers. De Jong was ordered to take charge of filling and launching the lifeboats, while the master strode off to his cabin to fetch the ship's papers. The *Tjisalak* actually had more lifeboats than she needed for the passengers and crew, three on each side, and de Jong had long intended that if the ship was struck by a torpedo he would fill the three boats on the lower side as the vessel settled into the sea. Walking over to port side No. 2, he began issuing orders. The passenger Captain Scotti, because of his experience at sea, was detailed to take charge of the boat, while de Jong, the Fourth Officer and some essential crewmen remained on deck. De Jong handed Scotti his knife and told him to cut the boat's lashings, except for a single line to hold the boat alongside until de Jong and the others could join Scotti and the others. Although there was no panic during the evacuation of the *Tjisalak*, when de Jong and the Fourth Officer got into the lifeboat they found that the Chinese members of the crew and those Indian lascars aboard 'sat down in the boat like being dead and we could not force them to do a single thing'.[4] Ignoring the attitude of these men, the Fourth Officer carefully placed a sextant and chronometer into the boat, and as de Jong looked back he could see that lifeboats Nos 1 and 3 were also fully loaded and about to be launched. Whilst this was going on the *Tjisalak* continued to sink further into the ocean as the list to port grew steadily worse. De Jong stepped back onto the deck and strode over to the captain, who was on the lower bridge, and reported to him that his boat was in the water and full. 'He told me to get into the boat also and get away from the ship. He was just preparing himself to get into the boat. I saw that he had his secret logbooks under his arm.'[5] When de Jong stepped back into his lifeboat, the water was lapping at the ship's main deck, and the swell was causing the lifeboat to smash time and again against the rail. With the Chinese seamen and the lascars refusing to take any orders or to cooperate for their own survival, de Jong recalled that only 'With great efforts we could keep clear the boat with the few Europeans.'[6] Time was running out and it was imperative that the three lifeboats cleared the ship's sides before she sank much lower. As de Jong struggled to get lifeboat No. 2 away, he was knocked off his feet several times by the violent impact of the boat against the ship's side. All the time this commotion was going on the ship's gun crew had remained at their station, firing into the distance. No. 3 lifeboat was standing by alongside the *Tjisalak* ready to take them off, while aboard No. 2, de Jong's orders for his crew to unship the oars and begin pulling fell upon deaf ears.

Without power, lifeboat No. 2 floated dangerously past the *Tjisalak*'s gun, which was still blasting away. De Jong and the handful of Europeans in his boat managed to get a few oars into the water and with a massive effort, rowed the lifeboat clear of the gun barrel. After the war a Dutch investigation of the sinking of the *Tjisalak* attempted to place the blame for the Japanese outrages subsequently committed against the crew and passengers onto the British gunners. The Dutch stated: 'The British gunners were only doing their duty, not knowing that by doing so they were blowing the last chance for survival of crew and passengers.'[7] In the light of the Japanese naval order of 20 March 1943, which authorized submarine commanders not to stop at the sinking of enemy ships, but to eliminate any surviving crew as well, whether the gunners fired on the submarine is irrelevant. The Japanese had been ordered to dispose of all survivors of the *Tjisalak*, with the exception of a few key personnel who would be held for questioning, and the blame for the tragedy has always been with the Japanese Navy.

Although now clear of the ship's gun, to their horror de Jong and the others discovered that their lifeboat was leaking heavily, so 'We started to bail the water out with buckets and pumps. A little later the ship went down with a sigh.'[8] At the last moment the gunners had jumped overboard and they swam to lifeboat No. 3. De Jong pulled the 3rd Engineer from the water, and he immediately grasped an oar and began helping the others to row clear of the sinking ship.

De Jong scanned the horizon for signs of their assailant and soon 'I could see the periscope of the sub on the port side at a distance of about a mile. We could see she was heading towards us and we soon could see three things sticking out of the water like periscopes.'[9] The submarine I-8 rose to the surface from periscope depth, a great bulk of a submarine weighing in at 2,600 tons, and Commander Tatsunosuke Ariizumi ordered his boat taken in close to the survivors gathered inside the three lifeboats.

The I-8 had already become a famous boat in the Japanese Navy when Commander Shinji Uchino had sailed the submarine all the way to German-occupied France in 1943 to deliver precious raw materials to the Nazi war machine, and a Japanese submarine crew trained to operate U-1224, a German Type IXC40 U-boat Hitler had presented to the Imperial Navy as a token of his friendship. The I-8 completed the trip to Brest and back to Kure, Japan, arriving home in December 1943 loaded down with the latest German military technology to assist the Japanese in developing new weapons to stave off defeat in the Pacific. Uchino and the crew of the I-8 had travelled an incredible 30,000 nautical miles.[10] Uchino had left the boat before the New Year, having been promoted to captain as a reward for his incredible seamanship. His replacement was Commander Ariizumi, soon to gain a reputation as a butcher and to soil the name of the I-8, already famous for a voyage of exceptional seamanship and endurance, turning it to one of infamy instead.

The *Tjisalak*'s captain brought his lifeboat, which only had Chinese sailors aboard, alongside de Jong's. The Fourth Officer and 3rd Engineer transferred into the captain's boat as the Chinese were refusing to cooperate with the rowing, and all eyes turned to the big submarine which was bearing down upon them. In a familiar replay of events, a voice shouted in English from the I-8's conning tower ordering the captain to identify himself. The captain did not move and the order was repeated by the Japanese officer. Reluctantly, the captain gingerly stood up inside his lifeboat and raised his hand. The Japanese officer ordered the captain to bring his lifeboat alongside the I-8. As the lifeboat came alongside, de Jong watched as the captain and the other Europeans aboard her clambered carefully up onto the submarine's deck. The lifeboat under the command of the Second Officer drifted further away from the submarine, as perhaps the men aboard already had a foreboding of danger, but de Jong followed the Japanese instructions and slowly brought lifeboat No. 2 alongside the I-8. The Japanese were quite animated, shouting for the merchant officers to report, and the Second Officer's boat followed de Jong towards the submarine.

When de Jong climbed aboard, the captain and the other Europeans had disappeared inside the submarine down an open hatch in the deck. Along with the 3rd Engineer, the Japanese ordered de Jong and his companions 'to sit down there [on the fore-deck] facing forward. We should in no case look back they told us. From all around they kept us covered. When I boarded the sub they took my knife away. I had my lifebelt on and luckily they forgot to take that away. My papers were packed in the inside of my lifebelt and they did not spot it.'[11] Within a few minutes the foredeck of the submarine was crowded with the Europeans, Chinese and

Indian lascars from the three lifeboats, all under armed guard from a clearly hostile collection of Japanese submariners.

> Two Japs were making us stand by in front of us, one with a revolver and one with a coil of rope. Again and again they shouted from the [conning] tower, 'Do not look back, because that will be too bad for you.' I got the impression that there was little discipline. Everybody just pleased himself and they all tried to get as many souvenirs as possible. So they took watches, papers and knives.[12]

De Jong sat and contemplated his situation. 'A little to the right before me was the 5th Eng. sitting. A little to the left and forward was the 3rd Eng. I got the impression that the Japs wanted to start all kinds of things at the same time. One was preparing himself to tie us up, another was fumbling with his revolver and so on.'[13] Although the Japanese were quite explicit in warning their prisoners not to look back, although curiosity caused most of them to do so. De Jong warned his men to stop and to keep their eyes forward as there was no use in antagonizing their captors. However, inside himself the Dutch officer knew that things were bad. 'I understood the end was there for all of us, and I told the Europeans near me. I told them to try to make the best of it. All of us sat down depressed.'[14] The 5th Engineer was barely able to contain his feelings, as he had escaped from the German-occupied Netherlands only to find himself now in the hands of the Japanese. Such were the peculiar fortunes of war. De Jong did not feel fear of what was to come as 'I had finished with my life and I felt abnormally calm.'[15] He was later to remark that every member of the crew of the *Tjisalak* behaved bravely and there was no screaming or begging for mercy from any of them.

From behind the cowed prisoners came the sounds of men fighting and the submarine got underway again, its large diesels throbbing, the screws beating the water into a foamy wake as the I-8 headed on an easterly course away from the wreckage and abandoned lifeboats. De Jong's mind seemed to have cleared from its previous melancholy and now raced with thoughts of escape.

> I was thinking now about jumping overboard, but I was surrounded by Chinese and I thought I had only a very small

chance. So I decided to stay and wait. What would happen now? Would they start to machine-gun us from the tower? Would they tie us up and then dive? It was very difficult to guess. To wait all the time was unbearable.[16]

De Jong's thoughts were broken by the Japanese ordering the 5th Engineer to his feet, who they told to start walking aft. Everyone heard a single shot as the young Dutchman was dispatched. De Jong was picked next.

One Jap was hanging on to my back when I walked aft. Maybe he wanted to pull off my lifebelt, maybe he wanted to prevent me from jumping overboard. Everywhere Japs were standing by with weapons. I realized that to dive with my lifebelt on would be very difficult and my chance was nil as I could not keep myself under with same. Whenever I should come into the water I would be riddled with bullets and probably die slowly. As I had to die anyhow I preferred a sudden death.[17]

De Jong was frogmarched further aft by his Japanese escort, past the conning tower and onto the aft deck.

At a distance of about 5 or 6 feet from the stern there was one Jap ready with his revolver. When I came alongside of him I stopped as I expected him to shoot me through the head. He pointed out to me however that I had to carry on. When I arrived at the very end of the deck, above the propellers I heard a bang and felt a terrific shock on my head and I toppled over into the water.[18]

The Japanese had deliberately chosen a place of execution directly above the churning propellers to make doubly sure that their victims would be killed. By a miracle, the falling de Jong narrowly missed the blades and floated off in the wake of the I-8, unconscious but nonetheless still alive, his lifejacket holding him up in the water.

When he regained consciousness he was floating upright in his lifebelt and the water around him was stained with blood from his head wound. The submarine was about a mile away in the distance. 'I was very down. I was afraid they would find out on the sub that

130

I was still alive and come and finish me off. To be executed once is pretty bad, but for a second time looked horrible to me.'[19] Inspecting his head gingerly with his fingers, de Jong discovered that the Japanese pistol bullet had not penetrated his skull. This fact raised his spirits, for his injury appeared to be survivable. 'Now I decided to try everything in my power to save my life.' Determined to avoid the roving I-8, which was making periodic sweeps through the dozens of bodies floating on the surface of the ocean, de Jong recalled that he 'nearly drowned by keeping my head under the surface' when he feigned death. [20] The massacre of the passengers and crew of the *Tjisalak* was still going on aboard the I-8, and de Jong now and again heard pistol shots as more were killed. Eventually, when the submarine disappeared out of sight towards the south, de Jong decided to head for the bulk of the floating wreckage 'to the West of me. So I decided to start swimming with the sun at my back until I could see some of the wreckage. I knew I had to be there before dark, would I have a chance? I did not take a rest but just swam as fast as I could.'[21]

By crude navigation, and a fierce determination to live, de Jong swam along in great pain from the salt water washing over his exposed head wound; he came upon some floating wreckage after about an hour. 'This gave me new hope and strength. I was out of breath and very tired but I kept on swimming. I was afraid I would not be able to reach the wreckage before sunset. Besides this the thought of sharks made me swim faster.'[22] Also in the back of his mind was the fear of the Japanese submarine coming back and discovering him still alive. 'After some time I again met part of a big raft and could sit down for a little while. I was exhausted. As far as I could see there were a few good big rafts together not far away.'[23] Some time later a totally exhausted de Jong swam alongside the rafts he had spotted earlier, but he found that he was too exhausted to clamber aboard. 'After having been hanging for ten minutes I was able to get on top of one of the rafts. Instantly I started to vomit heavily and the blood was running into my eyes. I felt simply miserable. Every time I vomited the wound started to bleed more and more.'[24] Sick, exhausted and bleeding, Chief Officer de Jong lay on the raft thinking that he was the only survivor of the *Tjisalak*. However, he was not alone for very long. A voice carried across the ocean, de Jong lifted his head and spotted a figure struggling through the water towards him. 'I shouted as loud as I could "Come on here, I cannot help you." After this I had to lie down again and vomit.' The second survivor who climbed aboard was the second wireless operator, a 21-year-old Briton surnamed Blears. 'He was exhausted. We nearly embraced each other.' Blears pulled out the raft's medicine box and treated de Jong as best he could, trying to make him as comfortable as possible until he had recovered from his severe concussion.

Blears' experience had been equally as horrendous as that of de Jong. The young officer had had tried to enlist in the Royal Navy at the age of seventeen, but being under age he had joined the Merchant Navy instead where his knowledge of Morse code meant he was appointed as a radio officer. Although offered a safe assignment, Blears had turned it down in favour of joining the Dutch ship *Tjisalak*, which required an English-speaking wireless operator. Blears witnessed far more of the brutal massacre perpetrated by the Japanese than de Jong. 'They were laughing,' recalled Blears of the Japanese sailors.

> They'd just go up and hit a guy on the back and take him up front, and then one of the guys with a sword would cut off his head. Zhunk! One guy, they cut his head halfway and let him flop around on the deck. The others I saw, they just lopped 'em off with one shot and threw 'em overboard.[25]

Incredible though it may seem, the Japanese officers in the conning tower overseeing the carnage were carefully preserving the moment for posterity. 'They were having fun, and there was a cameraman taking movies of the whole thing!'[26] Blears recalled. When Blear's turn came, he was struck with the flat of a sword and then dragged to his feet by Japanese sailors. Roughly, his wrists were then tied behind him, but cleverly Blears kept his wrists as far apart as possible when this was being done and he could feel afterwards that he would be able to free one of his hands. Marched towards the I-8's stern, Blears recalled that 'Two Japanese officers were waiting for us, one with a sword and the other with a sledgehammer.' Alongside Blears was another captive being led to his death, a Dutch crew member named Peter Bronger. Blears had no intention of dying in Japanese hands. 'When these guys came at us [the Japanese officers], I kicked with my foot and pulled my hand out (of the rope) right away and stopped the guy and dived off the submarine and dragged Peter with me.'[27] Rifle and machine-gun fire followed the Briton into the water and he tried to stay down deep as long as possible. On the second occasion that Blears surfaced he found that the submarine was now some distance away, though two Japanese sitting in deck chairs were taking pot shots at people in the water with rifles. Bronger was nowhere to be seen and Blears suspected that he had been killed by the sword-wielding Japanese officer before they both went overboard. In a similarly determined fashion to de Jong, Blears decided to swim back towards where the *Tjisalak* had foundered to look for a lifeboat or raft. A strong swimmer, a similar fear of sharks meant that he covered the distance to de Jong's raft in record time.

Blears let de Jong lie down and after bandaging the Dutch officer's wound, the radio operator placed a flag over de Jong's head to protect him from the sun. 'We both tried to relax a little,' recalled de Jong at the Tokyo War Crimes Trial. 'After a little while we heard shouting again, and shortly afterwards the 3rd Eng. hoisted himself into the raft. After we had all a little rest, we started to talk about what we should do next.'[28] The three officers could see empty lifeboats about one and a half miles away in the distance. Even further away the *Tjisalak*'s motorboat drifted, empty. De Jong suggested 'trying to get one of the nearest boats to go with that boat to the motorboat. After that we could prepare the motor-boat for a long trip and we could gather all the useful things from the other boats to sail some time in the evening.'[29] Bravely, both Blears and the 3rd Engineer volunteered to swim to the nearest lifeboat and row it back to the rafts to pick up the others. De Jong, as senior officer, declined to allow them because he feared patrolling sharks might have seized them. Instead, de Jong suggested that they try to row one of the rafts to the boats. As de Jong recollected, 'I could not do very much myself, as I suffered from cramp and vomited all the time . . . Both did everything they could for me. They fished a pillow out of the water and put that under my head. They worked hard and we really managed to get the big raft to the boats.'[30] On arrival the men discovered that the Japanese had stolen the marine chronometer and compass that the Second Officer had placed in one of the lifeboats, but by a miracle the Japanese had failed to find a portable radio set. The lifeboats were all leaking badly after having been shot up by Japanese machine-gun fire in an effort to sink any incriminating evidence of a war crime, so picking the best one Blears and the 3rd Engineer rowed the boat, with de Jong resting in the bottom, over to the motorboat. They were in for a disappointment for the motorboat was in a worse condition than the lifeboats, so the three survivors were forced to stay in the lifeboat and make the best of it. Rowing over to check the last lifeboat drifting in the ocean, the survivors heard shouting and spotted two figures in the sea. Rowing over to them, de Jong and his companions saved the 2nd Officer and an Indian lascar surnamed Dhange. The Indian was the only survivor among the twenty-two of his countrymen listed as passengers aboard the *Tjisalak*. The Japanese had tied the Indian seamen onto long ropes and then submerged the I-8, dragging the kicking and struggling men down into the depths, deliberately drowning them. Dhange was on the end of one of the lines and had managed to free himself from the rope and swim to the surface.

The lifeboat was equipped with wood-burning water distillers and de Jong ordered the others to try to haul aboard wooden hatch covers from the *Tjisalak* that were floating all about them. However, after all of their physical exertions so far that day, none had the strength to complete the task and de Jong decided instead that if it came to it he would burn the oars to provide fresh water. After scouring the abandoned lifeboats, which totalled five including the starboard boats dragged off the ship when the *Tjisalak* plunged beneath the waves, de Jong had to decide on a course to follow.

> We knew it was useless to try to get to the Islands to the west of us, as there is a current of about 50 miles to the east in this locality. By steering N.W. we hoped to make a good course North. Before we sailed we had a good look around us for some more possible survivors. As we had practically covered everything around the wreckage during the day, we could be pretty sure that we had not missed any other survivors.[31]

Day after day de Jong navigated the little lifeboat through the Indian Ocean by compass and sun bearings. 'Our intention was to keep plenty west afterwards so not to come in the gulf of Bengal. We had plenty of boat rations on board and ten tanks of drinking water, as we had unbolted the water tanks from the other boats. Furthermore, we had 2 compasses, 2 sets of sails, plenty of rope and canvas.'[32] Because of the vastness of the Indian Ocean, none of the survivors expected to be spotted by a friendly aircraft or rescued by a passing ship. Instead, de Jong and his companions were determined instead to save themselves and by careful navigation make landfall in three or four weeks. However, in the backs of their minds was the terrible fear of submarines. 'Our continuous fear was the sub. Life in the boat was pretty hard and the rain made it worse. We were soaked and could not dry ourselves. The cold let us suffer. We had to bail the boat out day and night.'[33]

Although they had a radio, the survivors held off from sending a distress call for two days, lest the Japanese submarine was still be in the area and having intercepted their message, come back to find and kill them. On 28 March they rigged the radio aerial and prepared to send their call for assistance. Suddenly, the 2nd Officer grabbed de Jong's sleeve and pointed astern.

> There was the sub coming. Just with its conning tower above the water. No doubt it was the same sub. A little later we saw a flash and when we were thinking what it could be we noticed a splash in the water. They were shelling us. We were absolutely sure now that it was the sub and we tried to prepare ourselves for a second death.[34]

Seven times the submarine fired at them, 'It was awful. We lowered the sail and waited for the end. Suddenly we saw the sub altering course and now we could see it was not a sub but a ship.'[35] Thinking that the mystery ship must be Japanese, perhaps a raider or supply vessel, the five survivors of the *Tjisalak* were astounded to discover that it was an American merchant ship bearing down upon them, guns blazing. The *James A. Wilder* had mistaken the lifeboat with its sail raised for a submarine conning tower and opened fire. Once they had realized their mistake, the gunners ceased fire immediately and the American ship picked up the exhausted survivors. Their ordeal at an end, de Jong, Blears and the others could only reflect upon their miraculous escapes from certain death, and mourn the other ninety-eight people who were never seen alive again after crossing the path of Commander Ariizumi and the murderous and sadistic crew of the I-8.

Chief Officer de Jong later officially wrote to the British

Admiralty, complaining about the lack of protection for merchant ships plying routes through the Indian Ocean that had led to several tragedies including not just the *Tjisalak*. He had also submitted some very novel ways that merchant crews could deal with Japanese submarines determined to kill every survivor from the ships they sank.

> In a case like ours [the sinking of the *Tjisalak*] there might have been a possibility to attack the sub with hand grenades. From several directions we could have closed with the boats and on a certain signal attack the sub with hand grenades. There is some danger in it of course as a few of the crew might escape with the sub and finish you off with shells from some distance. Another thing is that the first man who boards the sub takes a big bomb with him and blows himself up with the sub and all. This is not a very nice job, but in any case you take the Japs with you if you have to go.[36]

De Jong's final idea certainly has logic to it, though it would prob-ably have been very costly: 'The idea is to have a motor torpedo boat on board, camouflaged to look like an ordinary lifeboat. If the ship is torpedoed and the sub surfaces the motor torpedo boat should be able to finish her off.'[37] The Admiralty did not respond to any of de Jong's suggestions.

Notes

1. Statement of S.K. Chu, 2nd Mate, S.S. NANCY MOLLER, sunk 18 March 1944, Exhibit 2098, International Military Tribunal for the Far East, MB 1549, vol. 46, Exhibits (Macmillan Brown Library: University of Canterbury, Christchurch).
2. Ibid.
3. Ibid.
4. Statement of F. de Jong, Chief Officer, S.S. TJISALAK, sunk 26 March 1944, Exhibit 2099, International Military Tribunal for the Far East, MB 1549, vol. 46, Exhibits (MacMillan Brown Library: University of Canterbury, Christchurch).
5. Ibid.
6. Ibid.
7. Bezemer, K.W.L., *Geschiedenis van de Nederlandse Koopvaardij in de Tweede Wereldoorlog*, Part 2 (Elsevier: 1987), p. 1137.
8. Statement of F. de Jong, Chief Officer, S.S. TJISALAK, sunk 26 March 1944, Exhibit 2099, International Military Tribunal for the Far East,

MB 1549, vol. 46, Exhibits (MacMillan Brown Library: University of Canterbury, Christchurch).

9. Ibid.

10. For further details of the I-8's mission to France see the author's *Yanagi: The Secret Underwater Trade between Germany and Japan, 1942–1945* (Pen and Sword Maritime, 2005), pp. 60–7.

11. Statement of F. de Jong, Chief Officer, S.S. TJISALAK, sunk 26 March 1944, Exhibit 2099, International Military Tribunal for the Far East, MB 1549, vol. 46, Exhibits (MacMillan Brown Library: University of Canterbury, Christchurch).

12. Ibid.

13. Ibid.

14. Ibid.

15. Ibid.

16. Ibid.

17. Ibid.

18. Ibid.

19. Ibid.

20. Ibid.

21. Ibid.

22. Ibid.

23. Ibid.

24. Ibid.

25. *Honolulu Star-Bulletin*, Thursday, 29 March 2001.

26. Ibid.

27. Ibid.

28. Statement of F. de Jong, Chief Officer, S.S. TJISALAK, sunk 26 March 1944, Exhibit 2099, International Military Tribunal for the Far East, MB 1549, vol. 46, Exhibits (MacMillan Brown Library: University of Canterbury, Christchurch).

29. Ibid.

30. Ibid.

31. Ibid.

32. Ibid.

33. Ibid.

34. Ibid.

35. Ibid.

36. Ibid.

37. Ibid.

Chapter Thirteen

Death of the *Richard Hovey*

As the submarine was within a few feet of us we could
definitely determine that the men, who were lined up on its
deck as though they were on parade, were Japanese . . . They
were laughing and seemed to get quite a bit of sport out of
our predicament.

Lieutenant (jg) Harry Goudy, Gunnery Officer,
SS Richard Hovey

The IJN submarine I-26, under Lieutenant Commander Kusaka,
had slipped quietly out of Penang submarine base on 27 February
bound for the Arabian Sea on the far side of the Indian Ocean. The
I-26 was another famous boat in the Japanese Navy, being the first
submarine to have sunk an Allied ship on 7 December 1941 – the
day Japan attacked Pearl Harbor – 1,000 miles north-east of
Honolulu. It was here that the then skipper, Lieutenant
Commander Minoru Yokota, found and sank the *Cynthia Olson*,
an American merchant ship on her way from Tacoma, Washington
to Honolulu. In Hawaii a shore station registered a distress signal
from the vessel *before* Japanese aircraft arrived to wreck the US
Pacific Fleet, reporting that a submarine was attacking her. Of the
thirty-five crewmen aboard the vessel, none survived the attack.

Now, three years later, the new skipper, Kusaka, was taking the
I-26 out on the boat's eighth war patrol, having been given two
tasks to perform. Aboard the I-26 were ten members of a Japanese
military intelligence outfit called the Hikari Kikan. These men, all
Indian nationals, were going to be secretly landed in British India,
their task being to support the Indian independence movement and
destabilize the Raj. The Hikari Kikan worked closely with Subhas
Chandra Bose, an Indian nationalist who had escaped from British

custody in Calcutta earlier in the war. After making a daring escape across the Himalayas, Bose had gone to Germany via the Soviet Union in April 1941. He preached an aggressive independence war against the British in India and viewed the war in Europe as weakening Britain's control over the subcontinent. At the time he arrived in Berlin, German forces in North Africa had captured, almost intact, the 3rd (Indian) Motorized Brigade. The Germans assisted Bose with an intensive recruiting campaign, and within six months he had managed to collect a couple of thousand Indian servicemen which he formed into the Jai Hind, or Indian National Army, part of the German Wehrmacht.[1] After creating the Jai Hind, Bose had travelled by U-boat to the Indian Ocean and transferred to the Japanese submarine I-29 on 3 March 1943 for the journey to Japan. In Tokyo he intended to create a 'Provisional Government of Free India', and to recruit for what later became the Indian National Army, a collaborationist Indian military force created from prisoners of war held by the Japanese after the fighting in Burma and Malaya.[2]

Kusaka's orders were to drop off the ten Indian 'revolutionaries' close to the city of Karachi and he achieved this in early March without incident. The Japanese skipper's secondary orders were to begin raiding enemy communications in the Arabian Sea. The merchant traffic out of the oilfields of Iran to India, Ceylon and towards the Suez Canal was very busy, so Kusaka was optimistic of finding plenty of targets for his torpedoes.

On 13 March the I-26 attacked the 8,298-ton American tanker *H.D. Collier*, a Chevron ship loaded with over 100,000 barrels of petrol and aviation fuel that was sailing unescorted from Iran to Bombay in India. Struck in the stern by a torpedo, a fire broke out immediately. With the radio out of action, the crew took to the boats as the *Collier* went down, hastened by shellfire from the I-26, which had surfaced to finish off her prize. Kusaka struck again on 21 March, stalking and torpedoing the 8,117-ton Norwegian tanker *Grena*. Carrying only ballast, the *Grena* split in two and went straight to the bottom. Surfacing again, Kusaka ordered his gunners to open fire on the helpless survivors, but fortunately the Japanese failed to hit anyone and Kusaka ordered the I-26 back beneath the waves.

Only two days out from Bombay, the 7,176-ton American Liberty ship *Richard Hovey* was on her way back to the United

States. She was steaming, alone and unescorted, towards the entrance to the Suez Canal, and thence her course would take her through the Mediterranean before braving prowling German U-boats hunting convoys as she crossed the Atlantic. Captain Hans Thorsen had a ship full of people and cargo. Forty merchant seamen were under his command, as well as twenty-eight US Navy Armed Guards under Lieutenant (jg) Harry Goudy. The Armed Guards manned the ship's defensive guns located fore and aft. A single US Army cargo officer and a consular passenger completed the complement.

Unlike many of the other ships surprised and sunk by Japanese raiders throughout the region, Captain Thorsen knew that danger lurked unseen close by. The day before a report had been sent by radio to the ship from the Royal Navy authorities in Bombay warning skippers to be vigilant as a possible submarine periscope had been spotted in the area. Thorsen had placed the *Richard Hovey* onto a pre-planned zigzag course designed to throw off any prowling submarine, and had instructed Lieutenant Goudy to keep his men ready for action and alert. The Liberty ship was also equipped with anti-torpedo nets and Thorsen had ordered these lowered into the water, yet another possible defence against an enemy submarine. Lookouts were posted all about the ship, constantly scanning the water day and night for signs of danger, always conscious of the menace lurking somewhere in the deep beneath them.

The night of 28/29 March, though tense for the crew of the *Richard Hovey*, passed without incident, the only vessel sighted being an Arab dhow, an ancient sailing ship that had plied the rich trade routes between Arabia and India for centuries. The next morning was uneventful and by the afternoon the ship's company had begun to settle down to their routine. Meanwhile, aboard the I-26, Commander Kusaka watched the *Richard Hovey* powering through the calm sea through his attack periscope. Relaying speed, course and range coordinates of the enemy ship to his subordinates, Kusaka gave the order to fire. Three torpedoes burst from the submarine's bow tubes and rocketed off in the direction of the *Richard Hovey*. Released seconds apart, the Long Lance torpedoes fanned out to intercept the unsuspecting American ship. No one aboard the Liberty ship spotted the torpedoes running in the water, which was hardly surprising as the Japanese Long Lance was the most sophisticated torpedo in the world at the time – the Type 95 21-inch calibre torpedo had the longest range of any torpedo then in existence, a mighty 12,000 metres at a speed of 45 knots. The 23-foot 5-inch weapon could deliver a warhead considerably more powerful than the best American torpedo, initially 893lb of TNT and hexanitrodiphenylamine. What was truly revolutionary about the Long Lance was its propulsion system, which burned oxygen in turn to ignite kerosene, instead of the more conventional compressed air and alcohol used by every other navy in the world. This meant that the Long Lance not only had a greater range than other Allied torpedoes, the propulsion system also drastically reduced any telltale wake of bubbles in the water that would allow enemy ships to take evasive action.

The first torpedo blew an immense hole in the engine room, the blast killing the three men on watch; the fireball that shot up the ship's side threw cargo stored on deck high into the air and destroyed one of the lifeboats. The stern gun crew was showered with burning debris that severely injured one man who was dragged clear by his comrades. Seconds later, the second torpedo, to the tune of the ship's alarm klaxons sounding, blew up inside No. 4 hold. Moments later, the final metal fish ripped through No. 3 hold and detonated, causing the *Richard Hovey* to buckle amidships. Captain Thorsen gave the order to abandon ship and hastily packed his confidential papers inside a weighted bag that was thrown overboard to prevent their capture by the enemy. Radio operator Mathers stayed put inside the communications shack as long as he could, sending out a distress call on several frequencies, but no acknowledgements were received. 1st Officer Richard Evans took charge of filling the remaining three lifeboats.

Boat No. 4 was first away, loaded with fifteen men. No. 2 was next, containing seventeen men, and then No. 1 was launched under the command of 2nd Officer Turner. Captain Thorsen joined this boat and 1st Officer Evans got off in No. 4. Many men still remained aboard, including Lieutenant Goudy and his navy gunners. Two large life rafts were launched off the port side and Lifeboat No. 4 took one in tow that was packed with ten Armed Guards. Lieutenant Goudy and the remaining gunners clambered aboard the last raft and Lifeboat No. 1 threw them a line.

The *Richard Hovey* burned fiercely as the little flotilla of lifeboats and rafts lay off the ship some distance on the port side.

Someone spotted a large submarine periscope cutting through the water some way off and as the survivors watched the great bulk of the I-26 broke the surface. Figures soon crowded her decks and conning tower, and within minutes the submarine's deck gun began throwing shells at the wrecked Liberty ship. Some of the shells began to land in the water close by the survivors and it began to look to the Americans that the submarine was now firing directly at them rather than over their heads.

The I-26's diesels cranked into life and the submarine edged closer to the survivors' immobile crafts. Suddenly, the submarine's 20mm anti-aircraft cannon thundered to life, joined by light machine-gun fire, driving the stunned Americans over the sides of their boats and rafts into the water. The sea all around the survivors became a tumult of water spurts as the Japanese gunners plastered the area with flying lead. In common with previous Japanese attacks on survivors, Kusaka realized that the enemy sailors were using the lifeboats as cover to mask the fire of his gunners. The I-26's bows came slicing through the water, smashing heavily into Lifeboat No. 2. Evans and the other survivors back-pedalled madly to get clear of the great mass of the submarine passing close by them and from the shots which thudded into the water all around them. As the lifeboat capsized and partially submerged, without pausing the I-26 changed direction and smashed in Captain Thorsen's boat. From his position aboard one of the rafts, Lieutenant Goudy later wrote of his attackers: 'As the submarine was within a few feet of us we could definitely determine that the men, who were lined up on its deck as though they were on parade, were Japanese. They were in khaki uniforms and khaki caps.' Goudy also noted the plea-sure the Japanese were evidently getting from the attacks on the lifeboats: 'They were laughing and seemed to get quite a bit of sport out of our predicament.' In the conning tower, Goudy and many other survivors saw one Japanese officer holding a small movie camera to his eye, as he filmed the criminal actions of his colleagues.

After machine-gunning all of the lifeboats Kusaka called to the survivors from the conning tower bridge, asking for the captain. The soaked and terrified survivors had gingerly clambered back aboard their boats and rafts now that the gunfire had stopped. The boats had drifted quite far apart and the men in the water had managed to right Lifeboat No. 2, thirty-nine of them climbing

142

aboard the damaged boat. The Japanese fire, although prolonged, had not been effective in disposing of the survivors of the *Richard Hovey*, only wounding Deck Engineer Burns. In Lifeboat No. 1 Captain Thorsen rose slowly to his feet, joined by 2nd Officer Turner, Fireman Simms and Able Seaman Margetto. Japanese sailors indicated that the lifeboat should come alongside the I-26, and the skipper and his three comrades were roughly bundled down inside the submarine. A Japanese sailor climbed down inside the lifeboat and smashed the boat's radio. A line was then attached to the lifeboat and as the light began to fade from the sky the I-26's diesel struck up again as the submarine began to make off, dragging Lifeboat No. 1 in its wake.

In the meantime, 1st Officer Evans and twenty-four men remained in the water, using Lifeboat No. 4 as cover. It was getting dark. Because Evans's group had drifted some way from the rest of the survivors and because of the furious Japanese assaults launched on the other two lifeboats and raft, Evans believed that the Japanese had probably killed the remaining survivors. The ten US Navy gunners and thirteen merchant seamen with him clambered quietly back aboard the lifeboat when all had settled down. The boat was not only sitting low in the water with so many men crammed aboard, it was also full of holes made by Japanese machine-gun bullets. Even if Evans had managed to locate any more survivors, the extra weight might very well have sunk them. Some medical supplies and food were set adrift on the abandoned raft in case anyone was left alive and, starting up the lifeboat's small engine, Evans steered the boat away from the scene of the attack. The occupants of Lifeboat No. 4 were rescued three days later by a British Liberty ship, the *Samcalia*, and taken to Karachi (ironically the city where Commander Kusaka had landed the Indian Hikari Kikan agents earlier in the month).

The thirty-nine men left under the command of Lieutenant Harry Goudy, the Liberty ship's gunnery officer, were packed tightly aboard Lifeboat No. 2 and the pair of rafts after they found the one abandoned by Evans. Seamen immediately set about patching the boat up, as Japanese machine-gun bullets had drilled holes all through it and the boat was in danger of sinking. The two rafts were taken in tow and with men on the oars, the lifeboat began to make slow progress through the sea. Machine-gun bullets had torn up the boat's fresh water tanks, but an enterprising sailor named

Arthur Drechsler rigged up a still aboard one of the rafts and, using wood from the other raft as fuel, he managed to provide enough fresh water to keep his comrades alive for the seventeen days they were to spend adrift before they were rescued by another Liberty ship, the British *Samuta*, on 14 April. Only one man died during their ordeal, the young navy gunner who had been badly burned during the first torpedo explosion; he was buried at sea after a short religious service. Drechsler was later awarded the Merchant Marine Distinguished Service Medal for his actions.

Goudy, and many of the others in Lifeboat No. 2, felt that 1st Officer Evans had left the scene of the sinking of the *Richard Hovey* and the I-26's attack on the survivors with undue haste, and without first looking for survivors. An official complaint was made against him, but he was found not guilty of any wrongful actions by a US Coast Guard court of inquiry and the matter was quietly forgotten.

As for Commander Kusaka, he took the I-26 back to Penang, arriving on 25 April, and Captain Thorsen, 2nd Officer Turner, and Seamen Simms and Margetto were transferred to the local prisoner-of-war camp where they languished in terrible conditions until liberated at the war's end. Kusaka was brought before a military tribunal in 1946 and found guilty of war crimes. He was, however, only sentenced to five years' imprisonment in Sugamo Prison in Tokyo, an extremely light sentence for attempted murder. The I-26, which Kusaka left as commanding officer, met her fate in November 1944, sunk east of the Philippines with all hands lost.

Notes
1. The Jai Hind was renamed Infantry Regiment 950 in April 1943. From May to August 1943 it performed garrison duties along the coast of Holland, and then anti-partisan duties in France. After D-Day, the regiment (now administratively part of the Waffen-SS) retreated into Germany and eventually surrendered to American forces at Lake Constance in April 1945.
2. Adrian Weale, *Renegades: Hitler's Englishmen*, (Warner Books, 1995), pp. 212–14.

Chapter Fourteen

Running the Gauntlet

You are now my prisoners. Let this be a lesson to you that
Americans are weak. You must realize that Japan will rule
the world. You are stupid for letting your leaders take you to
war. Do you know that the entire American fleet is now at
the bottom of the Pacific?

Commander Tatsunosuke Ariizumi
Captain of the submarine I-8, 1944

After ordering the near complete destruction of the unarmed
passengers and crew of the Dutch merchant ship *Tjisalak* on 26
March 1944, Commander Ariizumi and the crew of the Japanese
submarine I-8 settled back into a game of cat and mouse as they
searched for another unprotected enemy merchantman to blast out
of the water. March dragged into April and then into June with no
targets encountered. By early July, with supplies of food and water
running low, Ariizumi would soon have to order the I-8 back to
base to resupply, but before that happened a plump target suddenly
presented itself on the horizon.

The American Liberty ship *Jean Nicolet* powered through the
gentle swell far out on the dark Indian Ocean. The air was hot and
humid even in the evening and many of the hatches were open to
allow what little breeze there was to circulate through the ship. The
vessel was sitting low in the water, her holds crammed with a heavy
cargo of military equipment bound for the Indian port of Calcutta.
She had steamed west after leaving San Pedro in California on 12
May 1944 and had called initially at Fremantle in Australia before
ploughing on into the Indian Ocean. In the ship's holds and lashed
securely to her decks were large pieces of heavy machinery, army
trucks, landing barges, steel mooring pontoons, piles of steel plate

and other assorted general war materiel. Captain David Nilsson was responsible for a full complement of crew and passengers. Forty American merchant seamen formed the crew of the *Jean Nicolet*, and twenty-eight US Navy Armed Guards manned the ship's small defensive armament. The total of 31 passengers aboard was made up of 6 officers, a medical corpsman and 12 enlisted men from the US Army, and there were 8 US Navy technical personnel and 4 civilians along for the voyage as well.

On the evening of 2 July, nearly two months out from California, the *Jean Nicolet* was approximately 700 miles south of the British colony of Ceylon and making for the port of Colombo for a short stopover before sailing on to Calcutta to unload. Unbeknown to Captain Nilsson his vessel was being stalked by a dangerous predator determined to prevent the Liberty ship from ever reaching India and delivering her valuable war cargo.

Aboard the Japanese submarine I-8 the control room was hushed as the skipper, Tatsunosuke Ariizumi, his eyes glued to the attack periscope, made his attack plot and issued orders to load two of the bow torpedo tubes. Ariizumi manoeuvred the I-8 into a perfect attack position on the starboard flank of the *Jean Nicolet* and prepared to unleash a pair of powerful Long Lance torpedoes. With a rush of compressed air the two torpedoes left the tubes seconds apart and powered through the waves, each travelling at over 40 knots, officers in the red-lit control room counting off the torpedo running times with stopwatches.

The first the crew of the *Jean Nicolet* knew of the presence of the huge Japanese submarine was an enormous explosion low on the starboard side, as the leading Long Lance detonated between Nos 2 and 3 holds. A massive plume of water erupted skyward and the ship immediately began to list to starboard as hundreds of tons of seawater engulfed the holds. Seconds later the second Japanese torpedo crashed into No. 4 hold, blowing a vast, jagged hole in the *Jean Nicolet*'s belly. Nilsson gave the order to abandon ship as the vessel appeared to be doomed. Crew and passengers grabbed life-jackets before frantically launching lifeboats and cork survival rafts into the ocean. In the radio room Augustus 'Gus' Tilden, the operator, quickly sent a distress call, informing Colombo and Calcutta that the *Jean Nicolet* had been torpedoed and was sinking at position 3° 28' S 74° 30' W, and the crew and passengers were taking to the boats. Every crewman and passenger got clear of the stricken ship alive, knowing that help would arrive at the scene within a few hours. Ariizumi, however, was determined to prevent the Americans from being rescued from their new predicament. As Nilsson and the others bobbed quietly on the surface of the ocean, the real threat to their lives was about to emerge quite literally from the dark depths below.

The surface of the sea appeared to boil, as white foam and masses of bubbles marked the ascent of the Japanese submarine from its concealed attack position. As water streamed from its conning tower and decks, hatches were thrown open with a metallic clang and the American survivors could see dozens of Japanese sailors emerging, many armed with rifles and pistols, all chattering excitedly. The submarine's diesel engines throbbed dully as the I-8 made its way steadily towards the lifeboats and rafts. Ominously, Japanese sailors on the conning tower trained light machine guns on the helpless survivors, as a powerful searchlight was played across the black water and settled on individual lifeboats for a moment like a baleful eye, before continuing to work its way around the scene as if the Japanese were carefully accounting for each and every survivor.

The familiar Japanese manner of dealing with survivors began to replay itself out all over again. A voice called out in English from the I-8, ordering the survivors to come alongside the submarine, and also demanding the name of the ship and the location of her captain and officers. The voice belonged to a Japanese-American, Harold Jiro Nakahara, who was what the Japanese termed a Nisei, or foreign-born Japanese. Nakahara had been born in Hawaii and he had been studying in Japan when the Pacific war had broken out. He had been drafted into the Japanese Navy as an interpreter and was never implicated in the subsequent crimes committed by his shipmates. In fact, Nakahara cooperated fully with the Tokyo war crimes trial after the war.

Following operational instructions, Commander Ariizumi intended to take the captain and radio operator prisoner for questioning, and dispose of the remaining survivors. Ariizumi would once again follow his murderous instructions to the letter, the chilling lines 'Do not stop at the sinking of enemy ships and cargoes. At the same time carry out the complete destruction of the crews of the enemy's ships'[1] burned into his mind. As mentioned before, the method by which the 'complete destruction of the crew' was to be achieved was left to the individual submarine commander's discretion. Ariizumi had evidently made it plain to his crew that the lives of the American survivors were of no regard to him, and that aside from securing the captain, radio operator and any other passengers or crew worthy of interrogation, the fate of the remainder was up to the submarine crew to decide. Japanese sailors armed with rifles, bayonets and improvised clubs made of steel pipes were preparing a reception committee aboard the submarine's deck.

Because it was dark and the lifeboats and rafts were being dispersed by the current all around the submarine and the abandoned *Jean Nicolet*, which was still afloat despite the catastrophic damage inflicted by the Japanese torpedo strikes, the Japanese did not manage to locate all of the survivors. Four Naval Armed Guards and a soldier would be the only survivors who would not board the I-8 that night, the darkness concealing them from periodic Japanese searches.

The first American to board the I-8 swam to the submarine and was hauled up by waiting Japanese hands. Seventeen-year-old William Musser, a mess room steward on the *Jean Nicolet*, was immediately frogmarched towards the bows between two Japanese sailors. Suddenly, one of his captors turned and struck Musser a savage blow across his skull with a length of steel pipe. The Japanese laughed as Musser staggered about concussed and terrified – taking careful aim with a pistol the same Japanese pulled the trigger and blew the American boy's brains out. Musser's body was then kicked over the side like a bag of refuse.

Ordinary Seaman Richard Kean climbed carefully onto the deck of the I-8 from his lifeboat, which following Japanese instructions had come alongside the submarine. Japanese sailors grabbed the terrified nineteen year old, frisked him for anything of value, stripped him of his lifejacket and then roughly bound his arms behind his back with rope. Kean too was led towards the bow, but before he got there a Japanese sailor drove a rifle bayonet deep into his stomach, and as Kean doubled over in agony another Japanese seaman brought the butt of his rifle down hard on the back of the American's head, crushing his skull and killing him instantly. The Japanese sailors then kicked Kean's body overboard as well.

Captain Nilsson had initially boarded one of the rafts with Lieutenant Deal of the US Naval Reserve, the officer commanding the Armed Guard detachment aboard the *Jean Nicolet*. The chief mate had come alongside in a motorized lifeboat, Nilsson had clambered aboard her and taken command. A light was visible aboard the abandoned Liberty ship and the conscientious captain had decided to go back to check the ship once again in case anyone still remained aboard her. The captain's lifeboat was headed towards the *Jean Nicolet* when the I-8 had surfaced and after cutting the lifeboat's engine, the crew had quietly rowed back to the raft. The I-8's 140mm deck gun was immediately trained on the abandoned ship and in the meantime the searchlight had picked out two lifeboats, one of them Captain Nilsson's; the submarine slowly cruised towards them.

Able Seaman McDougall was on the raft and as 'the submarine came alongside . . . we slipped into the water on the far side and clung on. For a time we could not see exactly what was happening, but we did see the submarine go astern and heard machine-gun fire.'[2] The I-8 unloaded the survivors from the lifeboats and rafts, and sailors then attempted to sink the empty boats with machine guns. The American tactic of attempting to hide from the attentions of the Japanese in the water was almost impossible, as the submarine came back and, using its searchlight, ordered the survivors back onto the raft. 'The submarine came alongside and threw a line to us. [Able Seaman George] Hess was the first man aboard and I was the second. They would only let us come aboard one at a time, amidships of the port side by the conning-tower.'[3]

The initial random murders of Musser and Kean gave way to an organized terrorization of the dozens of soldiers, sailors and civilians ordered aboard the I-8. McDougall recounted those first minutes on the Japanese submarine:

> When I climbed on to the deck I was told to remove my life jacket and to put up my Hands . . . While my hands were raised one of the Japanese sailors spotted my watch. He pulled my hand down and took the watch off my wrist. Then he saw my ring and tried to get it off my finger, but it was too tight. He drew his knife and as he appeared to be about to cut my finger off I managed to get the ring off and handed it to him.[4]

A gang of Japanese sailors robbed the cowed Americans of anything of value and as well as removing their lifejackets they also

149

ripped off the American servicemen's identity discs. Once frisked and robbed, each man's hands were bound behind his back, he was led onto the foredeck and forced to sit cross-legged with his comrades in silence. Any movement or sound was greeted with a rain of blows and slaps from the Japanese sailors watching the prisoners.

Captain Nilsson, radio operator Tilden and one of the passengers, Francis O'Gara, were taken below into the submarine. O'Gara was a representative of the War Shipping Administration (WSA) which actually built Liberty ships such as the *Jean Nicolet*, and he had been along for the voyage to India. A former sports writer for the *Philadelphia Enquirer*, O'Gara had spent two years at sea earlier in the war in the Merchant Marine before going to work for the WSA. In a somewhat surreal display, Commander Ariizumi, from his lofty position in the conning tower high above the ranks of huddled prisoners, occasionally harangued the Americans. The Japanese translator dutifully relayed his skipper's ramblings to the cowed Americans: 'You are now my prisoners,' shouted Ariizumi. 'Let this be a lesson to you that Americans are weak. You must realize that Japan will rule the world. You are stupid for letting your leaders take you to war. Do you know that the entire American fleet is now at the bottom of the Pacific?"

As the I-8 cruised about hunting for more survivors to haul aboard, the deck gunners fired three armour-piercing anti-ship shells into the *Jean Nicolet*, hoping to finally sink her. At one point a wave washed across the deck taking with it two seamen and Lieutenant Morrison Miller of the US Army. The two seamen would survive, but Miller, who had broken his arm during the abandoning of the *Jean Nicolet*, drowned. The ranks of survivors on the submarine's deck could hear activity behind the conning tower on the aft deck. Groups of Japanese sailors appeared regularly among the survivors and hauled an individual off out of sight; none of the Americans returned. The night air was soon rent with screams of agony and the sounds of violence, as the terrified survivors suffered untold mental anguish waiting to be snatched and led to an unknown fate. The *Jean Nicolet*'s carpenter did manage to take a quick glance behind the conning tower, and he reported quietly to the others that he had seen Ordinary Seaman King bayoneted twice and his body thrown overboard. The Japanese were certainly killing everyone who was taken. About ten or fifteen Japanese sailors had formed up in two lines on the aft deck and prisoners were being made to literally 'run the gauntlet' between them to their deaths. As each American was forced between the lines, Japanese sailors mercilessly struck the unfortunates with metal bars, rifle butts, fists and lengths of chain, while others stabbed or slashed at the victims with bayonets and knives. At the end of the gauntlet stood a large sailor armed with a rifle and bayonet whose job was to plunge his blade deep into the bleeding and bruised Americans and heave them bodily over the side like a man leaving hay with a pitchfork. Assistant Engineer Pyle managed to survive the gauntlet and later recounted what occurred:

Somewhere around midnight I was picked out and led aft . . . When I stopped for a second to take stock of the situation I was struck a terrific blow at the base of my head which caused me to feel a sensation similar to a bouncing ball. From there on, I was pushed along through two lines of Japanese sailors who rained blows upon my head and body with various objects, which I was too stunned or dazed to identify, although I was later told by my doctor that I had been cut with a bayonet or sword in the process. When I reached the end of the gauntlet I fell into what appeared to be a white foamy sea.[5]

Able Seaman Butler, a Naval Armed Guard, also managed to survive the gauntlet and later recounted his incredible story of survival: 'Soon they came and got me, and took me aft where . . . Japs were lined up abaft the conning-tower holding sabres, clubs, and lengths of lead piping. One Jap stopped me and tried to kick me in the stomach. Another hit me over the head with an iron pipe. Another cut me over the eye with a sabre.' Whilst these blows were raining down upon him, Butler, with his hands still firmly tied behind his back, escaped. 'I managed to break away, after I had gotten past the second one, and jumped overboard.'[6] Butler, Pyle and one other man were the only survivors of more than sixty who were led behind the conning tower. As for the remaining thirty or so survivors still huddled on the foredeck of the I-8, a new trial was about to commence for them.

The submarine's diving klaxon suddenly sounded above the sounds of violence and murder, the Japanese sailors immediately ceased killing the Americans and clattered back inside the casing, slamming the hatches shut firmly behind them. The remaining thirty survivors suddenly found themselves free of the sadistic attentions of the Japanese sailors, but sitting on the deck of a submerging submarine in the middle of the ocean with their hands firmly tied behind them. The reason Ariizumi had ordered the I-8 beneath the waves was a report from his radar operator of a plane rapidly closing on his position, a plane he correctly deduced to be a British rescue aircraft searching for survivors from the *Jean Nicolet*. Ariizumi simply left the thirty men to drown without the slightest thought. The plane was actually a Royal Canadian Air Force Liberator bomber flying far in advance of the British destroyer HMS *Hoxa*, which was herself steaming as fast as possible to rescue the survivors.

One American sailor had managed to secrete a small knife inside his shirt and as the I-8 began to dive this man frantically attempted to free the hands of as many of his comrades as he could. Amid screams and shouts the thirty men found themselves frantically thrashing about in the disturbed ocean caused by the submerging Japanese submarine. The sailor with the knife had managed to free the hands of about half of the survivors, but for those who did not quickly drown, the waters held a new danger as equally lethal as the Japanese – sharks.

The underwater explosions of the torpedoes and the death throes of the *Jean Nicolet* would have initially attracted sharks. The blood and bodies in the water from the Japanese massacre would have then drawn the sharks to the locality, and they would have begun feeding from the corpses floating lifelessly in the water. A new nightmare now unfolded for the remaining survivors as they listened to splashing all about them as sharks tore bodies to pieces, occasionally feeling powerful rough bodies brush past their frantically pistoning legs as the survivors trod water for hours on end. Shark skin is extremely rough and, along with the sharp edges of their fins, contact would have opened fresh scratches and wounds on the bodies of men already bleeding from cuts inflicted by their Japanese tormentors.[7] Inevitably, the scores of big oceanic sharks attracted to the area turned their attentions to the living and over the next fourteen hours, until rescue arrived in the form of HMS *Hoxa*, seventeen of the thirty survivors drowned or were taken by the patrolling sharks.

A group of swimmers, including Hess and McDougall, managed to stay afloat until dawn and swam close to the burning wreck of the *Jean Nicolet*. When the ship finally sank a life raft which had remained jammed in the rigging when the ship was initially abandoned was forced loose and the grateful survivors were able to take refuge on it. Salvation for the crew and passengers of the *Jean Nicolet* was slow in arriving for the thirteen men still alive of the thirty who had been sitting on the deck of the I-8 when it submerged. About 8.00am on the morning of 3 July a Liberator bomber roared overhead and dropped a small rubber dinghy into the sea. Designed for four men, seven survivors managed to climb aboard it and away from the ever- present sharks. Men were still dispersed across the ocean, some on rafts and others clinging to floating debris. Catalina flying boats attempted to locate the survivors and rescue them later that day, but an air search was too difficult and the attempt was called off. The unfortunate Americans spent another night without food or water, and with the constant fear of shark attack, until daybreak on 4 July.

Another big Liberator appeared in the sky overhead, roaring low over the survivors, and a short while later a ship was sighted on the horizon steaming towards their position. HMS *Hoxa* hove to amid the floating survivors, nets and lines were dropped over the sides and the remaining Americans were hauled to safety. The RAF dinghy and its seven occupants were rescued, along with thirteen others from rafts and three men who were clinging to debris. When the British were satisfied that everyone who was still alive had been found the *Hoxa* sailed for Addu Atoll in the Maldives, arriving without incident the next day.

British Naval Intelligence carefully debriefed all of the survivors, building up a detailed a picture of the events that had occurred, and the behaviour of Commander Ariizumi and his officers and men. The Royal Navy appropriately nicknamed Ariizumi 'The Butcher' for his various crimes – the evidence being prepared against the officer would hopefully be used in the future when Japan was defeated. After six days of questions, medical attention and some rest, the American survivors boarded HMS *Sonneti* and sailed to Colombo in Ceylon. On 27 July they boarded aircraft and were flown to Calcutta, their original destination all along. Of the one hundred passengers and crew aboard the *Jean Nicolet* when she departed from Fremantle, just twenty-three remained alive. Only two US Army enlisted men had survived, and along with a naval technician, they were assigned to duties in Calcutta. Ten merchant mariners and ten Naval Armed Guard survivors entrained for Bombay where they boarded the US Army transport *General William Mitchell* and sailed for San Diego, arriving on 6 October.

Three men were missing from the list of survivors, as no one had heard anything of Captain Nilsson, radio operator Gus Tilden or passenger Francis O'Gara since Ariizumi had ordered them taken below into the I-8. The fates of these men were only discovered after the defeat of Japan when O'Gara was found alive in September 1945 at Ofuna prisoner-of-war camp outside the Japanese city of Yokohama. The War Shipping Administration had assumed that O'Gara had been killed by the Japanese and had even named a Liberty ship in his honour. O'Gara filled in the blanks to US Navy investigators after the war and recounted a harrowing tale. After the I-8 had submerged, Nilsson, Tilden and O'Gara had been held as prisoners on board the submarine for a further forty-four days. The three men had been held separately, the crew often denying them food and water. All of them had also been subjected to regular beatings for no apparent reason other than to satisfy the crew's latent sadism. On 15 August the I-8 had arrived at Penang, a large island off the west coast of Malaya, and O'Gara and Nilsson had been taken ashore and imprisoned. Tilden was never seen again and it was assumed that his captors had executed the unfortunate radio operator at some point. Exactly one month later O'Gara was forced back aboard the I-8 and endured another ordeal as the submarine sailed to Yokohama. He never saw Nilsson again, but O'Gara surmised that the captain was placed aboard another submarine for transit to Japan, and that this submarine was sunk by the US Navy. As for O'Gara, he was hauled off as a slave labourer to the camp at Ofuna, where he remained until liberated nearly a year later.

One final merchant vessel was to fall victim to a murderous Japanese attack before the end of the war. The Liberty ship *John A. Johnson* was lumbering through the waves, her decks crowded with army trucks under heavy green tarpaulins, headed towards Honolulu. It was 30 October 1944 and the war had long since moved away from the American mainland, after hit-and-run attacks on merchant shipping during the early stages of the war by a pack of nine Japanese submarines that had fanned out and sat off the busiest American ports. No one aboard the *John A. Johnson* expected to encounter a Japanese submarine this far east from the main war in the Pacific, but the Japanese certainly had a surprise in store for them.

Following the Battle of Leyte Gulf, the I-12 under Commander Kameo Kudo had set out from Kure in Japan on 4 October with orders from the 6th Fleet to attack enemy merchant ships discovered between the Hawaiian Islands and San Francisco. Completed at Kawasaki's Kobe yard only five months before, the 2,943-ton I-12 was a Type-A2 submarine and the only one of her class. Basically identical in all regards to the Type-A1, the only difference between the I-12 and the earlier models was a decrease in her engine power, and an extended operational range of 22,000 nautical miles at 16 knots. This made the submarine the obvious choice to send back to the American west coast.

Kudo's orders, aside from attacking merchant convoys off the west coast, would also involve him backtracking to Hawaii, then sailing to Tahiti and finally to a point east of the Marshall Islands before returning home. It was an ambitious patrol considering the strength of American anti-submarine forces, but the Japanese high command evidently wanted to make the Americans believe that they were still capable of striking at the nation's doorstep.

Aboard the *John A. Johnson*, her crew of forty-one, twenty-eight US Navy Armed Guards and the single army officer who was in charge of the cargo knew none of this. The ship was sailing at a ponderous 9 knots, with all lights extinguished and was maintaining a strict radio silence – all quite normal. At 9.10pm the first torpedo came thundering into her starboard side, tearing loose the trucks stored on deck, and knocking the gunners and ships crew off their feet. Even though dealt a crippling blow, the Armed Guards, unaware of how badly damaged their ship was, raced to return fire at the unseen submarine. Seaman Harold L. Clark, one of the naval gunners, recalled: 'Lieutenant Yates came up and told me to help man the number 6 gun. I proceeded to the number 6 gun, and there sighted [the] explosion just astern of [the] ship. It looked like another torpedo. The ship began to break in two.'[8] The captain gave the order to abandon the *John A. Johnson* as the situation was clearly hopeless. The crew took to the lifeboats and rafts. 'We saw [an] object about three hundred feet away from us,'

155

recalled Clark. 'We signalled the object thinking it was another raft and it returned the signal. It came to the surface and turned out to be the submarine, and it started coming toward us.'[9] The crew, bobbing gently up and down aboard their survival craft, watched both the approaching submarine and their foundering ship as she broke into two sections that stayed afloat. Heavy army trucks were torn free from their moorings and slid down the upended decks into the ocean with a roar.

The I-12 surfaced and sailors rushed to man the deck gun. In the meantime machine guns had been brought up from below onto the I-12's conning-tower bridge. The submarine increased power, surging forwards, a great white-foamed bow wave rearing up, and as the dumbfounded Americans watched the stem of the I-12 slammed into one of the lifeboats, tumbling terrified survivors into the sea. Just then the clatter of machine-gun fire poured forth from the conning tower. Japanese seamen sprayed a murderous and indiscriminate fire onto the helpless men sat in lifeboats or swimming in the water, Japanese officers also taking potshots at the sailors with their pistols. Aboard Clark's raft they fearfully watched the approaching submarine, trapped and with nowhere to hide: 'About one hundred and fifty feet from us, [the] submarine machine-gunned us. I could see tracers going over our heads. We jumped into [the] water. Submarine passed by about one hundred and fifty feet. We swam back and got on the raft. Submarine circled and came back at us again.'[10] Rowing like men possessed, the crews of undamaged lifeboats desperately attempted to row clear of the submarine. The I-12, cruising on the surface like a huge grey shark, surged through the mass of lifeboats and rafts, the machine guns on the conning tower spitting lead at anything that moved. 'We dove into the water again,' recalled Clark, as the Japanese attacked his raft once more. 'This time [the] submarine hit the raft, and as it passed by they fired again with [a] machine gun, tracers hitting [the] water near me.'[11] The I-12 came close enough to the men in the water for Clark to notice 'Five American flags were painted on the port side of the bow. Men on the submarine were yelling 'Bonzi' [sic] and cursing at us.'[12]

Kudo later ordered his deck gunners to sink the floating sections of the *John A. Johnson* with shellfire, bombarding the wreck until it caught fire, exploding and sinking early the following morning. Six merchant seamen had been killed and many more wounded before complete darkness finally finished the Japanese attack, whereupon the I-12 submerged and made off from the scene of the crime. The flames and explosions resulting from the Japanese bombardment of the two sections of the *John A. Johnson* probably saved the survivors from the ocean. The crew of a Pan American Airways airliner spotted the flames far below them and managed to signal to the lifeboats, the pilot reporting the survivors' position to the US Navy in San Francisco. The USS *Argus* rescued the men at noon the day after the attack.

Kudo and the crew of the I-12 were not so fortunate. After the attack Kudo took his boat away from the west coast and headed into the mid-Pacific. He reported to the 6th Fleet in late December that he had managed to sink an enemy tanker and another freighter, though this claim has never been confirmed. The last anyone ever heard of Commander Kudo and the 113 other officers and men aboard the I-12 was a radio transmission picked up on 15 January 1945. Kudo reported that enemy forces north of the Marshall Islands had located his submarine. No one knows what fate befell the I-12 and the Japanese noted on 31 January that the vessel had been lost with all hands some time after the receipt of that final radio message.

Notes

1. Russell of Liverpool, Lord, *The Knights of Bushido: A Short History of Japanese War Crimes* (Greenhill Books, 2005), p. 214.
2. Ibid., p. 223.
3. Ibid., p. 223.
4. Ibid., p. 224.
5. Ibid., p. 225.
6. Ibid., p. 226.
7. Maniguet, Xavier, *The Jaws of Death: Shark as Predator, Man as Prey* (HarperCollins Publishers, 1992), pp. 115–30.
8. 'Sunk by Submarine, 1944.', EyeWitness to History, http://www.eyewitnesstohistory.com
9. Ibid.
10. Ibid.
11. Ibid.
12. Ibid.

Chapter Fifteen

Superior Orders

As far as I know Admiral Imamura never objected to these
orders for the execution of any of the prisoners of war . . . I
thought at the time that the affair was a bad thing . . . but I
could do nothing against orders from Fleet HQ.

Lieutenant Commander Okamoto
13th Special Naval Base Force, Singapore 1945

Captured aircrew were often subjected to severe punishments and
were usually executed by the Japanese Navy. As recounted earlier,
captured American naval aviators were brutally killed after being
plucked from the sea during the Battle of Midway in June 1942,
apparently as revenge for the battle going against the Japanese.

The execution of Allied aircrews was actually official Japanese
policy following Lieutenant Colonel Jimmy Doolittle's famous
surprise air attack on Japan on 18 April 1942, an event that deeply
shocked the Japanese government and people. Doolittle had led
sixteen specially modified US Army B-25 Mitchell medium
bombers off the aircraft carrier USS *Hornet* over 600 miles off
Japan, and had made history as the first air raid by the United States
against the Japanese Home Islands. The raiders had successfully
bombed targets in Tokyo, Yokohama, Kobe, Osaka and Nagoya
before fifteen of the aircraft crash-landed in occupied China (the
sixteenth landing in the neutral Soviet Union where plane and crew
were interned) – some of the crews managed to evade capture with
the assistance of the Chinese underground and Western missionaries. Unfortunately, some of the raiders were captured, tortured
and executed by the Japanese as revenge for their daring attack on
the heart of the empire. In the course of searching for Doolittle's
men the Japanese also murdered around 250,000 Chinese civilians,

largely as revenge (although the Japanese occupation army hardly needed an excuse to kill Chinese as they had been doing so in enormous numbers since 1937). The Doolittle Raid was an important psychological blow against Japan when America felt its back was against the wall between the bombing of Pearl Harbor in December 1941 and the naval victory at Midway in June 1942.

The Japanese reacted with predictable harshness to the Doolittle Raid by promulgating a dubious law making it an offence punishable by death or ten years imprisonment to launch air attacks on civilian targets, ignoring of course their own air campaigns against Chinese cities and other 'illegal' targets in Asia such as Singapore and Hong Kong. Japanese commanders in the field evidently took this law to mean all air attacks on all targets, both civilian and military. Although Japanese law demanded that captured Allied airmen be granted a military trial before sentence was passed, this legal nicety was mainly dispensed with and the unfortunate airmen were decapitated with swords after lengthy periods of often brutal interrogation and incarceration.

After the war there were several trials of Japanese naval personnel who had been involved in the deaths of Allied aircrew and many of the defendants were subsequently sentenced to death. One case in particular was taken as a legal standard, especially in its treatment of the defence plea of 'superior orders'. This was the so-called 'Jaluit Atoll Case', where members of the Japanese garrison forces in the Marshall Islands were placed before an American military commission and charged with the murders of three unarmed American airmen who were then their prisoners. The Marshall Islands, it will be recalled, were part of the so-called South Seas Mandate along with the Carolines and Marianas, former German colonies given to Japan in 1919 when the victors of the First World War dismantled the small German overseas empire. The charge against five IJN personnel was that:

> on or about 10th March, 1944, on the island of Aineman, Jaluit Atoll, Marshall Islands . . . [the accused] wilfully, feloniously, with malice aforethought without justifiable cause, and without trial or due process, assaulted and killed, by shooting and stabbing to death, three American fliers . . . then and there captured and unarmed prisoners of war in the custody of the said accused, all in violation of the dignity of

the United States of America, the International rules of warfare and the moral standards of civilised society.[1]

At the time of the murders, Jaluit Atoll was under the direct control of the Japanese Navy, and had been renamed the Jaluit Island Fortress. Jaluit, along with Wotje, Mille and Maloelap, were a series of defensive strong points designed to fend off any American amphibious assault against the inner island group of Kwajalein Atoll, an important Japanese naval base in the Marshall Islands. The South Pacific Mandate in 1944 was under the command of Admiral Boshiro Hosogaya, and the military facilities on the widely dispersed islands were utilized as bases for submarines and surface warships, as well as containing several significant Japanese airfields. Kwajalein Island was the southernmost and largest of the ninety-seven tropical islands making up Kwajalein Atoll, lying 2,100 nautical miles south-west of Hawaii.

In 1944, Jaluit Atoll, as one of the outer ring of defensive island groups protecting Kwajalein, was garrisoned by the Japanese 62nd Guard Unit numbering 547 naval ground troops under the command of Rear Admiral Nisuke Masuda. Also on the island was the 4th Establishment Department, a construction unit and an air unit, the total Japanese naval garrison numbering 1,584 men. The Imperial Japanese Army had also stationed the 2nd Battalion, 1st South Seas Detachment of 727 men on Jaluit, making the small coral and palm islands a formidable obstacle should the Americans have landed.

The American airmen who fell into Admiral Masuda's hands and were subsequently killed on his orders were playing their part in Admiral Chester Nimitz's invasion of the Marshalls in early 1944. Nimitz decided, wisely as it turned out, to simply bypass Kwajalein's outlying Japanese fortress islands, and to launch an amphibious assault directly onto Kwajalein itself, effectively driving a dagger into the heart of the South Seas Mandate. Vital to the success of the American plan, codenamed Operation Flintlock, was the reduction of an important Japanese airfield on Mille Atoll, so that Japanese aircraft could not interfere with the landings. US Navy and USAAF aircraft would batter Mille and other islands such as Jaluit, assuring American control of the air over Kwajalein when the 4th Marine Division under Major General Harry Schmidt and 7th Infantry Division under Major General Charles Corbett

160

stormed ashore on Roi-Namur and Kwajalein Island. Nimitz had effectively condemned Jaluit, Mille and Maloelap to wither on the vine, as the Japanese island garrisons would be left on the islands, cut off from supplies or reinforcements and subjected to repeated American air attacks until the final surrender in August 1945. B-24 Liberator heavy bombers and B-25 Mitchells, flying from re-captured Tarawa Atoll, carpet-bombed Mille and elsewhere, while P-40 Warhawks and P-39 Airacobras from Makin dropped down low to strafe and precision bomb.

The three American fliers brutally murdered by the Japanese on Jaluit were the survivors from a crashed B-24 or B-25 forced down by anti-aircraft fire close to the atoll in February 1944. Treated with usual casual Japanese brutality, the bound and blindfolded prisoners had been held on Emidj Island, where Admiral Masuda had his headquarters. In actual charge of the prisoners was Ensign Tasaki and for nearly a month the fliers languished in detention while Operation Flintlock progressed. A navy lieutenant was charged with interrogating the prisoners and information concerning the American offensive was beaten out of them in the presence of an interpreter.

At no point during their detention were the American prisoners placed before a military court, and in common with so many other similar cases, it appeared during the 1945 trial that Admiral Masuda simply decided one day that the prisoners would be executed. Masuda was not brought before the US Navy court because he had killed himself whilst in American detention, but he had written a statement in which he admitted ordering the fliers deaths. On 10 March, Ensign Tasaki released the three fliers into the custody of Lieutenant Yoshimura, they were loaded aboard a small boat and taken over to the nearby island of Aineman. Tasaki was fully aware that his prisoners were being taken away for execution. Under a heavy guard, the prisoners were loaded aboard a truck and driven to a cemetery, where they would die. Close by a large bonfire had been erected by Japanese sailors, ready to cremate the Americans' corpses after the executions had been carried out. Masuda was keen that no evidence remained of the crime. Travelling with the prisoners was the execution party, which consisted of Lieutenant Yoshimura, Ensign Kawachi and Warrant Officer Tanaka, armed with pistols and swords. In their defence, these three men argued that they had been reluctant to take part in the executions, but had been forced to do so, largely because of the strength of Admiral Masuda's personality. Their defence counsel, Lieutenant Commander Kozo Hirata of the IJN explained to the US Navy court why the Japanese servicemen had been unable to disobey an order they knew to be illegal. In an encapsulation of the standard Japanese defence of 'superior orders', Hirata described the absolute discipline and obedience which was expected from the Japanese forces – his explanation could be applied to any of the war crimes outlined throughout this book He quoted from an Imperial Rescript that stated: 'Subordinates should have the idea that the orders from their superiors are nothing but the orders personally of His Majesty the Emperor.'[2] Hirata claimed that the Japanese armed forces were exceptional among all the armed forces of the world in this respect, and, in defence of the actions of Yoshimura, Kawachi and Tanaka, it was therefore impossible to apply 'the liberal and individualistic ideas which rule usual societies unmodified to this totalistic [sic] and absolutistic military society'. Hirata pointed out that the order to kill the prisoners had been given direct by a rear admiral to 'mere Warrant Officers and Petty Officers'. If these subordinates had disobeyed, 'everyone would have fallen upon them,'[3] Hirata claimed.

Two of the American fliers were executed by shooting, while the third was beheaded by one of the accused; their bodies were then cremated and the ashes dumped into the sea. At the trial Ensign Tasaki was questioned as to why he had allowed his prisoners to be taken away from his custody to their deaths. Pleading 'superior orders', the young officer stated that he had merely acted on Masuda's orders, and the defence counsel argued that although Tasaki knew that the men were to be killed, this fact in no way placed him in the position of a participant in the commission of a crime.

In common with all other Allied trials of this nature, the Japanese plea of 'superior orders' was rejected by the court. Although the rejection of the plea was often substantially based upon American military law and judgements, the primary rejection was the rules promulgated by the Supreme Command of the Allied Powers for use in war crimes trials, the so-called 'SCAP Rules', mentioned earlier in this book. The Commander of the Marshalls Gilberts Area, Rear Admiral Harrill, directed Commodore B.H. Wyatt, President of the Commission that tried the Jaluit Atoll defendants, to use the SCAP Rules governing the trials of war criminals as a guide. They were a guide for substantive law and procedure on all issues arising from war crimes trials. One provision of the SCAP Rules (paragraph 16, sub-paragraph (f)) was applied to countering the defence of 'Superior Orders':

> The official position of the accused shall not absolve him from responsibility, nor be considered in mitigation of punishment. Further, action pursuant to order of the accused's [sic] superior, or of his government, shall not constitute a defence but may be considered in mitigation of punishment if the commission determines that justice so requires.[4]

The judgements handed down on three of the four guilty Japanese were severe. Ensign Tasaki, the prisoner's gaoler, was sentenced to ten years' imprisonment, a relatively light sentence because of the 'brief, passive and mechanical participation of the accused'. Lieutenant Yoshimura, Ensign Kawachi and Warrant Officer Tanaka were all sentenced to death and executed by hanging. As demonstrated by the secret nature of the executions of the Allied prisoners and disposal of their remains on Jaluit Atoll in 1944, senior Japanese officers remained concerned that their actions in killing airmen were illegal. They evidently feared punishment at some later time, and as the next case demonstrates, they were keen to cover up their terrible crimes and enforce a code of silence among their subordinates.

In July 1945, during a routine bombing raid on Singapore by USAAF B-24 Liberator aircraft, one plane was successfully engaged over Keppel Harbour by the anti-aircraft batteries on board the Japanese destroyer *Kamikaze* and the minesweeper *Toshimaru*. Badly damaged, the pilot ditched the stricken aircraft in the sea, the two Japanese warships picked up a total of seven survivors and took them to a small prison located at the Seletar Naval Base. Other Allied POWs had already been held at the prison, but the fourteen or fifteen former inmates had already been executed before the Americans arrived. Singapore was under the control of the 10th Special Naval Base Force, whose commander was Rear Admiral Imamura. In immediate charge of the prisoners at Seletar was Lieutenant Commander Okamoto, who subsequently appeared not to be overly enamoured with the task assigned to him.

Many of the Japanese concerned with the fates of the seven American airmen were tried by a British military court convened at Changi Prison on Singapore Island in December 1947. A navy cook, Harumitsu Oka, who witnessed some of the treatment meted out to the Americans, came forward and testified against his former superiors, breaking the Japanese wall of silence over war crimes, stating that those responsible for the subsequent murders 'should be punished for the good of Japan and humanity as a whole'.[5]

Oka's job was to feed the prisoners so he was able to observe their condition closely. 'When I went to see the flyers I noticed that one of them was an officer,' recalled Oka in 1947. 'He was wearing overalls with a zipper up the front and had a pair of cloth wings sewn onto it above the breast pocket. I was told that he was the pilot. The other members of the crew were wearing fatigues with combat boots but some had only shirts on above the waist.'[6] Commander Okamoto had the prisoners divided into two groups, separated into two huts at the prison. Oka stated that he peered into the huts and 'saw that they were lying on the floor with their hands tied in front of them and were blindfolded'.[7] One of the Americans had a deep gash on his leg from the crash-landing, but he was left to bleed all over the floor.

A young sub lieutenant named Kobayahi had been detailed by Okamoto to use his men to guard the prisoners, but after two weeks Kobayahi went to see his commander. Complaining that it was a nuisance providing men to guard the Americans when they could have been more usefully employed on other tasks, Kobayahi asked Okamoto what should be done with them. Okamoto telephoned Fleet Headquarters and spoke to Captain Matsuda on Admiral Imamura's staff, requesting instructions. The reply, when it came, was unequivocal: 'Execute them!'

Commander Okamoto evidently felt that the order to kill the American airmen was distasteful. In a statement to the British military court dated 11 June 1947, he wrote: 'I thought at the time that the affair was a bad thing and as a private individual thought these things were pitiful.'[8] Okamoto's sense of duty was strongly ingrained however, and in his defence he stated: 'I could do nothing against orders from Fleet HQ. I was not anxious to have the men disposed of. I was interested in the matter only because Lieutenant Kobayahi was unable to guard the men because of his operational duties.'⁹ Reluctantly perhaps, Okamoto ordered Kobayahi to kill the American POWs. In turn, Kobayahi ordered Petty Officer First Class Ton to carry out the actual executions.

On the morning of 4 or 5 August Seaman Oka witnessed Ton and four other petty officers board a truck at the naval base, each man carrying a sword. The truck was to take them to the place of execution at the Nee Soon rifle range, where the prisoners had been brought, and where other Japanese sailors waited. Ton invited Oka to join them in the truck, but Oka declined, later stating that 'I didn't like to participate in such things.' According to Oka, who heard about what happened at Nee Soon after the war from the Japanese participants when they were all interned together by the British, he saw the truck come back to camp at about 2.00pm. Oka later learned that about twenty-five Japanese sailors took part in the executions of the seven Americans. One, Petty Officer Hikiji, was a swordsmanship instructor, and using one of the prisoners as a living target, he decapitated the un-fortunate man to great applause from his awed audience. After the demonstration, the others were invited to participate in de-capitating the terrified prisoners, or as Oka related, 'to try their hand at it'. One of the prisoners managed to get away from his guards, and was chased by a sword-wielding sailor, who quickly caught up with him and cut off his head.

The bodies of the prisoners were dumped unceremoniously into a large pit specially dug for the executions, and the Japanese sailors returned to their normal routine at the base. Two weeks later Japan surrendered and in a panic Japanese officers ordered large amounts of documentation to be burned before the British arrived to re-occupy Singapore. All over the island large bonfires burned day and night and, using these as cover, Petty Officer Ton and the other executioners exhumed the American airmen's bodies, transported them to the Seletar Naval Base and cremated them on a huge bonfire on the central parade square. The ashes were then carefully collected and thrown into the sea.

With cold calculation, Commander Okamoto outlined the reasons why the seven Americans were executed. In his estimation, '(1) We could not send them back to Japan; (2) We could not guard them indefinitely; and (3) Although the general policy was to send POWs back to Japan or hand them over to the Army authorities, the orders of Fleet HQ had to be carried out.'¹⁰ If it was not for

Seaman Oka's conscience and his bravery in breaking the Japanese Navy's code of silence by coming forward in 1947, the fate of the seven Americans would probably never have been known.

Notes

1. *Law Reports of the Trials of War Criminals*, vol. 1, 'Case No. 6: The Jaluit Atoll Case' (His Majesty's Stationary Office, 1947), p. 72.
2. Ibid., p. 74.
3. Ibid., p. 74.
4. Ibid., p. 76.
5. Russell of Liverpool, Lord, *The Knights of Bushido: A Short History of Japanese War Crimes* (Greenhill Books, 2005), p. 75.
6. Ibid., p. 74.
7. Ibid., p. 74.
8. Ibid., p. 76.
9. Ibid., p. 76.
10. Ibid., p. 75.

Chapter Sixteen

The Rape of Manila

More shootings went on around the rest of the building.
From where we were we could hear victims in their death
agony, the shrill cries of children and the sobs of dying
mothers and girls.

Modesto Farolan, Acting Manager
Philippine Red Cross, Manila 1945

The fight for Manila, capital city of the Philippines, was one of the great street-fighting battles of the Second World War, rivalling Stalingrad and Berlin in its ferocity and destruction. Manila, once described as the 'Pearl of the Orient', a city famed for 300 years of Western architectural heritage centred around the 'mini-Vatican City' at its heart known as the Intramuros, was utterly destroyed. Although much of the city has been reconstructed, many of the original buildings have gone. The American drive to liberate Manila and the fierce Japanese resistance also resulted in a human tragedy of appalling scale and brutality. As they began to lose the battle the city's Imperial Navy defenders took out their frustrations on the local civilian population in an orgy of rape and murder rivalling that committed on the hapless population of the Chinese capital city of Nanjing in 1937. Japanese sailors ran amok deliberately torturing and murdering as many innocents as they could lay their hands on. It was truly Manila's *Götterdämmerung* and the Japanese Navy's darkest hour in the dying months of the war in the Pacific.

The Japanese Navy's greatest war crime was set in motion by the landing of Lieutenant General Walter Krueger's US 6th Army at Lingayen Gulf on 9 January 1945. General MacArthur had promised that the Americans would return following his defeat in

1942, and return they did with unprecedented firepower and determination. Krueger began immediately to drive south. On 31 January Lieutenant General Robert Eichelberger's 8th Army landed unopposed at Nasugbu in southern Luzon and began moving steadily towards Manila. Major General Joseph Swing's 11th Airborne Division was the strongest element in Eichelberger's command. In a daring parachute drop, Colonel Orin 'Hardrock' Haugen and the 11th Airborne's 511th Regimental Combat Team landed on Tagaytay Ridge on 4 February and spearheaded the northern advance.

The Japanese had done little to prevent American forces from advancing rapidly towards the capital and the converging American columns which set out on 4 February found intact bridges and shallow rivers to cross. But the Japanese were prepared to make the Americans fight for every inch of Manila, if necessary street by street and house by house. In overall command in the Philippines was General Tomoyuki Yamashita, the 'Tiger of Malaya', the famed general who with inferior numbers of troops had captured the Malayan Peninsula and Singapore from the British in February 1942. The Japanese 14th Area Army was subdivided into several 'groups', with the army troops garrisoning Manila consisting of Shimbu Group under the command of Lieutenant General Shizuo Yokoyama. Also stationed inside Manila was a large Japanese naval force covering the port and naval facilities across the city, known as the 31st Naval Special Base Force under the command of Rear Admiral Sanji Iwabuchi. The problem for the future of Manila was inter-service rivalry and insularity between the Imperial Army and Navy. Although General Yamashita was in overall control of the Philippines, the naval forces operating within 14th Area Army had a separate command structure, Iwabuchi reporting to his own service chief, Vice Admiral Denshichi Okuchi, the commander of the South-western Area Fleet in the Philippines. Okuchi, in turn, reported directly to the Combined Fleet in Japan, and not to General Yamashita. Yamashita realized that committing his forces to urban fighting against the Americans, with their superior air power, artillery and armour was foolish, and it would remove his ability to manoeuvre and strike at his opponent. There was also the problem of feeding upwards of one million citizens who were still inside the city when the Americans arrived, impossible for the poorly organized

Japanese logistics train to cope with. Therefore, Yamashita ordered General Yokoyama to pull his troops out of the city into the mountains of northern Luzon where a protracted defensive battle could be waged. Yokoyama had theoretical command over the Japanese naval troops in the city under Admiral Iwabuchi, and he ordered that the admiral withdraw his forces as well. When Vice Admiral Okuchi, Iwabuchi's superior, heard about Yamashita's withdrawal order, he in turn ordered Iwabuchi to defend to the last man the naval facilities and Nichols Field airfield in Manila. Okuchi informed Iwabuchi that the 31st Special Naval Base Force, along with ships' crews from Japanese vessels in the harbour, and assorted naval support staff, would be formed into one new unit called the Manila Naval Defence Force (MNDF).

Admiral Iwabuchi disobeyed his orders from General Yamashita to pull his forces out of the city, as he should have done, and he turned instead to Admiral Okuchi, his superior by loyalty and training, for instructions. It was a reflection of the deeply ingrained inter-service rivalry that even when sailors were placed under military command an admiral such as Iwabuchi could flagrantly ignore his orders and circumvent the chain of command. Yamashita and the army could do little about it. It was an unfortunate decision that would condemn many thousands of Filipinos, Japanese and Americans to death.

The MNDF was a motley collection of naval troops, ill equipped or trained to take on the cream of the US Army in Manila. Although the 31st Naval Special Base Force of infantry-trained sailors formed its core, the remainder of the personnel had virtually no infantry training other than some drill and weapon handling. The withdrawal of General Yokoyama's Shimbu Group of army troops saw the concomitant withdrawal of all armoured support, most of the heavy weapons and artillery in the city, and professionally trained land warfare officers. This left the 17,000 men of the MNDF to scavenge what weapons they could, aside from the reasonably well-armed 31st Naval Special Base Force. American Springfield 1903 rifles, long in storage in Manila after the 1942 defeat, were issued to Japanese sailors, and heavier machine guns, hand grenades, anti-aircraft cannons and field artillery were collected and distributed to the naval troops. Still, compared with the heavy equipment the Americans would shortly range against them, the Japanese sailors were only lightly armed. Their one great advantage was the fact the

169

Americans would have to engage them in urban warfare, enabling the Japanese to create hundreds of static defences, traps and obstacles for the Americans to fight their way through. The second advantage the Japanese had was that they were prepared to sacrifice their lives in the battle for Manila, and 17,000 men who had nothing to lose was a formidable opponent indeed.

On 3 February elements of the US 1st Cavalry Division under Major General Verne D. Mudge entered the northern suburbs of Manila, seizing a vital bridge across the Tuliahan River, the water feature separating American forces from the city proper. Japanese defences had been laid out to cover both sections of the city, a demarcation line running along the Pasig River through the heart of Manila. Army troops were involved in the defence, as General Yamashita had bowed to Admiral Okuchi's demand to defend the vital naval installations in the city, and placed under Admiral Iwabuchi's control a few thousand soldiers under the command of Colonel Katsuzo Noguchi. Called the Noguchi Detachment, they were ordered to dig in north of the Pasig. The defence of Manila was still, however, primarily a Japanese Navy affair. Iwabuchi deployed 4,500 of his men to support Colonel Noguchi north of the Pasig. A further 5,000, under Iwabuchi's direct command, would defend south of the Pasig, with 5,000 more in place to defend Fort McKinley and Nichols Field. A few thousand more naval troops were deployed on partially sunken ships in Manila Bay, or east of the city towards the main army troops, or Shimbu Group in the mountains.

With a bridge over the Tuliahan River in American hands, the first unit into Manila proper was a squadron of Brigadier General William Chase's 8th Cavalry Brigade, which drove into the massive campus of the University of Santo Tomas and immediate trouble. The university had been turned into a huge civilian internment camp during the Japanese occupation. The death rate among the prisoners had been slightly over 10 per cent, with 466 deaths out of a total prison population of 4,255. Chase's men broke into the camp at 9.00pm and fought the guards, while Sherman tanks crashed through the university walls. Placed under pressure, Lieutenant Colonel Toshio Hayashi retreated with his forty-six remaining men and a large contingent of internees to the Education Building. Demanding that he and his men be allowed safe passage to join Japanese troops in the south of the city, Hayashi threatened to slaughter his hostages unless the Americans agreed to his terms. On 5 February, the Americans reluctantly agreed, and the hostages were freed. After exchanging salutes the Japanese were escorted to their own lines. As chance would have it, Hayashi and his men went to the area around the Malacanang Palace, already occupied by American forces, and in the fighting that followed Hayashi and many of his men were killed. The rest ended up back at Santo Tomas as prisoners themselves.

As General MacArthur announced the imminent recapture of Manila, his divisional commanders reported stiffening Japanese resistance to the north and the south of the city. Iwabuchi's men had heavily fortified their sectors of the city, including the ancient heart of the city, the Intramuros, with barbed-wire entanglements, minefields, trench systems and road blocks. It was to take the Americans a month of bloodshed to clear the city of its Japanese Navy and Army defenders.

In the north General Griswold pushed elements of his XIV Corps south from Santo Tomas University towards the Pasig River. The 2nd Squadron of the 5th Cavalry was ordered to seize the intact Quezon Bridge late on 4 February, but the attempt was defeated by strong Japanese resistance and the Japanese blew the bridge. The next day the 37th Infantry Division began its move into Manila, Griswold dividing the city into two sectors, giving the 37th the western half and the 1st Cavalry the eastern. By 8 February units of the 37th Division had managed to clear out most of the Japanese from their assigned sector, but the methods they employed also killed thousands of innocent civilians. Because the Japanese were committed to a house-to-house resistance, when the American encountered dug-in defenders they simply levelled the building with artillery fire and tank support. Street after street was destroyed in this way, creating massive civilian casualties and destroying the city's infrastructure and architecture. The Japanese also contributed to the destruction and as units withdrew they blew up buildings as they went. The Japanese naval troops dug in on Provisor Island, an industrial centre on the Pasig River, put up a furious resistance that lasted until 11 February. Atrocities against the civilian population were also being committed by the Japanese, even as their lines were being threatened by strong American attacks. On 9 February, all the residents of the district of Ermita were ordered to assemble at Plaza Ferguson. By the late afternoon over 2,000 men, women and children of several different nationalities had gathered under a heavy Japanese guard. At 5.00pm a Japanese officer ordered that the men and male youths be separated from the women and younger children. Herded off to different parts of the city, twenty unfortunate girls were cut out from the main female group and sent to a Japanese officer's club located in a requisitioned restaurant named The Coffee Pot. The Japanese fed the girls and gave them drinks, before they were herded off to the nearby Bay View Hotel. Imprisoned in various rooms throughout the hotel, over the next four days and nights Japanese officers and other ranks were given free access to the terrified girls, who were dragged from their rooms and repeatedly raped.

Time was running out for the brutal Japanese occupation of Manila. In the east, General Mudge's 5th Cavalry was involved in some heavy fighting, and the 7th and 8th Cavalry fought bitter battles to wrest control of two water supply complexes from the Japanese in the north of the city. By 10 February the Americans had crossed the Pasig and were consolidating their hold over most of the city. However, the Japanese still strongly defended the Intramuros, Nichols Field and Fort McKinley. The 11th Airborne Division had been halted before the airfield since 4 February, where Japanese naval troops, strongly supported by their limited field artillery, had held the Americans in check. Nichols Field finally fell to the American paratroopers on 11 February, a significant victory that allowed General Swing to complete the encirclement of Manila by day's end on the 12th. Trapped like rats, the Japanese continued to resist fiercely, but they also now decided to initiate an orgy of rape and murder within the areas of the city still under their control, in what came to be called the Manila Massacre.

Vice Admiral Okuchi, commander of the South-west Area Fleet, now safely headquartered with General Yamashita at Baguio City, received a radio message from the surrounded Rear Admiral Iwabuchi on 18 February: 'I am overwhelmed with shame for the many casualties among my subordinates and for being unable to discharge my duty because of my incompetence . . . Now, with what strength remains, we will daringly engage the enemy. Banzai to the Emperor!' There would be no Japanese surrender, as Iwabuchi radioed: 'We are determined to fight to the last man.' The Japanese defenders now had nothing to look to except their own deaths in battle, and for many this grim prospect seems to have contributed

172

to a feeling that they could do what they liked to the hapless civilians waiting for liberation, and do so with remarkable degrees of bestiality and sadism.

The slaughter of innocent Filipino men, women and children was official Japanese policy. At the International Military Tribunal for the Far East a file of orders issued by the Manila Navy Defence Force between December 1944 and February 1945 was entered into evidence. One of the Japanese documents read: 'Be careful to make no mistake in the time of exploding and burning when the enemy invades. When killing Filipinos, assemble them together in one place as far as possible thereby saving ammunition and labor.' Ordinary Japanese sailors were under no illusions about how they should treat the city's population. Many diaries kept by Japanese soldiers and sailors were captured by American forces after the war ended, and some of this damning material was entered as evidence at the Tokyo War Crimes Trials. According to one such diary, kept by Warrant Officer Yamaguchi, 'We are ordered to kill all the males we find. Mopping up the bandits from now on will be a sight indeed.' Yamaguchi's diary continues in this matter-of-fact way describing the murders he and his men were committing each day. 'Our aim is to kill or wound all the men and collect information. Women who attempt to escape are to be killed. All in all, our aim is extermination.'

Inside the once beautiful Intramuros walled city, pounded into ruins by the Americans, the fighting went on until 28 February. The ancient and well-built buildings provided excellent cover for the defenders, necessitating yet more destruction by the Americans who simply blew up everything in their path that exhibited any sign of resistance, killing thousands more civilians. As one historian has commented, 'American lives were understandably far more valuable than historic landmarks.' Behind the Japanese front line, naval troops were also running amok, raping, pillaging and burning on a massive scale. At the Manila German Club many civilians had taken shelter from the incessant American bombardment of the Intramuros. Japanese naval troops surrounded the building, sealed it off by means of a wall of inflammable material, poured petrol over this barricade and then ignited it. As the German Club went up in flames, many of the people inside tried to break out and escape. Japanese sailors were waiting for them. Impaled on bayonets, some were also shot dead. Women who made it through the flaming barricade were dragged screaming into nearby ruined buildings where Japanese sailors gang-raped them. Some were carrying children, but the Japanese bayoneted these babies in their mother's arms before assaulting them. After being raped many times the Japanese sailors often cut the women's breasts off with bayonets; some had petrol poured onto their hair and ignited. The activities of the Japanese at the German Club were repeated on countless occasions throughout the remaining areas of Manila under their occupation, and with many degrees of bestiality.

On 7 February advancing American forces came upon evidence of Japanese bestiality at the corner of Juan Luna and Moriones Streets. Scattered about on the pavement, lying in the grass beside the road, or clustered in ditches of water were the mutilated corpses of forty-nine people. About one-third of the victims were women, and one-third were babies or very young children. All had been shot, bayoneted or beheaded and due to the state of undress of the women it was clear that many had been raped before being murdered. Later that same day the Americans discovered a further 115 bodies scattered about the grounds of the Dy-Pac Lumber Company, located close to the railway station. The bodies were mainly piled up in ditches, the Americans noting that most of the adults and older children had had their hands tied behind their backs before being shot or bayoneted to death. The infants among the dead had not been bound, but none had been spared. Among the dead were children as young as two years; some of the female victims had been pregnant. In some cases Japanese troops had cut the foetuses out of their mother's bellies before killing the victim. The absolute barbarity of the Japanese committing these atrocities was commented upon by US Army medical officer Dr John H. Amnesse, who treated some of the massacre survivors. As well as bayonet wounds, young girls had had both of their nipples amputated from their breasts, and Amnesse also treated a two-year-old boy who had had both of his arms cut off by the Japanese. Some children as young as five were nursing bayonet stab wounds and severe burns caused by sadistic Japanese troops for no other reason than to inflict pain and suffering on infants.

Modesto Farolan, acting manager of the Philippine Red Cross, described how on 10 February a squad of Japanese marines entered the Red Cross Building and butchered everyone they could find. The doctors, nurses, patients with young babies and refugees

174

seeking shelter were all bayoneted or shot to death. Nurses pleaded for the lives of mothers holding young babies, but the Japanese ran both mother and child through with bayonets before they ransacked the building searching for food and supplies. Farolan recounted:

Dr. de Venecia, a voluntary surgeon, was preparing with an attendant two cases for operation. Miss Rosario Andaya, a nurse on volunteer duty, was out in the main corridor keeping order among the large crowd that filled the building to over-flowing. As we heard the noise of rifle fire in every section of the building, Miss Andaya screamed for mercy to spare the lives of a mother and child beside her. Before we knew what had happened, a soldier with drawn bayonet came into the temporary combined officer room-ward where I was. Dr. de Venezia who had just walked over to my corner, Misses Loverize and de Paz, both nurses, and an attendant, ducked into our respective corners for safety. First, Dr. de Venezia was shot twice while he was seated at his corner. The soldier next aimed at the attendant beside him but missed her. She threw herself over to where the two nurses had covered them-selves with mattresses beside my desk and saw two patients crouching underneath. One bayonet thrust finished each of them. Another bayonet thrust at the girl that had escaped the first shot caught Miss de Paz underneath. Looking underneath my desk, the soldier fired two shots at me but the bullets passed between my feet, scraping the bottom rim of my Red Cross steel helmet. After me, he shot a young mother with her 10-day baby, along with her mother, the baby's grand-mother.[1]

The survivors listened in terror as 'More shootings went on around the rest of the building. From where we were we could hear victims in their death agony, the shrill cries of children and the sobs of dying mothers and girls.'

Benito Legarda, who was eighteen at the time of the battle, recalled many years later what he had witnessed: 'Women were raped and sliced with bayonets from groin to throat and left to bleed to death in the hot sun.' No mercy was shown by the Japanese for these non-combatants. 'Children were seized by the legs and had their heads bashed against the wall. Babies were tossed into the air and caught on bayonets. Unborn fetuses [sic] were gouged out with bayonets from pregnant women.'[2]

At St Paul's College some 250 civilians were deliberately rounded up by the Japanese and forced into the damaged building. All of the doors were then solidly shut and locked to prevent escape. The people gathered inside noticed that there were three chandeliers wrapped in blackout paper hanging inside, with electrical wires trailing off outside. The Japanese certainly appear to have enjoyed the suffering they caused, for some time later some sailors entered the college with biscuits, alcohol and sweets, and placed these on a large table underneath the chandeliers. The Japanese told the captives that they were safe where they were and perhaps they might like some food and drink. After the guards withdrew a large portion of the civilians went to the table containing the food and drink, but had barely taken a bite when the three chandeliers exploded above them. The Japanese had deliberately booby-trapped the lights with explosives, and placed the table and its bait in the perfect position to cause the maximum number of casualties. Outside, the Japanese opened fire with machine guns into the building and some began throwing hand grenades through the windows broken by the explosions. Panic ensued, and as many endeavoured to escape through a hole made in the wall by the explosives, they were mown down by machine-gun fire.

According to the father superior of La Salle College, the Japanese arrived on 12 February. Twenty marines led by a single officer forced their way into the building, at that time occupied by seventy civilians including thirty women and young girls, children, four adult family heads and fifteen Catholic monks and a priest. The Japanese immediately set about killing everyone, running from room to room shooting people, stabbing them with bayonets and swords and sexually assaulting the young women. According to the father superior, 'When the Japanese had finished, they threw our bodies into a heap at the foot of the stairs. The dead were thrown over the living. Not many died outright, a few died within one or two hours, the rest slowly bled to death. The soldiers retired and we heard them later drinking outside. Frequently they returned to laugh and mock at our suffering.'[3]

Many of the Japanese raped young women and girls who were

bleeding to death from gunshot and stab wounds. 'That night I managed to extricate myself from the dead bodies and hid behind the high altar of the chapel, where I was joined the next morning by eight or ten others still alive . . . The soldiers ransacked the building and all the sacred vessels were stolen.'

On the Wednesday evening, when they were satisfied that everyone was either dead or mortally wounded, the officer ordered his men to set fire to the chapel before departing. 'One of the brothers, who was dying, succeeded in putting it [the fire] out. The following afternoon the Americans captured the college and took the few survivors out.'[4]

Carolina Coruna, a 22-year-old nurse witnessed two large-scale massacres in the city centre. As she recounted for US Army investigators later, 'On each occasion, Japanese firing squads composed of about 10 soldiers armed with automatic weapons lined up the civilians at the intersection of Victoria and General Solano Streets and mowed them down with point-blank fire. Womenfolk of the victims who ran out to plead with the soldiers were killed in cold blood before they even reached the soldiers.' Demonstrating the callous behaviour of individual Japanese troops in Manila, Coruna recounted a further tale of horror:

> I was living within the walled city with a family named Velez on Anda Street. One night a Japanese sentry came to our house. He called into the shelter where five were seeking shelter, 'Are there any men inside?' I can speak a little Japanese. I came to the doorway and told him, 'There are only women and a two month baby.'

The Japanese gruffly ordered the women to keep the baby quiet. Then, for no apparent reason he shot Coruna.

> As I turned he fired and I fell, shot in the legs and paralyzed from the hips down. I feigned death, with eyes open, watching the sentry. He entered the shelter and approached Mrs. Velez who held the baby in her arms, trying to cover its mouth so it wouldn't cry out. The soldier advanced with fixed bayonet and thrust the blade into the child's head. Mrs. Velez screamed in anguish and the soldier fired in her face, killing her instantly. Then he shot and killed Mrs. Velez's sister. From

that moment on I do not have a very clear recollection of the events that followed.[5]

At the Spanish Consulate many neutral nationals and refugees had gathered seeking protection. Spain was a neutral country, but the Japanese ignored the large Spanish flag flying outside the building and opened a concentrated fire through the doors and windows in a deliberate attempt to kill the occupants. When the building burst into flames, desperate people fled into the garden where a heavily armed Japanese reception committee was waiting for them. Over fifty people were either burned alive in the building or stabbed to death by bayonet-wielding Japanese troops in the consulate garden. The Japanese destroyed 90 per cent of Spanish buildings in Manila, including the Casino Espanol and its library, and the House of the Auxilio Social and Patronato Escolar Espanol, these buildings being torched.[6]

A respected urological surgeon and lecturer on the history of medicine at the University of the Philippines, Dr Frankel, described for American war crimes investigators the grisly massacre of innocents perpetrated at the College of Medicine building. Inside, Dr Frankel and about 190 men, women and children were herded into one of the rooms at the college. The Japanese then surrounded the terrified people with furniture soaked in petrol and set the barricade alight. Anyone who managed to escape the flames was shot and killed. Dr Frankel, his sister and one other person did manage to survive the conflagration, and were able to give a statement of what the Japanese had done.

The very last pocket of Japanese resistance was the ruins of the Finance Building, which the Americans pounded with heavy artillery until all were dead inside. It was 3 March 1945, a month since American forces had first entered the northern suburbs. The death toll was fearful. Approximately 100,000 Filipino civilians were deliberately killed by Japanese forces and many thousands more by American efforts to recapture the city. Nearly 16,000 Japanese died, most of them naval troops, accounting for virtually their entire garrison. The Americans lost 1,010 killed and 5,565 wounded during the month-long fight in the fiercest urban fighting of the Pacific War.[7] Although criticized by the post-war Filipino government and others for the destruction they wrought on the city, an American battle report suggested: 'The destruction stemmed from the American decision to save lives in a battle against Japanese troops who had decided to sacrifice their lives as dearly as possible.' General MacArthur could proudly state at the Malacanang Palace after the battle: 'Your capital city, cruelly punished though it be, has regained its rightful place – a citadel of democracy in the East.'

The man deemed responsible for all of this suffering was General Tomoyuki Yamashita, commander of the Japanese 14th Area Army. When the war ended in August 1945, Yamashita and 50,000 troops were still resisting the American advance from their positions in the mountains behind the town of Baguio. Originally the 'Tiger of Malaya' had had an army of 300,000. Yamashita was placed on trial even though he had withdrawn his army from Manila before the Americans had arrived, and had given orders that the city was not to be defended. With the death of Admiral Iwabuchi in the fighting in the city, Yamashita, as his nominal superior, would carry the can for the Imperial Navy's butchery of civilians. 'The trial certainly brought out all of the horrors of the closing days of Japanese authority in Manila,' recalled journalist Dennis Warner, who attended the 1945 trial. 'But because the case was so hastily prepared, much of the evidence related to what had happened in the city during February 1945. It seemed to some of us reporting on that trial that General Yamashita could scarcely be held accountable, even for command responsibility, in that terrible period.'[8] After a trial lasting forty-two days, Yamashita was found guilty of war crimes committed by the admirals not under his direct control, and he was executed by hanging on 23 February 1946 close to the ruins of Manila. Yamashita certainly bore responsibility for war crimes committed by army troops in the surrounding countryside against so-called 'guerrillas' during the closing stages of the war, and the British were keen to prosecute him for the murders of Chinese and Allied troops and civilians following the fall of Singapore in 1942. Yamashita, in his defence, argued that he bore no responsibility for the behaviour of the Imperial Navy in Manila *after* he had withdrawn his forces. The tribunal, however, found him guilty because the Manila Naval Defence Force was *part* of Yamashita's 14th Army. As Warner commented, 'Justice on this occasion was perhaps not very kind.'[9]

The scale of Japanese atrocities in the Philippines came close to their activities in occupied China in the numbers of people butchered and the material damage they inflicted on the nation. The Tokyo Trial listed seventy-two large-scale massacres and 131,029 murders as a bare minimum figure for Japanese war crimes victims in the Philippines. An incredible 14,618 pages of sworn affidavits concerning the Philippines were taken by American investigators, and each detailed a separate atrocity. Sorting out who was guilty and who bore responsibility over the guilty was difficult, given the short period of time allotted for war crimes trials after the war ended. Remarkably few Japanese responsible for the actual murders were ever tried, with most of the convictions and/or imprisonments or executions of those Japanese officers guilty of breeches of 'command responsibility' being that they had failed to control their men.

Notes

1. *Law Reports of Trials of War Criminals, Selected and Prepared by the United Nations War Crimes Commission*, Trial of General Tomoyuki Yamashita, vol. IV (His Majesty's Stationary Office: 1948).
2. 'Battle of Manila reduced "Pearl of the Orient" to rubble', by Karl Wilson, *Manila Times*, 15 August 2005.
3. Ibid.
4. Ibid.
5. Ibid.
6. Escoda, Jose, *Warsaw of Asia: The Rape of Manila* (Giraffe Books, 2000).
7. Plenty, Herbert, *Manila Monody: The Rape and the Rampage* (Athena Press Ltd, 2006).
8. 'The Tiger and the Rape of Manila' by Dennis Warner, *International Herald Tribune*, 3 February 1995.
9. Ibid.

Chapter Seventeen

Retribution and Revenge

Japan is a divine nation, centred on the Emperor.
Yoshiro Mori, Prime Minister of Japan, 2000

The scale of Japanese crimes across Asia and the Pacific are difficult to quantify accurately, indeed the exact figures are disputed
and probably will never be known. In China alone, the Japanese
massacred approximately 8.4 million 'non-military' persons
(according to the Chinese government), a crime greater than that
of the Nazi Holocaust against the Jews but today virtually
unknown outside China. To the Chinese today the crimes of the
Japanese still figure prominently in Asian diplomacy and society,
and the government has made great efforts to educate the younger
generation about the nation's dark past (though historical accuracy
is not always the main goal). The attitude of successive post-war
Japanese governments to the nation's wartime record has
continued to stir great animosity towards Japan by its neighbours,
particularly China and South Korea, as the wounds of war and
occupation remain open and painful in Asia. The enormous figure
of Chinese dead includes, as mentioned earlier, over 300,000
soldiers and civilians who were brutalized and killed in the city of
Nanjing on the Yangtze River inland from Shanghai in 1937–8
during what came to be called 'The Rape of Nanking'.

In order to create what the Japanese termed the 'Greater East-
Asia Co-Prosperity Sphere', Japanese propaganda claiming that
Imperial forces were emancipating the millions of Asian peoples
then under Western colonial control, the Japanese murdered 30
million Filipinos, Malays, Vietnamese, Cambodians, Burmese and
Indonesians, and of this extraordinary figure approximately 23
million were ethnic Chinese. Throughout the war, the Japanese

often reserved their most horrific acts of bestial violence for Chinese wherever they found them across Asia. The task of sorting through the mountains of corpses left by the Japanese and apportioning blame on individuals was to be a massive and onerous task for the Allies.

Less than a year before the surrender of Nazi Germany, the United Nations War Crimes Commission formed a Far Eastern and Pacific Subcommittee as the Allies geared up to begin gathering evidence against alleged Japanese war criminals. Formed in May 1944, the Subcommittee's work would not really begin for some time to come, as Japan was still stubbornly resisting Allied efforts to defeat her. Because of the nature of the membership of the Subcommittee, its legal and diplomatic members drawn from a total of eleven nations,[1] administrative and executive tasks fell on the shoulders of the Allied authorities who actually had military control over liberated countries. In the Far East, it fell to General Douglas MacArthur, Supreme Allied Commander, to order the establishment of an International Military Tribunal for the Far East (IMTFE) in January 1946, more commonly known as the 'Tokyo Trials'.

Often, to demonstrate the treatment of Allied prisoners of war by the Japanese a simple comparison is made with those prisoners held by the Germans during the same period. Although exact figures vary, for example, a little over 27,000 American military personnel were captured by the Japanese during the Second World War. Dr Charles A. Stenger, formerly of the Veterans Administration, is one of several academics who have conducted the comparison. According to Stenger, 93,941 American military personnel were captured by the Germans between 1941 and 1945, and of that figure only 1,121 died in captivity, or just over 1 per cent. In comparison, of the 27,465 American military personnel held by the Japanese, 11,107 died in captivity, a death rate of over 40 per cent. The appalling death rates among British, Commonwealth and Dutch POWs were equally as high, as shown in the table opposite.

The IMTFE was concerned with the big picture and the 'big fish' – this refers to those Japanese government and military officials who had planned and waged aggressive war in Asia and the Pacific between 1941 and 1945. These leaders were tried for three types of crimes: 'Class A' (crimes against peace), 'Class B' (war crimes)

Table 1: Deaths of Commonwealth and Dutch POWs in Japanese Captivity.[2]

Country	Total deaths	Prisoners	Death Rate %
Australia	7,412	21,726	34
Canada	273	1,691	16
United Kingdom	12,433	50,016	25
New Zealand	31	121	26
Dutch (white)	8,500	37,000	23
Totals	**35,756**	**132,134**	**27**

and 'Class C' (crimes against humanity), committed during the Second World War. The first classification refers to the leaders' joint conspiracy to start and then wage war, while the latter two classifications refer to atrocities. Subordinate and junior officers, many of whom actually conducted the killings personally, or at least ordered them, were to be dealt with separately from the IMTFE by a series of tribunals established by the victorious Allied powers throughout the former Japanese Empire. Importantly, the crimes committed by Japanese forces in China and Korea between 1937 and 1945 were not dealt with by the IMFTE, and instead the Chinese authorities instituted thirteen tribunals themselves – 504 Japanese were convicted by these bodies and 149 were subsequently executed. The IMFTE convened on 3 May 1946. Twenty-five former Japanese military and political leaders were charged with 'Class A' crimes, the most famous being the former prime minister General Hideki Tojo, and a further 300,000 Japanese were charged with 'Class B' or 'Class C' crimes at dozens of tribunals throughout Asia and the Pacific. The Australians, due to the fact that so many of their servicemen and nationals had fallen into Japanese hands during the war, were particularly interested in seeing some measure of justice meted out to those responsible for war crimes. Australian military courts charged 924 Japanese nationals with war crimes and of these 496 were convicted and given prison terms. Another 148 were found guilty of murder and executed.

The British also conducted extensive war crimes trials in twenty-three cities in Asia, based upon the regions of Singapore, Malaya, North Borneo, Burma and Hong Kong. South-East Asia

Command, under Vice Admiral Lord Louis Mountbatten, was placed in charge of investigating and prosecuting Japanese war criminals, primarily concerning war crimes against former British POWs. The British collected 35,963 witness statements, as well as questioning local residents. Responsibility for collecting much of this material was with E Group of Force 136, a section of the Special Operations Executive (SOE). The local populations of areas that had been under Japanese occupation at the time of the alleged war crimes were of primary importance to the British investigation. Frederick Bellenger, Financial Secretary to the War Office, commenting at the time, wrote: 'Although the military administration is anxious to bring to justice the perpetrators of such crimes, their success in doing so is largely dependent upon the willingness of the local population to come forward with reports.'[3] The first British trial opened in Singapore on 21 January 1946 and by May 8,900 suspects were under arrest, although less than 1,000 of these were ever brought to trial. The problem was that the British investigation was hampered by a lack of staff and funds. British efforts were concentrated instead on repatriating servicemen, rather than hunting for justice for those who would never return. Although British foreign secretary Ernest Bevin stated in February 1946 that 'regarding the Far East, I agree that high priority should be given to trials of minor war criminals',[4] this was largely to be an unfulfilled ambition. After 1947 the number of staff investigating Japanese war crimes was reduced and the final trial in Singapore came to an end in December 1948. In the end the British executed 174 Japanese for war crimes.

The US Navy was much more active throughout the Pacific in prosecuting suspected Japanese war criminals (and much better funded than the British), convening military commissions at Guam and Kwajalein (such as the Jaluit Atoll Case, referred to in Chapter 15). An excellent example of post-war investigations into Japanese activities was the US Navy's dogged determination to uncover the truth of what had occurred on Truk in the Caroline Islands (part of the pre-war Japanese Mandated Pacific Islands), wartime headquarters of the Japanese 4th Fleet. The Office of the Director of War Crimes gathered evidence from a wide range of sources and not just from naval forces in the field. Released prisoners of war were questioned, battle reports and killed and missing-in-action reports were consulted, local civilians interviewed, Japanese prisoners questioned and forensic evidence gathered (such as the bodies of Allied servicemen that the Japanese had concealed). As mentioned before, as the war drew to a close the Japanese had very thoroughly 'cleaned' their records, removing any incriminating documents and destroying vital evidence that would have demonstrated the commission of war crimes.

The US Navy, after liberating Truk, initiated an immediate investigation into possible war crimes, but turned up nothing. It appeared initially as though the 4th Fleet had abided by the Geneva Conventions in its treatment of POWs. For three months the Americans carefully questioned thousands of Japanese and local Trukese, but no questionable acts surfaced. It was all too good to be true, of course, and naval investigators knew that something was amiss. It simply did not add up and certainly looked extremely suspicious to Brigadier General Robert Blake, commander of US occupation forces. Blake knew of Japanese atrocities committed everywhere else they had been, so it stood to reason that war crimes must have occurred on Truk. He ordered investigators to continue digging. The Americans decided to use a ruse to allow one of their men to infiltrate the Japanese camp. On Truk, as elsewhere throughout the Japanese wartime empire, Koreans had been conscripted and forced into labour battalions in support of Japanese fighting troops. A Korean-American named Da Young managed to infiltrate a group of Korean prisoners from a labour unit being held by the Americans on Truk, and ingratiated himself with certain individuals. Soon, the truth of what had occurred on Truk during the war began to emerge. His conversations with various prisoners revealed that the Japanese 4th Fleet had engaged in a massive cover-up of war crimes, and just before the end of the war had warned their own personnel, the Koreans and locals that if they spoke to the Americans about what had occurred retribution would be taken against them. This 'wall-of-silence' technique was attempted by the Japanese everywhere they had perpetrated crimes and was to prove particularly effective in silencing any Japanese servicemen who were troubled by what they or their colleagues had done during the war. Through the use of their Korean 'spy', the Americans were able to identify and isolate several Japanese prisoners; following this action many Koreans and local Trukese believed that the Americans were now in possession of all the facts and several came forward with further information.

The process of collecting evidence was slow and painstaking, as the US Navy carefully built up cases against individual Japanese naval officers until they were confident in charging them formally and placing them before a military commission.

The Americans afforded the Japanese accused every protection of their rights under the law, including the presumption of innocence until proven guilty, something which the Japanese had failed to exercise in their own trials of Allied personnel and local inhabitants throughout their empire. Japanese defence lawyers worked closely with the defendants and the accused were allowed to gather evidence themselves to present before the commission. The US Navy was interested in achieving convictions against those Japanese who had been in positions of command, using the theory of 'command responsibility', and to convict these men of failing to control their subordinates who had murdered and mistreated prisoners of war in their care.

A total of 137 Japanese officers were tried and 129 were convicted of war crimes. Notable among those convicted was Lieutenant Shinji Sakagami who had strangled to death two American POWs with his bare hands. Another was Surgeon Captain Hiroshi Iwanami and eighteen members of his medical staff who, in a series of perverted medical experiments similar to those conducted by German SS doctors in concentration camps in Europe, had murdered six POWs by injecting them with streptococcus bacteria which caused blood poisoning, and of wrapping tourniquets around the arms and legs of prisoners for long periods, often resulting in death from shock. Iwanami had also dissected the prisoners' bodies, including decapitating them, and boiling the flesh off their bones so their skeletons could be used as medical exhibits. The prisoners' internal organs had also been preserved for study by the doctor. Captain Masaharu Tanaka and Lieutenant Commander Yoshinumi Danzaki were found guilty of murdering seven POWs on Dublon Island, the prisoners being beheaded, stabbed or beaten to death. More horrifying medical experiments came to light, resulting in the conviction of Surgeon Commander Chisato Ueno and eight of his staff for the murder of an American prisoner who they drugged with chloroform, strapped to an operating table and then dissected him while the man was alive. When Ueno and his colleagues had completed their dissection, the prisoner was taken out of the hospital on a stretcher whilst still alive and placed on the ground next to a freshly dug hole. A navy dentist, Ensign Takeshi Enriguchi, drew his sword and decapitated the prisoner, and then the mutilated corpse was pushed into the hole and buried.

Vice Admiral Hara of the 4th Fleet was the senior Japanese convicted of war crimes, being sentenced to six years in Sugamo prison in Tokyo for 'command responsibility' offences. For those convicted of murder, the sentence of the Commission was death by hanging. On the island of Guam in May 1947 the US Marines had erected a large wooden hut near the radio station, inside which were two gallows side-by-side, allowing for the execution of pairs of prisoners. The final two Japanese war criminals to be executed were Rear Admiral Shimpei Asano, commander of the 41st Guard Unit, and the aforementioned Surgeon Commander Ueno. One hundred and twenty-seven of their fellow war criminals had preceded them to this place. It was 31 March 1949 and at a given codeword the two men were taken from their cells on Guam, their hands securely cuffed behind their backs. Escorted by Marines to a waiting jeep, the pair was driven the short distance in the failing evening light to the execution hut. Marched inside, a Marine corporal stood ready to execute them, rows of chairs facing the dual gallows, where witnesses and officials sat silently watching the proceedings. The admiral and the naval surgeon were swiftly escorted up the nine steps to their respective gallows. The hand-cuffs were removed by Marines and replaced with leather straps secured around the condemned men's torsos, designed to pin the arms against the sides of the body, and another around their legs. A black hood was tugged over each man's head followed by the rope noose and the order to proceed with the execution was given. Due to his rank, Admiral Asano was hanged first, followed at 8.26pm by Ueno. A lever was pulled by the executioner, the floor of the gallows dropped open and Ueno fell through, his passage swiftly arrested by the rope which terminated his life.

For other Japanese, war criminals or not, the revenge of those they had abused was not conducted through courts and military tribunals. With the war over in the Netherlands East Indies, the Dutch were determined to re-establish their colonial rule and fresh troops were dispatched from the Netherlands to accomplish this task. They were to face the rise of Indonesian nationalism which the Japanese had fostered during the occupation and there were some cases of locals killing recently released white civilian internees of the Japanese and former POWs. The situation was so serious for freed Dutch civilians that due to a lack of manpower the Dutch government actually asked the Japanese guards to protect the prisoners until they could be relieved by Dutch colonial forces. In a bizarre twist of irony in some places across Indonesia, white civilian internees, 26,233 of whom had perished under Japanese occupation in the East Indies, now relied upon their tormentors to keep them alive. Once sufficient Dutch troops were in control of some areas, the Japanese troops were disarmed and in a display of massive retaliation, 236 were killed in the first nine days after liberation. Hundreds of other Japanese soldiers were interned in camps on Java and Timor where their Dutch guards recreated the appalling conditions under which the Japanese had imprisoned Dutch nationals. Torture and summary execution were employed and if any prisoner was unable to work he was beaten to death. In this manner the furious Dutch killed over 1,000 Japanese troops. Once they had tired of this form of retaliation the Dutch simply released the surviving Japanese prisoners and left them to make their own way back home.

In China, which had suffered more than any other country in Asia from the brutal Japanese occupation, summary justice was handed out to many Japanese soldiers and sailors captured by the enraged Chinese citizenry. In the city of Hankou in the north-east twenty-six Japanese soldiers were rounded up by Chinese civilians on 19 August 1945, four days after the unconditional surrender. Having suffered an occupation of virtually indescribable barbarity and savagery since 1937, the Chinese were in no mood for legal niceties. These Japanese prisoners represented eight years of terror. A massive crowd gathered to watch the executions. Four Japanese were forced to their knees and in a replay of what they had done so many times to innocent Chinese prisoners, they were beheaded. Another group of four were tied to wooden posts and shot in the back of the head. Four more had their arms and legs broken and amputated when they were conscious; they were then left to bleed to death. Four more were castrated, their genitals stuffed into their mouths, and their hands and feet were also cut off. The ten remaining Japanese prisoners each had their eyes gouged out before Chinese soldiers bayoneted them to death in an eerie replay of the tortures the Japanese had visited upon millions of Chinese soldiers and civilians. All of these terrible tortures and executions were merely reproductions of what the local Chinese had seen their Japanese overlords do to their friends and relatives. The two examples cited from Indonesia and China were not unique – thousands of Japanese servicemen, guilty or not of appalling crimes, were similarly dispatched before the formal process of trials and tribunals began in earnest.

Notes
1. Australia, Belgium, China, Czechoslovakia, France, India, Luxembourg, the Netherlands, Poland, Great Britain and the United States.
2. Data courtesy of the Far East Prisoners of War Association (FEPOW).
3. The National Archives (TNA): Public Record Office (PRO) WO203/4927A.
4. Bevin to Attlee, 5 February 1946, The National Archives (TNA): Public Record Office (PRO), WO32/12197.

Afterword

Throughout the course of this book mention has been made of the many nameless members of the IJN who were not investigated or prosecuted for war crimes after the war, even though witnesses named particular vessels involved in massacres perpetrated at sea, or other sources named naval units and individuals involved in crimes committed on land. Several reasons can be introduced that go some way to explaining why so many Japanese were able to commit awful crimes during the war and escape any punishment. One reason was, as we have seen, a lack of resources to have enabled some of the Allied nations to hunt down and prosecute suspected war criminals. There were also problems associated with translation that made any investigations and trials long-winded affairs, as the Allied powers went through the motions of granting the Japanese defendants transparent trials under the rule of law. Insufficient numbers of translators meant that delays occurred during the process of investigation and/or trial, and the military commissions and tribunals were under increasing pressure from their national governments to bring the war crimes prosecutions to a close. Japan would become an ally of the United States and other countries she had so recently warred against, the idea being that a strong demilitarized Japan would become an important block against the spread of Soviet-inspired communism throughout Asia. The attention of the victorious Allied powers was soon diverted away from chasing down war criminals in a friendly country trying hard to forget its imperialist past by the Korean War, which broke out in 1950. Japan was an important base for American and Allied military forces fighting North Korea and China, and the Japanese economy benefited immeasurably from this association. Geo-political considerations rendered the search for Japanese war criminals embarrassing and best forgotten. The Allied powers could demonstrate that they had punished wartime Japanese aggression by pointing out the numbers of Japanese convicted of war crimes and either executed or imprisoned, and they could make comparisons with the Nuremberg Trials of prominent Nazis in Germany. But the 'Tokyo Trial' was not on the scale of its German cousin. It might be argued that 'war weariness' by the end of 1945 meant that there was little appetite amongst those whose job it was to make sure the guilty were punished to actually do so compre-hensively. Instead, a series of *prominenti* were hanged or imprisoned, and the job of catching the men who actually murdered was left to individual nations, many of whom, Britain in particular, were near bankrupt after years of war.

The rise of nationalism amongst the indigenous inhabitants of many of the European colonies occupied by the Japanese during the Second World War was also a contributory factor that meant most Japanese escaped prosecution. France, Britain and the Netherlands all returned to their Asian colonies to try to re-establish their rule after 1945. Only the British were ultimately able to in Hong Kong and Singapore, and for a while in Burma and Malaya. French Indo-China was eventually to convulse with another brutal war that would last until the 1970s, and the Netherlands East Indies would reinvent itself as Indonesia. The Allied war crimes trials had been primarily interested in the crimes the Japanese committed against white people: white POWs, white colonists. Very little though has been made of the devastation wrought by the Japanese armed forces against the indigenous peoples of China, Indonesia, Malaysia, the Philippines, Burma or a multitude of islands throughout the vast Pacific, and the white soldiers and civilians who had been imprisoned by the Japanese largely returned to the West at the earliest opportunity after their liberation. Similarly, the Japanese were disarmed and transported back to Japan where their labour was required to rebuild the country as an American-inspired bulwark against communism. Half a world soon separated the abused and the abusers, and has remained so to this day.

Many of the Japanese sailors who appear on the pages of this book, and who committed such terrible deeds over sixty years ago, are still alive today. There is no individual like Simon Wiesenthal, or organization such as Yad Vashem or Mossad that hunts for these men in the hope of bringing them to justice before they die, or at the least names and shames them for what they are. No one has bothered these men in over six decades. In Germany it is a crime to deny the Holocaust, yet Japan (whose position is outlined in Appendix 1) does not even consider those who were convicted and executed in Tokyo, or elsewhere in Asia and the Pacific, by the Allies to be war criminals. Her government issues regular apologies for the wartime behaviour of the Japanese people, and that appears to be the best anyone can hope for.

For those interested in exploring further the subject of Japanese war crimes, several excellent works exist that should be required reading. The seminal and authoritative book *The Knights of Bushido: A Short History of Japanese War Crimes* by Lord Russell of Liverpool is one of the most significant early works to document the subject. [1] More recently, Lawrence Rees has documented the terrible human price of war in Asia and the Pacific in *Horror in the East: The Japanese at War 1931–1945*.[2] One book which has stirred considerable controversy is *The Rape of Nanking* by the late Iris Chang, covering one of the modern world's worst atrocities. [3] Some Japanese historians have begun to reassess their nation's wartime record, and of particular significance is Toshiyuki Tanaka's *Hidden Horrors: Japanese War Crimes in World War II*,[4] translated by John W. Dower. Some sections of this book detail the various war crimes trials conducted after the war in the Far East, and a significant work devoted to this subject is the excellent *Judgment at Tokyo: The Japanese War Crimes Trials* by Timothy P. Maga. [5] For those who wish to understand more about the wartime Imperial Japanese Navy and the deployments and operations mentioned in this book, consulting *A Battle History of the Imperial Japanese Navy* by Paul S. Dull would be a good starting point. [6] To understand further the how's and why's of the Allies' terrible run of defeats in Asia at the beginning of the war that placed so many of their soldiers and sailors into Japanese hands, Bernard Edwards' *Japan's Blitzkrieg: The Allied Collapse in the East 1941–42* tells the story in more detail than is possible in this book.[7]

Notes

1. Russell of Liverpool, Lord, *The Knights of Bushido: A Short History of Japanese War Crimes* (Greenhill Books, 2002).
2. Rees, Lawrence, *Horror in the East: The Japanese at War 1931–1945* (BBC Books, 2001).
3. Chang, Iris, *The Rape of Nanking: The Forgotten Holocaust of World War II* (Basic Books Inc., 1998).
4. Toshiyuki Tanaka, translated by John W. Dower, *Hidden Horrors: Japanese War Crimes in World War II* (Westview Press Inc., 1997).
5. Maga, Timothy P., *Judgment at Tokyo: The Japanese War Crimes Trials* (University of Kentucky Press, 2001).
6. Dull, Paul S., *A Battle History of the Imperial Japanese Navy 1941–45* (US Naval Institute Press, 1978).
7. Edwards, Bernard, *Japan's Blitzkrieg: The Allied Collapse in the East 1941–42* (Pen & Sword Books Ltd, 2006).

Appendix 1

'War Crimes' and the Japanese Government Today

Former Japanese Prime Minister Ryutaro Hashimoto was quoted in 1996 responding to criticism of his paying homage to Japanese war criminals at the Yasakuni Shrine in Tokyo, 'Why should it matter any more?' The atrocities committed by individuals and units of the IJN discussed throughout this book are normally termed as 'war crimes' by the international community of nations, and by most academics and researchers in this field. What is baffling is that in Japan today they are not recognized as such. In fact, the Japanese Justice Minister in 1994, Nagano Shigeto, stated with confidence that 'The Pacific War was a war of liberation.' A year later, in 1995, 221 members of the Diet, the Japanese parliament, backed a resolution that stated in part: 'The Pacific War was a war to liberate colonised Asia.' Dozens of examples can be found of senior Japanese political figures and academics who remain in denial concerning Japan's wartime record, especially concerning the atrocities that her armed forces caused. History textbooks in schools have been routinely altered by the Japanese government, keen to portray Japan as the victim in a war it started, and not to educate young people about what really occurred. Successive Japanese prime ministers, including most recently Junichiro Koizumi, have regularly paid homage to Japan's war dead at the infamous Yasukuni Shrine in Tokyo, where alongside millions of Japanese servicemen many 'Class-A' war criminals are also memorialized, including Hideki Tojo. These issues have caused outrage in the countries that suffered greatly under Japanese occupation, drawing particular approbation

194

from China and South Korea. It is indeed an extraordinary situation where some Japanese, even leaders, are able to pervert historical fact and deny the terrible holocaust that Japan unleashed on Asia and the Pacific between 1937 and 1945. No parallel can be found and if compared with Germany, the position of the two nations could not be more dissimilar.

The Japanese government's position today is clear on the issue of war crimes. Because Japan never signed any of the Geneva Conventions its actions during the Second World War did not violate international laws. In 1929 the Japanese government signed the Kellog-Briand Pact, which renders its actions between 1937 and 1945 liable to charges of 'crimes against peace'. This charge was levelled against the Japanese Class-A War Criminals tried by the International Military Tribunal for the Far East, otherwise known as the Tokyo Trials, such as General Hideki Tojo, convened between 1946 and 1949. The problem with the Kellog-Briand Pact is that it contains no enforcement clause stipulating penalties in the event of a violation, so Japan does not recognize it today.

In 1945 Japan accepted the terms of the Potsdam Declaration which ended the Second World War in the Far East. In Article 10 of the Declaration, two kinds of 'war crime' are alluded to: the violation of international laws, such as the maltreatment of prisoners of war, and obstructing democratic tendencies among the Japanese people. Japan, however, continues to refuse to recognize those convicted at the Tokyo Trials and other trials as criminals, although it has accepted the judgments made in the trials and in the 1952 Treaty of San Francisco (which formally ended the state of war between Japan and the United States). This is because the 1952 Treaty does not mention the legal validity of the tribunal.

The current position of the Japanese government is quite confusing and contradictory. It accepts the judgment and sentences set by the Trial as *demands*, but it does not accept the legal validity of the Tokyo war crimes tribunal. Put simply, the Tokyo Trials and other war crimes trials have no standing in Japanese law. The Japanese can allude to 'victor's justice', as Japan accepted the terms of the Potsdam Declaration to end the war, and as a condition for acceptance it had to agree to a number of conditions including the incarceration and/or execution of those deemed responsible for the war. These people were defined as guilty by a tribunal organized by the victorious Allied powers, not the Japanese.

The post-war Japanese constitution allowed violations of the defendants' legal rights, such as execution, if proper legal procedure was followed, in the general public interest. Therefore, the executions and incarcerations were valid under the new constitution, but illegal under Japanese criminal law, and remain so to this day. Men convicted as war criminals after the war are not defined as such in Japan today, but their execution or incarceration is regarded as legally valid. Many point to this legal confusion as further evidence of a Japan unwilling to own up to its wartime crimes, and it further fuels calls for a more responsible and sensitive approach by the Japanese government towards history.

Appendix 2

German U-boat War Crimes

On only one documented occasion during the Second World War was a German U-boat skipper responsible for the cold-blooded murder of unarmed Allied merchant seamen after he had sunk their ship. In this particular case, known as the *Peleus* Massacre, the officers responsible for the murders were subsequently tried and convicted.

On 13 March 1944, U-852 under the command of 35-year-old Lieutenant Commander Heinz-Wilhelm Eck intercepted the 4,695-ton Greek merchant ship *Peleus* in the South Atlantic. The crew totalled thirty-five men of many nationalities including Russians and Chinese who were transporting a cargo of ballast from Freetown to Buenos Aires. Eck had tracked the *Peleus* until darkness had fallen, and then, after closing up the range between his U-boat and the merchantman, he had fired two torpedoes at her whilst surfaced. The *Peleus* was completely ripped apart by the detonations, which killed perhaps half of the crew, and the ship abruptly sank. For the survivors left clinging desperately to wreckage or life rafts, no one expected what followed from a German submarine. U-852 slowly nosed into the field of debris. It appeared from his post-war interrogation that Eck was primarily interested in recording his kill and required the name and tonnage of the ship in order to do so. Two survivors were hauled aboard the U-boat and the necessary information recorded, before they were returned to the water unharmed. Eck then told the survivors to turn off all the lights fitted to their survival equipment and life rafts, in order to give his U-boat a head start in exiting the vicinity before Allied ships arrived. This was a ruse, however, for although

Eck argued at his post-war trial that he had ordered his men to open fire with machine guns in order to sink the remaining large pieces of wreckage, including the life rafts, in order that no evidence of the sinking should be discovered, this was rejected as a fabrication. It appears that Eck was concerned that any seamen who were rescued by the Allies would betray the presence of his U-boat in the South Atlantic, a fact which he wished to conceal as thoroughly as possible. U-boats were under orders from the commander of the German Navy, Grand Admiral Karl Dönitz, not to take survivors on board, for the simple reason that space and provisions would not permit such humanitarian gestures. Dönitz had issued several orders forbidding displays of humanity lest commanders unnecessarily risk their boats, so survivors were always left to fend for themselves, many never to be picked up.

On this occasion Eck ordered machine guns, machine pistols and hand grenades to be brought topside, and for the next five hours he mercilessly 'cleaned up' the scene of the sinking, with most of the survivors from the *Peleus* being shot to death in the water. Even the U-boat's 37mm and 20mm anti-aircraft guns were turned on the helpless men in the water. To add to the disgrace, U-852's medical officer took part in the massacre. Eventually Eck lost interest in attempting to sink the life rafts, which were remarkably resistant to machine-gun bullets, and U-852 slunk away into the night. It was only because three men survived the massacre and a further forty-nine days adrift before being rescued by a Portuguese neutral, that this heinous crime became known to the Allied authorities. Eck's actions were universally condemned by the U-boat service, and personally by Dönitz himself at the Nuremberg War Crimes Trial.

At his trial in Hamburg in the autumn of 1945, Eck argued in his defence that he had ordered his crew to disperse floating wreckage with machine-gun fire, and that any civilian deaths among the survivors were accidental or the result of the overzealous following of his orders by his crew. On 17 October 1945 Eck was found guilty of war crimes, along with U-852's executive officer, Lieutenant August Hoffmann. The Chief Engineer, Lieutenant Commander Hans Lenz, the medical officer, Lieutenant Dr Walter Weisspfennig, and a leading seaman, Wolfgang Schwender were also found guilty. Lenz was sentenced to life imprisonment and Schwender to fifteen years (Schwender was released from prison on parole in 1951, and Lenz in 1952). Eck, Hoffmann and Weisspfennig were sentenced to death and executed by a British firing squad on 30 November 1945.

The action by Eck was the only known massacre carried out by the German Navy's U-boat service during the Second World War and was widely condemned throughout the German military after the war. Donitz resisted Hitler's idea of killing unarmed merchant ship survivors as a method of wearing down the Allied war machine as dishonourable to the Navy. However, the German example of this kind of behaviour does demonstrate that German naval officers and men could commit outrages against the laws of war in the same way as their Japanese allies. What set them apart was the general unwillingness of the vast majority of officers to accept such a massacre doctrine as a legitimate method of fighting the enemy. Unfortunately, Allied propaganda from the Second World War has proved hard to eradicate from the truth of what happened and erroneous stories of German U-boats machine-gunning defenceless Allied seamen have remained embedded in the public consciousness. Notably, recent films, for example *U-571*, have perpetuated this myth in order to demonize what was essentially the least brutal of the various military forces of Nazi Germany. The evidence for this form of crime simply does not exist, and the punishments given to Eck and his companions were widely applauded by former U-boatmen at the time and long afterwards.

Appendix 3

Japanese Navy Human Medical Experiments

As mentioned earlier in this book, the US Navy successfully tried and executed several IJN medical corps personnel who were found guilty of murderous medical experiments on the island of Truk. However, in November 2006 a former Japanese Navy medical officer spoke to Japanese media admitting that he had been ordered to take part in medical experiments on humans while stationed in the Philippines in late 1944, demonstrating that the practice was more widespread throughout the IJN. According to a welter of press reports all over the world, Akira Makino, aged eighty-four, was a former officer in the Japanese Navy's Medical Corps No. 33 Patrol Unit stationed at Zamboanga airfield on Mindanao Island in December 1944.[1] Makino says that he was ordered to conduct medical experiments on a wide variety of local men, women and children, mirroring the well-documented experiments conducted on Chinese and Allied prisoners by the Japanese Army's Unit 731 in northern China during the same period, which resulted in the deaths of over 10,000 people during germ warfare tests. Makino told the Kyodo News Agency that experiments on live prisoners began at Zamboanga shortly after he arrived in December 1944, and recounted that the first experiment he took part in was the dissection of two local men accused of being American spies. A school had been turned into a hospital by the IJN, and Makino stated that the two men were stripped and then tied to operating tables. Many such 'operations' were conducted over several months and although assistants covered the prisoners' faces on some occasions with ether-soaked cloths to render them unconscious, it may be the case that some procedures were made without anaesthetic. Makino was ordered to conduct spurious surgical procedures on the first two victims, along with Japanese Navy medical students and qualified doctors. Makino related: 'I thought "What a horrible thing I'm doing to innocent people even though I'm ordered to do it".'[2] Overall, the experiments included amputating arms and legs, suturing blood vessels and abdominal dissections, and Makino stated that at least thirty men, women and children died as a result. After each experiment the victims were strangled with a rope and their bodies were buried at secret locations.[3] The reason for these experiments appears to have been training purposes. All files pertaining to these horrific medical abuses were destroyed by the IJN before the Americans arrived. Makino stated that he felt unable to refuse to cooperate in the experiments because he had been ordered to do so by a senior medical officer, a classic case of 'superior orders', recalling: 'I would have been killed if I had disobeyed the order. That was the case in those days.'[4]

The naval experiments came to an end in February 1945 and the invasion by United States forces in March forced the eventual dispersal of those who had taken part in the murders. With little to fear from any possible war crimes prosecution as would probably be the case in Europe regarding Nazi medical crimes, Makino, when asked why he had suddenly revealed this information sixty years after the event, was quoted as saying: 'I want to tell the truth about the war to as many people as possible. If I'm given the opportunity, I'll continue to testify in atonement.'[5] Whether further revelations concerning IJN medical experiments will come to light following Makino's statement is unknown, and due to the Japanese carefully destroying evidence soon after the commission of these crimes, the extent of IJN medical experimentation will probably remain a secret.

Notes
1. 'Japanese man admits human experiments',
   http://www.NEWS.com.au, 26 November 2006
2. Ibid.

201

3. 'Japan's navy conducted medical experiments on Filipinos during war', *International Herald Tribune*, 25 November 2006.
4. 'Japanese man admits human experiments', NEWS.com.au, 26 November 2006.
5. Ibid.

Sources and Bibliography

Archives

Australian War Memorial, Canberra
'Summary of Japanese massacres of Australian POWs in Ambon 6–20 February 1942', NAA A 705/15 Item 166/43/989.

Minute to the Secretary, Department of the Army, 16 May 1942, NAA A 5954 Item 532/1.

Official Notification of the death of F/O William White DFC, 28 June 1946, NAA A705/15 Item 166/43/989.

MacMillan Brown Library, University of Canterbury, Christchurch, New Zealand
Statement of P.H. Rees, Chief Engineer, M.V. SUTLEJ, sunk 26 February 1944, Exhibit 2096, International Military Tribunal for the Far East, MB 1549, vol. 46, Exhibits.

Report of attack of S.S. ASCOT, sunk 29 February 1944, Exhibit 2097, International Military Tribunal for the Far East, MB 1549, vol. 46, Exhibits

Statement of S.K. Chu, 2nd Mate, S.S. NANCY MOLLER, sunk 18 March 1944, Exhibit 2098, International Military Tribunal for the Far East, MB 1549, vol. 46, Exhibits.

Statement of F. de Jong, Chief Officer, S.S. TJISALAK, sunk 26 March 1944, Exhibit 2099, International Military Tribunal for the Far East, MB 1549, vol. 46, Exhibits.

Affidavit of Sugamo Prisoner 4A-24 Mii Junsuke sworn on 30 May 1946, Exhibit 2104, International Military Tribunal for the Far East, MB 1549, vol. 46, Exhibits.

National Archives of Australia, Canberra
'Japanese air raids on Darwin and northern Australia, 1942–43', Fact Sheet 195.

2nd Australian War Crimes Section Interrogation Reports, Sugamo Prison, Tokyo 1949
Executions of Australian and Dutch POWs, Laha Airfield, Ambon Island, February 1942, 'Interrogation report of Yoshizaki, Saburo', File 85H. 851, 85K.
Executions of Australian and Dutch POWs, Laha Airfield Ambon 1942, Continuation of investigating a second massacre, 'Interrogation report of Kanamoto, Yoshizaki', File 85H. 851.

The National Archives (Public Record Office), Kew
(PRO) WO203/4927A.
(PRO) WO32/12197.

United States Marine Corps Historical Archives
1. 'Total Listing of Casualties and Disposition of Wake Island Personnel, 1941–1945', File 1L.

Published Sources
Bayly, Christopher and Harper, Tim, *Forgotten Armies: Britain's Asian Empire & the War with Japan* (Allen Lane), 2004.
Beaumont, Joan, *Gull Force: Survival and Leadership in Captivity 1941–1945* (Allen & Unwin), 1988.
Bezemer, K.W.L., *Geschiedenis van de Nederlandse Koopvaardij in de Tweede Wereldoorlog*, Part 2 (Elsevier), 1987.
Bloomfield, David, *Rabaul Diary: The Escape of a Lark Force Man* (Australian Military History Publications), 2001.
Chang, Iris, *The Rape of Nanking: The Forgotten Holocaust of World War II* (Basic Books Inc.), 1998.
Cohen, Stan B., *Enemy on Island, Issue in Doubt: The Capture of Wake Island* (Pictorial History Publishing Company, Incorporated), 1983.
Cook, Haruko Taya and Cook, Theodore F., *Japan at War: An Oral History* (New Press), 1993.
Dictionary of American Naval Fighting Ships, vol. II (US Naval Historical Center), 1963.
Dictionary of American Naval Fighting Ships, vol. VI (US Naval Historical Center), 1976.
Dong, Stella, *Shanghai: The Rise and Fall of a Decadent City* (William Morrow), 2000.

Dower, John, *War Without Mercy: Race and Power in the Pacific War* (Pantheon Books), 1986.

Dull, Paul S., *A Battle History of the Imperial Japanese Navy 1941–45* (Naval Institute Press), 1978.

Durschmied, Erik, *Unsung Heroes: The Twentieth Century's Forgotten History-Makers* (Hodder & Stoughton), 2003.

Edwards, Bernard, *Japan's Blitzkrieg: The Allied Collapse in the East 1941–42* (Pen & Sword Books Ltd), 2006.

Escoda, Jose, *Warsaw of Asia: The Rape of Manila* (Giraffe Books), 2000.

Felton, Mark, *Yanagi: The Secret Underwater Trade between Germany and Japan 1942–1945* (Pen & Sword Maritime), 2005.

——, *The Fujita Plan: Japanese Attacks on the United States and Australia during the Second World War* (Pen & Sword Maritime), 2006.

Gamble, Bruce D., *Darkest Hour: The True Story of Lark Force at Rabaul – Australia's Worst Military Disaster of World War II* (Motorbooks International), 2006.

Gay, George, *Sole Survivor* (Midway Publications), 1983.

Harrison, Courtney T., *Ambon Island of Mist: 2/21st Battalion AIF (Gull Force): Prisoners of War 1941–45*, (T.W. & C.T. Harrison), 1989.

Herman, Arthur, *To Rule The Waves: How the British Navy Shaped the Modern World* (Hodder and Stoughton), 2005.

Hoyt, Edwin P., *Japan's War: The Great Pacific Conflict* (Da Capo Press), 1989.

The Japanese Story of the Battle of Midway, ONI Review, (Office of Naval Intelligence), 1947.

Johnson, Carl, *Little Hell: The Story of the 2/22nd Battalion and Lark Force* (History House – Jenkin Australia Publishing Ltd), 2004.

Keay, John, *Last Post: The End of Empire in the Far East* (John Murray (Publishers), 1997.

Lamont-Brown, Raymond, *Ships from Hell* (Sutton Publishing), 2002.

Lavo, Carl, *Back from the Deep: Strange Story of the Sister Subs "Squalus" and "Sculpin"* (US Naval Institute Press), 1995.

Law Reports of Trials of War Criminals, vol. 1 (His Majesty's Stationary Office), 1947.

Law Reports of Trials of War Criminals, Selected and Prepared by the United Nations War Crimes Commission, Trial of General Tomoyuki Yamashita, vol. IV (His Majesty's Stationary Office), 1948.

MacArthur, Brian, *Surviving the Sword: Prisoners of the Japanese in the Far East, 1942–45* (Random House), 2005.

Maga, Timothy P., *Judgment at Tokyo: The Japanese War Crimes Trials* (University of Kentucky Press), 2001.

Maniguet, Xavier, *The Jaws of Death: Shark as Predator, Man as Prey* (HarperCollins Publishers), 1992.

Marder, Arthur J., *Old Friend, New Enemies: The Royal Navy and the Imperial Japanese Navy, Strategic Illusions 1936–41* (Clarendon Press), 1981.

Michno, Gregory F., *Death on Hellships: Prisoners at Sea in the Pacific War* (Pen & Sword Books Ltd), 2001.

Milligan, Christopher S. and Foley, John C.H., *Australian Hospital Ship Centaur: The Myth of Immunity* (Nairana Publications), 1993.

Morley, James W. (ed.), *A Fateful Choice: Japan's Advance into Southeast Asia* (Columbia University Press), 1980.

Nila, Gary, *Japanese Special Naval Landing Forces: Uniforms and Equipment 1932–1945* (Men-at-Arms, Osprey), 2006.

Parshall, Jonathan and Tully, Anthony, *Shattered Sword: The Japanese Story of the Battle of Midway* (Potomac Books Inc.), 2006.

Perrett, Bryan, *Last Stand: Famous Battles against the Odds* (Weidenfeld Military), 1992.

Plenty, Herbert, *Manila Monody: The Rape and the Rampage* (Athena Press Ltd), 2006.

Rees, Lawrence, *Horror in the East: The Japanese at War 1931–1945* (BBC Books), 2001.

Russell of Liverpool, Lord, *The Knights of Bushido: A Short History of Japanese War Crimes* (Greenhill Books), 2002.

Smith, Colin, *Singapore Burning: Heroism and Surrender in World War II* (Penguin Viking), 2005.

Tanaka Toshiyuki, translated by John W. Dower, *Hidden Horrors: Japanese War Crimes in World War II* (Westview Press Inc.), 1997.

Urwin, Gregory, *Facing Fearful Odds: The Siege of Wake Island* (University of Nebraska Press), 1997.

Weale, Adrian, *Renegades: Hitler's Englishmen* (Warner Books), 1995.

Woodburn Kirby, Major General S., Addis, C.T., Meiklejohn, J.F. and Wards, G.T., *The War Against Japan: The Loss of Singapore*, Official Campaign History vol. I (History of the Second World War: United Kingdom Military), (Naval & Military Press Limited 2004).

Wukovits, John, *Pacific Alamo: The Battle for Wake Island* (New American Library), 2004.

Newspapers and Journals

BBC History Magazine
China Daily
Honolulu Star-Bulletin
International Herald Tribune
Journal of the Australian War Memorial

The Manila Times
Military History
National Geographic
Naval History
New York Times
Proceedings
Shanghai Daily
The Times
World War II

Websites

BBC History, http://www.bbc.co.uk/history.

Combined Fleet, http://www.combinedfleet.com.

Dictionary of American Naval Fighting Ships Online (DANFS), http://www.hazegray.org/danfs.htm.

EyeWitness to History, http://www.eyewitnesstohistory.com.

George Duncan's Massacres and Atrocities of World War II, http://members.iinet.net.au.

Historynet website, http://www.historynet.com.

Hubbs, Major Mark E., 'Massacre on Wake Island', http://www.ussyorktown.com/yorktown/massacre.html.

NEWS.com website, http://www.NEWS.com.au.

'On Eternal Patrol – Lost Submariners of World War II', http://www.oneternalpatrol.com.

'The Sinking of the *Centaur*', Commonwealth Department of Veterans' Affairs, http://www.dva.gov.au.

'Two Mysteries of the Edsall', USS *Edsall*, 'Josh', DD-219, http://www.geocities.com/CapeCanaveral/Galaxy/3070/jjedsall.htm.

War Crimes Committed by the Imperial Japanese Navy, http://www.users.bigpond.com/battleforaustralia/JapWarCrimes.html.

U-boat.net website and discussion forums, http://www.u-boat.net.

Index

208